LITERARY REVISIONISM
AND THE
BURDEN OF MODERNITY

LITERARY REVISIONISM
AND THE
BURDEN OF MODERNITY

Jean-Pierre Mileur

University of California Press
Berkeley
Los Angeles
London

University of California Press
Berkeley and Los Angeles, California

University of California Press, Ltd.
London, England

© 1985 by
The Regents of the University of California

Library of Congress Cataloging in Publication Data

Mileur, Jean-Pierre.
   Literary revisionism and the burden of modernity.
   Includes index.
   1. Criticism. 2. Bloom, Harold. 3. Poetry.
4. English poetry—History and criticism. I. Title.
PN81.M526 1985   801'.95   84-2768
ISBN 0-520-05236-6

Printed in the United States of America

1   2   3   4   5   6   7   8   9

For Kelly
beloved

CONTENTS

ACKNOWLEDGMENTS

I wish to thank John Guillory and my colleagues at the University of California, Riverside, Steven Axelrod, John Ganim, Edwin Eigner, and Robert Essick, who read and commented upon this book at various stages and gave encouragement and support to its grateful author. My thanks also to the Committee on Research of the University of California, Riverside, which provided funding for the preparation of the manuscript.

NOTE ON ABBREVIATIONS

For convenience, the following abbreviations will be used when referring to frequently cited works:

A   Harold Bloom. *Agon: Toward a Theory of Revisionism.* Oxford: Oxford University Press, 1982.

AI   Harold Bloom. *The Anxiety of Influence.* Oxford: Oxford University Press, 1973.

BPEP   W. J. Bate. *The Burden of the Past and the English Poet.* New York: Norton, 1972.

CW   Geoffrey Hartman. *Criticism in the Wilderness: The Study of Literature Today.* New Haven: Yale University Press, 1980.

EC   Henry Chadwick. *The Early Church.* New York: Penguin Books, 1967.

GG   Elaine Pagels. *The Gnostic Gospels.* New York: Random House, 1979.

GR   Hans Jonas. *The Gnostic Religion.* Boston: Beacon Press, 1958.

HD   Adolf von Harnack. *History of Dogma.* 7 vols. in 4. Trans. Neil Buchanan. New York: Dover Books, 1900.

KC   Harold Bloom. *Kabbalah and Criticism.* New York: Seabury Press, 1975.

LI   Michel Foucault. "Language to Infinity." In Don-
        ald F. Bouchard, ed., *Language, Counter-Memory,
        Practice*. Ithaca: Cornell University Press, 1977.

MAP   Harold Bloom. *A Map of Misreading*. Oxford: Ox-
        ford University Press, 1975.

MM   Sigmund Freud. "Mourning and Melancholia." In
        The Complete Psychological Works of Freud, ed. and
        trans. James Strachey, vol. xiv. London: Hogarth
        Press, 1964.

NBLS   Neil Hertz. "The Notion of Blockage in the Litera-
        ture of the Sublime." In Geoffrey Hartman, ed.,
        Psychoanalysis and the Question of the Text. Balti-
        more: Johns Hopkins University Press, 1978.

ONT   Adolf von Harnack. *The Origin of the New Testa-
        ment*. Trans. J. R. Wilkinson. London: Williams &
        Norgate, 1925.

P   Abraham Heschel. *The Prophets*. 2 vols. New
        York: Harper & Row, 1962.

PR   Harold Bloom. *Poetry and Repression: Revisionism
        from Blake to Stevens*. New Haven: Yale University
        Press, 1976.

RS   Thomas Weiskel. *The Romantic Sublime: Studies in
        the Structure and Psychology of Transcendence*. Balti-
        more: Johns Hopkins University Press, 1976.

   Where poetry or prose by Collins, Gray, Wordsworth, or
Shelley is quoted, citations refer to the following editions:

Poetical Works of Gray and Collins, Ed. Austin Lane Poole.
Rev. Leonard Whibley and Frederick Page. Oxford: Oxford
University Press, 1937.

Wordsworth: Poetical Works. Ed. Thomas Hutchinson. Rev. Ernest de Selincourt. Oxford: Oxford University Press, 1936.

Shelley: Poetical Works. Ed. Thomas Hutchinson. Rev. G. M. Matthews. Oxford: Oxford University Press, 1970.

INTRODUCTION

Simply put, our post-Enlightenment dilemma and the burden of our modernity involve the apparent necessity of a
choice between the best interests of the past and those of the
present and future. As we will see, the fine critic and literary
biographer Walter Jackson Bate argues passionately that this
is a false dilemma, that there is no law of the arts determining that a deep appreciation of and involvement with the
great achievements of the past is inimical to creativity in the
present. Historically, however, the last two hundred and
fifty, perhaps three hundred, years have been remarkable for
the persistence of this belief (or fear) in both criticism and
literature. Today, as readers, teachers, and authors, we are
all familiar with and in some way influenced by the idea that
modern society and literary achievement are somehow antithetical, that we moderns are permanently alienated from the
nurturing sources of creative genius.

In our particular version of the battle between the Ancients and the Moderns, the familiar (ultimately Arnoldian)
defense of the tradition usually invokes the argument that at
the end of the Renaissance or thereabouts essential values
and beliefs identified with religious culture began to be sublimated into a developing secularism. The chief vehicle of
this sublimation was the tradition of secular letters, which
eventually emerged as an embattled repository of essential
values, alienated within but still speaking with some authority to modern society. Thus, the study of literature is justi-

fied as a means of renewing from generation to generation our contact with an essential source of values and as a primary means of individual and collective self-examination. Surely the great majority of American and British critics, whatever their present convictions, founded their careers in the shadow of this credo and to varying degrees continue to depend upon it.

Precisely because of this dependence, certain difficulties with such a defense of literary culture have come to seem particularly damaging to literary and critical practice alike. We began by citing the fear (the conviction in some quarters) that the use of literature as a means of instruction and source of value—that is, as a kind of cultural superego—has a devastating effect on its more anarchic, archaic role as a source of creative expression and renewal. This same respect for literature that seems to work against literary creativity also ruthlessly subordinates criticism to the "great" literature it examines. Unfortunately, a criticism largely confined to explications of authorial intention is powerless to address any of the problems apparent in its own practices or to reassess the role of literature in a modern society.

It is no secret that a great many literary people look on modern society with disfavor and tend to find confirmation of literature's role as a privileged source of values, a higher activity, in its distance from the vulgarity so apparent elsewhere. But such a view has certain (generally) unintended consequences. First, it implicitly devalues the contemporary as somehow tainted by its very modernity in relation to works safely insulated by time, which are more suitable objects of an essentially nostalgic impulse. Second, valuing literature *because* of its alienation from modern society can create an ironical, de facto alliance between literature's orthodox defenders and those who believe that the true genius of our modernity lies in commerce and technology and that, therefore, where literature cannot be made into a commodity or an instrument of propaganda, it should be segregated in the schools where it can be respected when it seems useful and condescended to for its pretensions when it does not.

There can be little doubt that our dependence on the idea that the value of literature is based, at least in part, on its alienation from modernity has done much to promote the irrelevance we purport to fear. Perhaps more threatening, however, is our ideological dependence on literature's alienation from itself. The notion of secularization includes the conviction that the forms and values of belief can be used and their salutory effects preserved in the absence of belief. Indeed, they are seen as more useful when disengaged from what is, after all, at worst mere superstition, at best something inherently limited by the impossibility of agreement. When literature becomes the repository of these secularized values, it too is viewed (and learns to view itself) ambivalently, as a means of instruction and self-examination and, like values themselves, as something tainted by the limitations of belief.

This ambivalence takes the form of a rigid distinction between criticism and literature that performs two contradictory acts of segregation simultaneously: (1) what is enlightened in literature is distinguished from what is suspect by including only the former in the legitimate subject matter of a disciplinary criticism; and (2) what is derivative and mutable (that is, subject to the conditions of our modernity) is distinguished from what is original and timeless. So literature is at once suspect and the origin of value, and criticism is at once the expression of our enlightened secularity and hopelessly inferior. Among the most bizarre results of our ambivalence is the fact that our conception of the usefulness of literature no longer requires that any more of it be written—a fact that has not been lost on contemporary authors. What I have called the familiar or Arnoldian defense is now so institutionalized as to constitute a seldom-spoken dogma, providing the largely implicit social and moral rationale for a variety of critical practice. This "dogma" manifests itself as an orthodoxy largely in the shared stance of outraged defender of the faith greeting potential challenges to the views I have outlined above. As if we had not already encountered irony enough, one consequence of the very success with which the orthodox defense (from now on, this is how I will refer to this particular combination of critical concept and moral stance) has been internalized even outside the academy is that knowledge of or engagement with literature is irrelevant to the firm (if abstract) conviction of its value.

These are metacritical, cultural difficulties that critical intentionalism, or the New Criticism, for all its contributions to close reading, is too self-limited to deal with. So the stage has been set for some time for an upheaval in the study of literature—an upheaval that seems to have arrived in the form of an influx of European ideas and methods (structuralism, deconstructionism, Lacanian psychoanalysis, *Rezeptionsästhetik*, etc.), accompanied by certain homegrown challenges to the hegemony of the New Criticism (revisionism, reader response criticism, pluralism, etc.).

Amid all the confusion, the charges and countercharges, claims and counterclaims, one thing is becoming clear: there can be no serious argument over whether simply to reject the orthodox defense, for, contrary even to its own protestations, it is now less a statement about the tradition than the tradition itself for at least the past one hundred years. Any Anglo-American criticism with pretensions to historical accuracy or canonical ambitions, whatever its metacritical orientation, must recognize that many of the "greats" have written in the shadow of and affirmed the principles of the orthodox defense and that, for better or for worse, it is a part of the professional identity of the individual critic. Thus, the best metaphor for our relation to the tradition is an Oedipal one—what can no longer be denied must be incorporated on the most favorable possible terms. This difficult wisdom (along with all our evasions) is the founding insight of Harold Bloom's revisionism.

According to Bloom, revisionism is best characterized by the poet's desire to discover an original relation to truth and thus to open the tradition and its texts to his own experience. As a process, revision involves a re-seeing, leading to a re-valuing, leading to a re-aiming. This last step might as accurately be called a reconciliation or restitution since, as the above definition implies, revisionism aims not at transforming truth and the tradition it sustains so much as reconciling us with it in an altered relationship. Bloom's historical model for such a revisionism is provided by religious heterodoxies such as the Jewish Kabbalah, which aims at opening up through revisionary interpretation a monolithic tradition and its seemingly complacent God to the people's present suffering, all the while taking pains to avoid any final, catastrophic loss of faith. For this reason, revisionism, however radical it may appear to be, is grounded in an intensely conservative attempt to defend the tradition from the consequences of its shortcomings.

If we are to fully comprehend the complexity of revisionism as a literary critical stance, we must resist the natural temptation to characterize it simply as an attack on the orthodox defense of tradition rather than on the tradition itself, for, as we have already noted, they are no longer easily or clearly distinguishable. Bloom, for example, insists strongly that statements about the tradition, attacks and defenses alike, are themselves a part of the tradition. In this way, he questions the ease with which the orthodox critic uses literature without being implicated in its fictionality—an ease ultimately based on that doubleness created in the tradition by the notion of secularization. But criticism itself, even literature as we conceive it, is based on secularization, so Bloom's revisionary insistence on the unity of the tradition after Milton is ultimately inscribed within a larger, orthodox historical design differentiating an earlier, more fertile phase of the tradition from a fallen modernity. Bloom's position, like all revisionisms, invites charges of self-contradiction, as it seems at one moment to attack orthodoxy while backhandedly affirming it at another. Such appearances are the inevitable product of a mind striving for creative freedom within a powerful tradition that has already been internalized as an aspect of creative identity.

Bloom's literary history, like Freud's psychoanalysis, recognizes that relations with the tradition are overdetermined, quite capable of sustaining internal contradictions, and only partially circumscribed by the comforting logic of either/or. To religious heterodoxy and Freudian psychoanalysis Bloom adds Nietzsche's philosophical deconstructions to complete the formidable arsenal he trains against the orthodox idealization of literature and literary relations—our cherished belief that poetry is the domain of light, something to be aspired to for the highest and most humane purposes.

In his now-famous tetralogy (*The Anxiety of Influence, Kabbalah and Criticism, A Map of Misreading,* and *Poetry and Repression*) Bloom makes his attack on our tendency to idealize literature by confusing it with the humanizing project itself. True to the double structure of revisionism, what frequently may seem like an attack on literature is firmly inscribed within a passionate love of poetry and an anxious concern for its fate. The young poet, Bloom argues, is chiefly distinguished by his more violent rebellion against the inevitability of death and consequent "Gnostic" drive "to be elsewhere." Specifically, this drive takes the form of the desire to be original, to surpass the achievements of his great precursors, and to transform the tradition in his image. Tragically, the very conditions of poetic election stand between the poet, or ephebe, and the fulfillment of his ambition.

Every poetic identity originates in the poetry of a precursor; there, for the first time, the young poet or ephebe (as Bloom calls him) discovers his desire to be a poet and the conviction of his potential. Thus, poetic identity is, from the beginning, as tied to the precursor as the child to the parent. Yet the very stature that allows the precursor to stand for the poet's own limitless poetic desire also makes him *the* representative of the authority of the tradition. The precursor is both a nurturing influence and a blocking agent, and the ephebe's relationship with him is marked by an incurable ambivalence.

In his famous revisionary ratios (clinamen, tessera, kenosis, daemonization, askesis, apophrades) Bloom traces the life cycle of the strong (that is, Bloomian) poet through a progressive series of defenses designed to evade the influence and authority of the precursor and assert the power and independence of the younger poet. In their rather self-conscious eclecticism, the very names of the ratios comprise a heterodoxy, and each strives to assert an identity between a poetic relationship or situation, a Freudian defense, a rhetorical figure or trope, and a concept drawn from religious or philosophical heterodoxy. Thus, poetic relationships and Bloom's own criticism are both inscribed within the heterodox tradition-within-a-tradition.

Certainly de-idealizing poetic relationships as defenses and the facility with which Bloom leaps from poetry to rhetoric, to psychoanalysis, to religion, to philosophy, and back again would have raised some eyebrows, but the intensity of much of the criticism that has been leveled at Bloom has much to do with two further aspects of his theory. First, since the elevation of literature is a bulwark of orthodox humanism, Bloom's identification of poetry with frequently archaic heterodoxies breaks down the distinction between orthodox and heterodox upon which the apparent ideological coherence of literary humanism (or any other system of belief from Christianity to quantum mechanics) is based. In Bloom's writings, orthodoxy and heterodoxy are not antithetical, or even symbiotic; they are antithetical *and* symbiotic. Thus, the familiar conceptual landscape of humanism is strangely altered.

Second, there is Bloom's sense of the inevitability of the poet's failure—a failure that stands for the failure of the humanizing project of secularization itself. Bloom argues that in apophrades, the final stage in the life cycle of the strong poet, he

> holds his own poem so open again to the precursor's work that at first we might believe the wheel has come full circle, and that we are back in the later poet's flooded apprenticeship, before his strength began to assert itself in the revisionary ratios. But the poem is now *held* open to the precursor, where once it *was* open, and the uncanny effect is that the new poem's achievement makes it seem to us, not as though the precursor was writing it, but as though the later poet himself had written the precursor's characteristic work.
>
> (*AI*, 16)

This looks very much like the wished-for, humane conclusion to the drama of poetic relations, in which the poet is, in the fullness of his mature strength, reconciled with the precursor and the tradition, which he can now afford to give their due. Yet Bloom seems finally unwilling or unable to assert the reality of this ending. The key moment, in which the ephebe becomes essential to the precursor and to the tradition, remains in the realm of "seems," an "effect" rather than a reality. In the last, decisive moment, poetry falls short of desire, not just in the poet's career, but in Bloom's argument, which is finally unable to assert positively the reality of what we desire from poetry or for it.

This is not surprising since Bloom's poetic psychology and his literary history militate against the fulfillment of poetic desire. Because poetic identity is so closely identified with the precursor, any diminution of the precursor that is more than mere seeming involves a consequent diminution of the later poet as well. In poems themselves, Bloom argues, apophrades is associated with metalepsis or transumption—a figure granting the later priority over the earlier. But, for a variety of reasons, he goes on to assert that poets after Milton are prevented from matching his success with this trope—no poet can surpass his precursor as Milton did his.

From the idea that poetry and individual desire are permanently separated, it is only a short step to the conclusion that the entire project of literary humanism—to find and/or create in literature an embodiment of a perfected human desire, against which we can measure and adjust ourselves and our institutions—is doomed to failure, is already a failure. This is the point at which Bloom's explicit theorizing rejoins the darkest, seldom-spoken fears of more orthodox critics.

It is no wonder that so many have reacted so violently against Bloom's views. Yet his melancholy over the eventual failure of poetry as we now conceive it, his dark view of literary history, coexists with a powerful yearning toward a poetic absolute, a visionary hope. Writing from within a tradition he finds critically deficient but which has already appropriated to itself our most powerful means of expression, Bloom represents his desire in the form of an intense negation of desire wherever it coincides with orthodoxy's weak idealizations. The provenance of this strategy—its dangers and its possibilities—is the burden of this study.

In Chapter 1, the first section, "The Failure of Secularization," continues and elaborates the argument sketched above, taking as its text Geoffrey Hartman's revisionary comparison in *Criticism in the Wilderness* of Bloom's revisionism with the more widely understood stance of T. S. Eliot. After Bloom, Hartman has the most complete and powerfully articulated revisionist stance in American criticism today. The juxtaposition of the two allows us to use each to point out the complementary strengths and weaknesses of the other, while giving us a clearer, more complete sense of revisionism's complaint against and relationship with more orthodox criticism. Despite their differences, and despite Hartman's greater involvement with and sympathy for the deconstructionism of Jacques Derrida, both men aim at transforming our understanding of the concept of secularization in terms that take into account recent developments in Europe but ultimately answer to the peculiar nature of the Anglo-American literary/intellectual tradition, so different from those of France and Germany.

In the second section, "Asceticism, the Kabbalah, and Gnosis," I explore the complexities of Bloom's treatment in *Kabbalah and Criticism* and *Agon* of these venerable heterodoxies as ancestors and analogues of his own revisionism. Bloom uses this relationship between his particular brand of critical modernism and archaic modes of interpretation to break down the barrier, represented for orthodoxy by secularization, between our rational, disinterested criticism and their highly interested and "superstitious" criticisms. In Bloom's accounts, the relationship is reestablished between interpretive questions and the dynamics of belief, the challenge of hope, the risk of despair. In this way, Bloom seeks to reinject an archaic urgency into the problematic of secularization and to make the divinatory element in literature once more a reputable topic of discussion.

Asceticism is Bloom's primary paradigm for the negative representation of desire common to the Kabbalah, Gnosticism, and modern revisionism. It also involves the perilous turning of desire against itself, which accounts for the bifurcated structure of revisionism in general and of Bloom's in particular. The uneasy relationship between the conservative and radicalizing elements of the revisionary stance is half-examined and, where Bloom's self-awareness falters,

half-acted out in his treatment of the tension between the
mainstream Kabbalah, an essentially conservative attempt
to revitalize the tradition in response to contemporary conditions, and a gnosticizing tendency internal to it, an essential part of its motive force, which threatens to subvert and
overturn tradition entirely. In this section, we see Bloom's
conflicts merge with those of the Kabbalists, and the tradition assumes an uncanny aspect of wholeness quite unfamil-
iar to us, accustomed as we are to taking refuge in the
fiction of an isolate modernity.

By the end of our basic examination of critical revisionism in Chapter 1, we find ourselves carried onto what is, at
least for the overwhelming majority of modern literary critics, alien ground: the origin of our Western tradition in the
convergence of and conflict among orthodox Jewish, Greek,
Gnostic, and Christian tendencies. Necessarily then, much
of Chapter 2 presents the exposition of the new broadened
context that Bloom brings to literary critical debate.

Thus, we begin with a historical review of the main
tenets of Gnosticism in its role as the heterodoxy posing
the greatest threat to emergent Christianity. What this review reveals is that from the very beginning, our tradition
is interpretive, revisionary rather than original, and that the
Gnostic tendencies eventually branded heretical are indistinguishable from the motive power for a Christianity clearly
distinct from Judaism. Both of these facts pose serious challenges to the notions, widely accepted as common sense,
that literature precedes and takes absolute priority over
interpretation and that gnosticizing tendencies such as
Bloom's are antitraditional.

The recognition that orthodox and heterodox are, in our
tradition, equally "original" provides the basis for a still
broader contextualization of contemporary critical conflict as
an episode in the history of canonicity, which is as ideologically central to the secular as it was to the sacred literary

tradition. What begins in the section "The Canon: Sacred and Secular" as a historical exposition of the origins and consequences of the formation of the authoritative Christian canon is modulated by means of discussions of Marcion, Freud, and Bloom's concept of transumption into the literary question of whether any later work can really fulfill or subsume into itself any earlier one—as, for example, the New Testament claims to fulfill the Old. Bloom denies that the New Testament fulfills the Old just as he denies that transumption, the rhetorical figure by means of which the later poet overcomes the influence of his precursors, has been fully available to any poet since Milton. As it turns out, transumption is variously Bloom's trope for the fulfillment *and* the failure of poetic desire, for the process of secularization, and for canonization.

The failure of transumption after Milton raises the question of whether true canonization is possible today, which brings us to a discussion of Michel Foucault's "library" as an alternative metaphor for the nature and source of modern literary authority. With an origin and an end firmly established, we return in the section "Canon and the Sublime" to a historical discussion of the consequences in the eighteenth century of the accession of the secular canon to central cultural authority, focusing on the new burden of the past, documented in Walter Jackson Bate's *The Burden of the Past and the English Poet,* and on the subsequent Romantic revisions of the vogue of the sublime examined by Thomas Weiskel in *The Romantic Sublime.* This discussion not only provides the middle term, linking earlier versions of canonicity to the library; it also provides background for the readings of Gray, Wordsworth, and Shelley that follow.

Chapter 3, "Romantic Losses," seeks to ground firmly in poetic practice the historical and theoretical themes developed in the earlier discussion—canon, the negative representation of desire, transumption, etc. In tracing the linked themes of desire and loss from Gray to Wordsworth to Shelley to Bloom, we can also plot the emergence of our modern, highly problematical relationship with originality as something we exalt and strive for mightily but which we no longer believe possible, at least not in any form that answers to the intensity of our desire. And thus we are finally brought to recognize that Bloom stands directly in the line of the great Romantics as the new and even more stringent practitioner of gain-through-loss.

It is frequently the case that gnosticizing and highly individual criticisms like Bloom's are most easily grasped when they are being put to use in some (perhaps equally gnostic) project. Thus, I have diverged from Bloom and substantially revised his literary history by regarding the decline of literature and the future end of poetry as necessary fictions—that is, they may still be true but they are, in any case, an essential part of our understanding of our own secularity and therefore not reliable witnesses. Bloom's conceptions of literary authority and creative desire remain firmly bound to a canonicity that he suspects may no longer be possible and that prevents him from venturing into the realm of the library to confront the challenge of reconceiving the hoped-for for very different conditions.

We need not repeat the error of exaggerating and mystifying our own modernity, of creating still another version of "secularization," in order to see that our enabling fictions have a momentum of their own, which may have carried us so far that it is now easier to reconceive literature than to continue defending it in its present form.

I wish to call into question Bloom's claims about the gloomy prospects of literature because they mark the point at which the intense identification of critic with poet gives way to a new distance—a shift in perspective that obscures even from Bloom his place in the Romantic tradition. The text that seems to me to stand luminously behind Bloom's ultimate de-identification with the poet is the "Arab dream" of *The Prelude* (Book V). In the dream, Wordsworth is at first the companion of a bedouin who carries with him the shell of a pure, absolute poetry. Suddenly, there is a sharp change in perspective, and Wordsworth is a distant spectator as the Arab flees before "the fleet waters of a drowning world." In this moment, Wordsworth declares for a poetic of sublimation and for his natural self and against the poetry of the absolute ancestral Word—of apocalyptic transformation. In this moment, he becomes modern, individual, original, and forever alienated from the poetic past. No matter how great a poet he becomes, that greatness cannot be reassimilated into the tradition on any terms but its own.

The de-identification built into the role of critical spectator is what distinguishes the critic from what he reads, criticism from literature; it is also the means by which we disqualify ourselves from the risks and rewards of striving within the tradition in exchange for the more solipsistic pleasures (and anxieties) of modern individuality. De-identification is an aspect of the genre in which we are writing rather than a statement about any actual distinctively modern state of affairs—merely a means of momentarily stabilizing the endless reversability of insides and outsides, orthodox and heterodox, that marks the tradition we all share. Yet we must concede that, since Wordsworth, criticism has largely succeeded in making real that modernity, that collective originality, it purports to describe. We are cut off and, as with any self-amputation, the condition seems permanent, even though the necessity of endlessly repeating the operation in the act of criticism suggests otherwise.

My obvious sense of Bloom's critical importance would not alone be enough to justify this book since, recently and at substantial length, others have explicated the essentials of Bloom's theory—Frank Lentricchia's *After the New Criticism* (1980) and Elizabeth Bruss's *Beautiful Theories* (1982) are two examples that come immediately to mind. Despite their strength in other ways, however, these efforts seem to me to lack any real sympathy with Bloom's project, any sense of its underlying significance. To put it as straightforwardly as possible, they apparently do not understand why anyone would want to write in such a way—inviting accusations of self-contradiction, esotericism, irresponsibility, etc.—and not in some other, more reassuring manner. It is this kind of comprehension I seek to supply, the kind we expect of ourselves when we read literature.

Bloom's work presents the spectacle of a historically established tradition of revisionism so worked over by a powerful creativity that nothing seems untransformed. Yet that creativity arises out of and returns to reside within the revisionism it augments and transforms. Bloom is a genuinely literary figure, not the least because our very conception of modernity tends to involve that intersection of literature with revisionism that he articulates. Striving to make an impact from within an authoritative tradition, the modern work of literature—poetic, novelistic, or critical—necessarily appears in some dimension as a commentary on its own predicament, the predicament of modernity.

As I have tried to suggest, I intend more here than an explication or critique of Bloom's views. To a wider, more skeptical audience, Bloom is most important because the entire phenomenon of revisionism shines luminously through his writings as through a prism. Bloom projects, more clearly and variously than anyone, the contradictions and conflicts inherent in our combination of a worshipful stance toward a high cultural orthodoxy and a tendency to identify greatness with the heterodox. This is the larger issue I seek to examine and from which, for the moment and to his credit, Harold Bloom cannot be clearly distinguished.

I

REVISIONISM AND CRITICISM

Since the publication of *The Anxiety of Influence* in 1973 introduced the heterodox religious terminology of the revisionary ratios (tessera, apophrades, etc.), Harold Bloom's theory of poetic revisionism and his own critical revisionism have been steadily refined. Along with this refinement and commencing with *Kabbalah and Criticism* (1975) there has been an increasing emphasis on ideas and terms originating in the Kabbalah, Gnosticism, and Neoplatonism until, in *Agon* (1982), Bloom is frankly professing an allegiance if not to Gnosticism then to gnosis.

Clearly, Bloom's commitment to gnosis is itself a revisionary gesture, apparently aimed at reoriginating criticism on some ground untainted by what Bloom and his friend and ally Geoffrey Hartman both consider the tired Neoclassicism of contemporary critical language. In Bloom's case, however, the revisionary project is undermined by a deep affinity for that melancholy view of poetic possibility— everywhere present in the works of the Sensibility Poets, submerged but still powerful beneath the countervailing optimism of the great Romantics—which is the key element in the literary tradition it seeks to revise. It is this fear, perhaps even conviction, that the myth of poetic entropy is stronger than that of poetic regeneration that causes him to share the literary history of Walter Jackson Bate's *The Burden of the Past and the English Poet*. Paradoxically, it is through Bate's very Longinian idealizing of literary greatness that his book becomes another instance of the malaise it describes. And it is similarly instructive that Bloom's revisionism, weighed down by his melancholy, can offer us no more optimistic a model of literary history.

From early predictions of the end of poetry in *The Anxiety of Influence* to forebodings about the death of textuality itself at the end of *Agon,* Bloom's revisionary poetic has been haunted by a melancholy with its historical and literary roots in the peculiar contradictions of eighteenth-century humanism. This melancholy seems to function as Bloom's own Covering Cherub, cutting off his vigorous, often exuberant criticism from any corresponding vision of literary possibility. Even worse, Bloom's very brilliance as a critic seems to prevent any examination of the relationship between his success as a revisionist and his underlying pessimism.

That Bloom's unprecedented success in challenging methods and assumptions based on weakly platitudinizing defenses of literature and criticism issues in nothing more positive forcefully reminds us that at the center of the whole post-Enlightenment tradition is the extreme difficulty of envisioning or even presuming a future for letters. This alone justifies the most careful examination of Bloom's work. But he also offers us this problem in a highly suggestive form, epitomized, I think, in the ambiguous status of his Gnostic and Kabbalistic terminology.

Insofar as he wishes to present himself as a critic, Bloom is surely not exhorting us to *believe* in the Kabbalah or Gnosticism when he employs their language and ideas. Yet these are languages of belief. Nor when he says, for instance, that the Kabbalah is the model for all subsequent revisionary poetics does Bloom appear to mean that revisionary critics, like Kabbalistic interpreters, interpret in order to preserve the possibility of belief. If he does mean this, it is at least obvious that the activity of criticism itself seems to require some distinction between the aims of sacred and secular interpretation, between their belief and ours. In short, such terms are always figures or, as Bloom would have it, tropes. Despite the variety of rhetorical articulations that Bloom imposes on this relation (I am thinking here of *A Map of Misreading*), all such tropes seem ultimately to refer us back, as the very ground of their possibility, to the enormously problematical notion of secularization.

Secularization or, as he sees it, the failure of the Enlightenment project of translating traditional religious values into a secular context, is a central concern of Hartman's *Criticism in the Wilderness*. The idea that religious values or ways of valuing can and have been translated more or less intact into a rational humanism through the historical process of secularization is fundamental to a tradition of critical discussion about the nature and value of literature including Matthew Arnold in the nineteenth century and M. H. Abrams today. Hartman is further distinguished as one of our most insightful commentators on the work of Bloom, and *Criticism in the Wilderness* contains his most sustained and broadly contextualized treatment to date of Bloom's revisionism and of his own. We now turn to that discussion as our starting point.

THE FAILURE OF SECULARIZATION

Fundamental to Hartman's purpose in *Criticism in the Wilderness* is a contrast between the tradition as understood by Bloom and by T. S. Eliot. In order to draw this comparison, he goes all the way back to Bloom's first book, *Shelley's Mythmaking* (1959), in which, he says, Bloom uses Shelley against Eliot much as Northrop Frye uses Blake. Shelley is "inserted into the line of great poets from whom a 'total form of vision' might be descried," yet his particular religion is "too radical for a Christian-Humanist synthesis," so Bloom turns to "a Jewish revision of late German Romanticism: to Martin Buber." Out of Buber's I-Thou distinction,

Bloom identifies Shelley's mythmaking with a lyrical process or relation, rather than with a static and determining "synthesis or redemptive iconography" (*CW,* 102).

But for all its emphasis on relation or process, Hartman argues, Bloom's understanding of Shelley remains deeply inconsistent since his historical reflection establishes Shelley's poetry "as a source of value by placing it in a monumentalized tradition"—that of the "great" tradition of English visionary poetry since Spenser. Although Bloom claims that Shelley stands "in a free relation to the mythmaking 'spirit' present before all myth," the value of that freedom is established only with reference to the highly iconographic myth of the great visionary tradition (*CW,* 103).

In his second book, *The Visionary Company* (1961), Bloom turns the imaginative freedom of Shelley's mythmaking into a critique of the old academic view of the Romantics as poets of nature. And, in his third book, *Blake's Apocalypse* (1963), "Bloom still insists on the freedom of the Romantic poet who creates new myths from old or 'revises' in a transcendent way Milton or the Bible." Yet this "protestant" liberty mingles with a Gnostic theme: the poet's suspicion of both imagination and nature, so that the notion of the precursor poet and the demiurge converge (*CW,* 104–5). Once this convergence occurs, Bloom's faith in the regenerative, mythmaking powers of visionary poetry begins to erode until, with *The Anxiety of Influence,* he is openly predicting the coming end of poetry.

If the "mythmaking 'spirit' present before all myth"— the visionariness present before there is a tradition of vision—is indeed inaccessible, then not only is the Romantic response to the pessimism of the late eighteenth century called into question, but the very purpose of the revisionary project as well. For if Hartman and the later Bloom are right, they can hardly be aiming at the reorigination of criticism outside (or before) the dominant tradition. Or, if they are, what they hope to achieve in the long run is not yet apparent.

Hartman's examination of Bloom's position today is placed in the context of a long treatment of Carlyle's *Sartor Resartus*, in which he argues that what is crucial for our understanding of that work is its "recovery of the relationship of criticism to enthusiasm—to the religious question—and its understanding of what is common to criticism and fiction" (*CW*, 50). In these matters, Carlyle is presented as a genuine precursor of the revisionist critics of today.

Hartman goes on to argue that criticism differs from fiction by making the experience of reading explicit. By intruding and maintaining the persona of the editor, reviewer, or reader, our struggle to identify or not with imaginative experience, usually a story, is worked through in the act of criticism. What this explicit examination of the reading experience reveals is that the psychological drama of reading centers on an "aroused merging: a possible loss of boundaries, a fear of absorption, the stimulation of a sympathetic faculty that may take over and produce self-alienation" (*CW*, 50).

It is this fear of merging, of falling into the text, that is responsible for the clear line between commentary and literature that contemporary criticism is beginning to blur. If we try simply to deny the reality of such an anxiety of merging, we risk a distancing defense, claiming that "all origins are fake or contaminated or (at best) motivating fictions." This defense, Hartman suggests, parallels Gnosticism's distinction between origin or pure good and the world—our world—created by a usurpatory demiurge (*CW*, 51) and raises yet again questions about the relation of criticism to fiction to theology. One might even say that it reveals the relationship between criticism and fiction to be a theological issue at base.

What Hartman refers to, of course, is the way in which

the Gnostics denied the orthodox account of origins by turning it inside out, by assigning events antithetical values, thereby avoiding a final fall into, for example, the text of Genesis. Of course such a liberating distance from the fictions of orthodoxy can lead to the extreme Gnostic optimism of Wordsworth's "by our own spirits are we deified." As Hartman points out, however, Wordsworth ends "But thereof come in the end despondency and madness"—the "dark obverse of the quest for originality and autonomy" (*CW,* 51).

Bloom, Hartman argues, approaches Gnosticism from its darker, Freudian side (*CW,* 52). In Bloom's view, expressed in his notion of misreading, every writer is a demiurge, defensively falsifying the canonized text of another writer/demiurge. Initially, in *Blake's Apocalypse,* Bloom regarded Blake as the arch-revisionist, defying the Bible itself, who used Gnostic arguments to deny ultimate authority to the biblical writings. Eventually, however, Bloom turned against this Gnostic optimism when he came to see that Blake was no less self-deceived than every writer who makes this claim.

If we step back for a moment, we can see that Hartman's treatment implies two very interesting points. First, it implies that the attempt to reoriginate—to return to a time before the creation, which is also a time before the first, creating word is uttered—is an attempt to return through the precursor text to the origins of textuality itself, in order to get outside the historically and culturally determined and determining paradigm of the text and repossess it as pure possibility. Blake's is a struggle to gain control over the power of textualization itself, and Bloom's conclusion that this is impossible, even for Blake, is also to conclude that it is impossible for consciousness to escape the paradigm of the text, as problematical and history-burdened as it is.

Second, Hartman's treatment further suggests that the notion of a single decisively authoritative reading (including the one intended by the author) is also dependent upon the belief that it is possible to get back beyond the historical origin of the text to that point at which we can determine the preconditions not only of the coming into being of texts but also of their readings.

Speaking for himself, Hartman presents critical reading as a defense against the "author/demiurge of that strange, wonderful, seductive reality we call a fiction" (*CW*, 52). More immediately, this may be seen as a defense against the danger of falling into the text. But it can be argued, as conservative critics will, that if we treat critical reading as a defense against the imposition of a demiurgic fiction, we merely open the way for the imposition of our own demiurgic fictions. From this point of view, which I think Hartman ultimately may share, critical reading might be seen additionally as our defense against the consequences of a successful defense against the author/demiurge—the danger of becoming demiurgic ourselves.

In Bloomian misreading, the danger of becoming demiurgic is what cannot be avoided. Bloom does not seem to grant criticism the lingering objectivity that Hartman does. Bloom's insistence that poet and critic alike as misreaders inevitably assume the demiurgic role suggests that we have already fallen into the text—that, like the Gnostic demiurge or Blake's Urizen, we are doomed to inadequate creation within a master text of which we have lost sight and thus cannot successfully revise.

Misreading, intended as a defense against identifying with demiurgic creation, is actually an indication that that identification has already been forced upon us as the precondition for entering the play of texts, which is why misreadings fail finally to be fully transumptive, to emerge into the new origin of a new tradition. This suggests in turn that, for Bloom, the text or textuality is demiurgic in relation to consciousness or, more precisely, to desire. In this context, each text represents, as a misreading, a gesture in the direction of a liberating gnosis that is defeated, either, as was just suggested, by the demiurgic nature of textuality or, more frighteningly, by a disorder in the very process of desiring.

Freud provides Bloom with his model(s) for the disordering of desire or demiurge-as-quality-of-consciousness, yet Bloom diverges from Freud in denying sublimation as a second chance. Perhaps Bloom's focus on the later, darker, and more literary Freud of *Beyond the Pleasure Principle* (1920) and after, and his insistence that Lacan is right in saying that it is Freud's literariness that is essential, indicate that underlying the disordering of Freudian desire is the demiurgic nature of the text.

This raises a question as to why Bloom insists on being a critic and writing from within or between texts. His melancholy may well be a consequence of this choice, although we can once again reverse our conclusion of the previous paragraph by pointing out that the choice reflects disordered desire as an attribute of critical consciousness rather than of the demiurgic nature of textuality.

Perhaps it is this inability to decide whether text or consciousness is responsible, whether the situation is contingent or inherent, that distinguishes Bloom from his Gnostic precursors as a Gnostic seemingly without hope, fallen into the great tradition and its Bible and unable to get past the alienation that is our inheritance from the eighteenth century in order to discover a modern, optimistic gnosis.

Hartman avoids these difficulties by placing his own emphasis not so much on the need to defend against the author/demiurge as against the arbitrary and disorienting power of fictionality: "Fictions, in this light, are fabulations that make us aware, by a kind of contagion, of the artificial or magical force of all constructions, including those of science" (*CW,* 52).

Both Bloom's misreading and Hartman's fictionality bring us back to the problem of secularization. If, as we have already observed, the distinction between a language of belief, however interpretive, and a secular critical language makes tropes of all translations from one to the other, then what Hartman's subversive fictionality threatens to reveal is the inauthenticity of the connections between secular activities and the archaic sources of the values justifying them. Similarly, Bloom's misreading is ultimately based on the failure of the secular to subsume the sacred. In Bloomian misreading, the misreading never becomes a fully transumptive trope of the original; it remains haunted by the now-daemonized form of the precursor. Thus, the very notion of misreading argues the failure of secularization, suggesting also that precisely where secularization fails is in relation to desire—our desire to envision a new end, appropriate to a secular age, for self and society. As long as the notion of secularization itself is not directly challenged, as Hartman seeks to do, this failure of desire to be satisfied necessarily appears either as a disordering of the process of desiring—a conclusion to which, as we will see, Bloom is led in *Agon*— or as evidence that the modern, secular world is permanently divorced from human values.

Such an understanding of what is implied in the concept of misreading also helps to clarify the reasons for Bloom's exceeding vagueness about when the present age of anxiety and necessary misreading began: the difficulty is identical with the difficulty of deciding when "secularization" began. Also, Bloom's own tendency to link the archaism of religious languages of belief with Freud's anthropological (*Totem and Taboo*) and instinctual (*Beyond the Pleasure Principle, Ego and Id,* etc.) versions of archaism seems, in many ways, representative of secular attempts to appeal to the archaic as an origin and authority for contemporary values, even while insisting that such appeals are merely "metaphorical." We might even go so far as to speculate that criticism is the very form of this ambivalence and that the traditional distinction between criticism and literature aims at defending secularization by maintaining the pretense that archaic/secular, superstition/knowledge, and ideology/fact are rendered clearly distinguishable by virtue of the fact that society underwent such a historical process of secularization.

Elsewhere in *Criticism in the Wilderness,* in a discussion of Wordsworth's "Resolution and Independence," Hartman contends that Wordsworth is tempted by the "quirkiness" of his own imagination to see the leech gatherer as an omen of a "more-than-natural intimation of a more-than-natural way of sustaining one's life." The threat is that Wordsworth will be misled by his own imagination to lose his bearings and see "heaven in a leech-gatherer and infinity in a handful of leeches" (*CW,* 30). This danger of being misled or deceived is also, according to Hartman, at the bottom of our need for complex reading as a defense against fictionality, all of which suggests that the Romantic imagination represents the first step in that internalization of the problem of fictionality that culminates in the dissemblings of the Freudian unconscious. Nor, I think, can we help but wonder if this fear of being deceived is not itself a historical product of the Enlightenment, with its emphasis on the accessibility of truth, the power of reason, and the inevitability of progress.

In any case, approached from this direction, Bloom's Freudianism stands revealed not as an arbitrary, retrospective imposition on Romantic and Victorian poetry but as a historical argument in itself, an admission that no critic, however vociferously he insists on the distinction between fiction and commentary, can excuse himself from the problematic of fictionality of which Romantic literature and Freudian psychoanalysis are equally a part. In addition, the mixture of theological and psychological ideas that many critics profess to find so disorienting in Bloom's work ex-

presses a recognition, also historical in nature, that, as a
defense against the disorienting powers of fiction, complex
or critical reading makes no sense except in terms of a history linking the whole question of the relationship between
text and commentary, fact and fiction, to the religious origins of our culture. It makes no sense because, as many
members of society have discovered, we can defend our conception of reality equally well (if not better) by refusing to
read at all or by confining our reading to a fiction so debased
in the direction of wish-fulfillment that it cannot possibly
pose any threat. The recognition of this fact, however subliminal, is somewhere near the root of the myriad predictions of the future end of literature that abound in literary
history from the eighteenth century all the way up to Bloom
himself.

If all this is true, we cannot but wonder why society
continues to maintain a mercenary army of professional
readers, a kind of standing audience, which it pays a respect-
able wage to do its serious reading and to continue grappling
with the difficult relationship between fiction and reality.
Here again, the answer must be historical; indeed, it is history itself. For try as they might, science and its Caliban,
social science, have failed to eliminate the need for the metaphor of history. The progress of knowledge still has little
relationship to the progress of society and culture in many
important respects. And so much that we are and hope to be
can still only be explained or justified historically.

History is itself the most powerful metaphor of our culture, and by "history," I mean that sense of events
connected and haunted by a sense of an invisible, perhaps
arbitrary, intentionality and not the easy assurance of progressivism. I mean that history that begins in a special relationship to the originating text of our history and culture,
the Bible. Our continuing dependence on the notion that
events have the power to confirm or discredit ideas and

actions bears witness to the failure of the Enlightenment project of secularization, of banishing archaism, and of separating the future decisively from the past. The battle between the Ancients and Moderns still goes on. Authority, where it does not depend upon simple force, still depends upon this history and its vehicle, the text, which have their common origin in the archaism that rational, secular, technological society has failed to abandon but succeeded in segregating in university departments of humanities, where students briefly do a kind of cultural national service before receiving their honorable discharges.

Events are haunted by this qualitative presence just as all texts are haunted by the specter of fiction, and events and texts are bound together historically, culturally, by the fear of deception—that finally, flatly, simply, we are deceived by experience and expectation alike; that our words, even our thoughts and feelings are lies; that God has not chosen the people of Israel or any other people; that judgment will never come; that time is leading us nowhere.

In essence then, Hartman argues, Bloom's revisionary ratios represent an attempt to codify the defense mechanisms that are equally characteristic of the creative writer and reader by virtue of a common tradition (*CW*, 53)—a tradition bestowing on each as an essential part of his own creative identity an awareness of the other's role in all its complexity. Nowhere does Bloom suggest that knowing that we read and write defensively excuses us from defensiveness. In this, Bloom is true to the history of knowledge or, to put it another way, to history as knowledge: good books do not necessarily make good people. He is much more honest than those who take recourse to the less vexing defense of insisting on a clear distinction between literature and criticism, which pretends that the destabilizing contagion of fictionality can be confronted generically, with the additional salutory benefit of excusing those who wrap themselves in the mantle of culture from responsibility for seeing to it that somebody (who is not paid for doing so) wants to or should want to read what they write.

Lest this seem merely another anti-intellectual attack on academic men of letters, let me hasten to add that the same defensive division frees other, nonacademic, writers from any responsibility for seeing to it that anyone *should* want to read what they write. The familiar game of mutual disparagement played by the representatives of the high and the popular cultures disguises a deep and fundamental cooperation, which yields to each precisely the kind of authority it most desires.

This superficial warfare between an authority based on high culture and a pure knowledge and that based on popular culture and pragmatic knowledge is at least as old as the conflict between Gnostic and orthodox tendencies in the early church, and it is a part of the history that the Enlightenment sought unsuccessfully to render irrelevant. However, to admit that the fiction/commentary distinction and its consequences are also genuinely historical is not to say that all such ideas are equally productive of a positive experience of events as history. In this case, it can be argued that Bloom's theological/psychoanalytic conception of our defense against history is more genuinely a part of the history of our self-consciousness about history than the fiction/commentary distinction, which is much more heavily implicated as a primary ideological vehicle in secular humanism's interest in obscuring such historical awareness. This is to say that, given a chance, the metaphor of history does yield a knowledge that answers to the qualitative demands that all men make on experience—but only if the element of self-deception, which is historically a part of all historical explanation, does not become too obtrusive. Any mode of historical explanation operates to privilege some questions and obscure others. But if the questions obscured come to seem more important than those privileged, the validity of histori-cal explanation itself comes into question.

Hartman continues to urge the importance of Bloom's attempts to bring into secular literary criticism parallels from heterodox religious movements, especially Gnosticism, as a means of revealing the heterodox (that is, Gnostic), self-sub-verting tendency in orthodox critical practice. In Bloom's psychotheology, Hartman argues: "The sourcy demiurge has to be at once incorporated and repressed by the new poet-demiurge," and "literary autonomy is conceived as a freeing of oneself from an influential master by a [self-] cur-tailment of sacrifice." "According to Bloom then," Hartman continues, "poetic history, at least since Milton, unfolds as a series of sacrifices" (*CW*, 53). This is so, but it is important to remember, as Hartman himself has already pointed out, that the freedom purchased by this sacrifice is illusory; there is no return to origins. Approaching this from a slightly different angle, we can see how Bloom's argument suggests that those critics who regard the revisionists' refusal to ac-cept any clear distinction between commentary and literature as a profanation of the Great Tradition do so in order to defend themselves from the knowledge that, historically, their particular brand of literary humanism has been haunted by the fear not that culture will be profaned but that no profanation will be sufficient to free a rational, secular study of letters from the archaism of literature.

Hartman sees in Bloom's revisionary ratios something akin to what is suggested by Walter Benjamin's "Theses on the Philosophy of History," which he quotes as follows:

> One would have to picture the angel of history like this. His face is turned toward the past. Where *we* perceive a chain of events, *he* sees one single catastrophe which keeps piling wreckage upon wreckage, and hurls it in front of his feet. The angel would like to stay, awaken the dead, and make whole what has been wrecked. But a storm is blowing from Paradise; it has got caught in his

wings with such violence that the angel can no longer close them.
This storm irresistably propels him into the future to which his
back is turned, while the pile of debris before him grows sky-
ward. This storm is what we call progress.

$(CW, 53-54)^1$

Benjamin suggests that the storm of progress blows the angel along too fast for the present to be used up in the living
or for the past to be redeemed in the present. As a result, the
past accumulates, burdening and threatening the future.
And, indeed, the refusal of the past to go away or to be
superseded has been the most vexing problem of historical
progressivism. Benjamin goes a step farther, however, suggesting that the progressive modern's emphasis on the future
actually enhances the power of the past by daemonizing it.
This brings us back, once again, to the reason for the inevitable illusoriness of the freedom purchased from the precursor by the younger poet's act of self-curtailment. The intensity of engagement involved in the precursor's subversion
daemonizes him and gives him a superadded power even in
defeat.

Hartman approaches the center of his interest in Bloom
when he compares him to Eliot in light of the observation:
"That criticism is a contemporary form of theology will
seem sadly obvious to those who object to its inflation"
(CW, 54). When Eliot calls his earliest collection The Sacred
Wood, he confesses what was to be a lifelong concern with
the relation of criticism and poetry to religion. In The Use of
Poetry and the Use of Criticism (1933) he recognizes that, since
the Romantics, the literary act has come " 'to be conceived
as a sort of raid on the absolute and its result a revelation.' "
(Eliot is quoting Jacques Rivière.) Yet, Hartman points out,
Eliot remains unclear as to "whether we preserve the sacred

---

1. This is Hartman's revision of Harry Zohn's translation in *Illumina-
tions*, ed. Hannah Arendt (New York: Schocken, 1969).

wood by staying outside or by raiding it," although he does at least acknowledge "that the greatest writers of the modern period have considered trespass or profanation inevitable" (*CW*, 54).

Even though a book like *Kabbalah and Criticism* scarcely seems to belong to the same world of discourse as Eliot's, *Kabbalah* is the Hebrew word for "tradition":

> The sacred wood in this instance is the Bible as "received" by medieval interpreters calling themselves Kabbalists, who claim that their understanding of the sacred text is a literal and orthodox one. It is clear, however, that they have penetrated the wood—now more like a jungle—and are wildly, sublimely conscious of the danger of profanation.
>
> (*CW*, 54)

Now Hartman reaches the center of his own argument:

> Profanation, as in Kafka's famous parable, is structured into the critical ritual, into the model as contemplated or applied. "Leopards break into the temple and drink the sacrificial chalices dry; this occurs repeatedly, again and again: finally it can be reckoned on beforehand and becomes part of the ceremony."
>
> What this means when we consider a canon of secular authors rather than the Bible is that the "spiritual form" (Blake) of the dead writers returns upon the living, like those leopards. It has to be incorporated or appeased by tricks that resemble Freudian defense mechanisms. And in this there can be no progress, only repetition and elaboration—more ceremonies, sacrifices, lies, defenses. That we esteem these is the woe and wonder that Bloom constantly commemorates. The literature of the past is an "unquiet grave."
>
> (*CW*, 54–55)

This certainly returns us to our earlier observation, that the problem for the secular critic is not to avoid profanation but to find a profanation sufficient to his purposes. Yet, incredibly, Hartman's analogy between the critical and the temple ritual ignores completely the whole point of Kafka's parable: the failure of the profanation to transform the religious ritual into something else. So how do we make the leap to the "critical ritual"? And what a multitude of crucial questions is avoided "when we consider a canon of secular authors rather than the Bible," not the least of which is by what means and at what cost the notion of canon is translated into so radically different a context. This is even more surprising since Hartman is perfectly aware of the difficulty, both critical and historical, with such acts of secularization-by-analogy. If *Criticism in the Wilderness* can be said to have a single theme, it is the confusion resulting from secular criticism's refusal to acknowledge or confront the lingering archaism of its own theological origins.

Despite his best efforts (which are very good indeed), Hartman is ultimately enmeshed in the same analogy he seeks to critique by a lingering belief that in the self-consciousness represented by criticism lies salvation from our present confusion. If Hartman seems perilously close here to orthodox idealizing, he remains distinguished as a revisionist by his insistence that it is not literature-as-defense but criticism as an awareness of literature-as-defense that offers us our best hope. Hartman achieves this qualified hope, a positive representation of the relationship with tradition, by accepting a final, tentative identification with the aims, if not the methods and rationalizations, of critical orthodoxy.

By contrast, Bloom's more extreme, more gnosticizing revisionary thrust refuses to find within the orthodox critical tradition any representation adequate to his desire, his aims for literature and criticism. Thus, his only recourse is to negative representations, dark forebodings of the end of poetry that serve as the negative signs of a wished-for new order. When representation and desire are set at odds in so radical a way, there arises the curiously indulgent melancholy, part pain and part pleasure, that marks much of Bloom's writing. In this context, we can see that Hartman is not quite right when he describes Bloom's loss of faith in the visionary possibilities of poetry. It would be far more accurate, I think, to say that under the pressure of an increasing awareness of the contradictions in the Romantic tradition and in the criticism that has grown out of it, Bloom has been driven to erect a massive system of negative representations in order to keep a visionary hope alive in the face of the manifest failings of the received tradition.

Hartman then argues:

> For Eliot, however, this return of the dead is limited by a trust in the established religious ritual and an urbane thesis of personal integration. The thesis is not naively progressivist, yet it flatters our capacity to bear or recreate the past without the distortion or *sparagmos* that Bloom insists is necessary. "The poet has," Eliot declares, "not a 'personality' to express, but a particular medium, which is only a medium and not a personality, in which impressions and experiences combine in peculiar and unexpected ways."
>
> (*CW*, 55)

How is it that "a trust in the established religious ritual" is a defense against religious archaism?—unless, of course, we assume that the nature and function of religious and critical ritual is fundamentally the same—that the demons haunting the religious mind are the same as those that haunt the secular, critical mind. But can it not be argued with equal cogency in light of the whole project of secularization that the demon haunting the enlightened mind is religion as a response to the secular mind's own archaic demons, demons which can no longer be acknowledged as such because they are aspects of an outmoded religious sensibility? It can, of course, be argued that ritual is religion's defense against itself or that, for Eliot, it is a discipline that protects him from the Romantic temptation to pursue the absolute. But this is to adopt a curiously alienated, post-Enlightenment perspective, a perspective that pays homage to the discipline of the past while emptying it of its distinctive content. This suggests that our primary means of flattering "our capacity to bear or recreate the past without the distortion or *sparagmos* that Bloom insists is necessary" is a covert, secularizing process of analogy that finally operates to obscure but not banish key distinctions. Consider, for example, the "return of the dead."

From a critical, secular viewpoint, the presence of the great dead is a perpetual problem, haunting every aspect of the living writer's practice. We may argue that the notion of resurrection is simply a way of buying off the dead and securing the present for ourselves with the promise of a future compensation. But clearly the religious person, sheltered in the church and shielded emotionally and intellectually by the doctrine of resurrection, is not in the same position of exposure as the secular artist. His problem is how to bury the dead; his religious counterpart's problem is how to resurrect them.

Eliot's primary defense against the past is, as Hartman points out, his formalism, of which an attachment to ritual is one aspect. Yet such an attachment to religion is, for a modern mind, fraught with contradictions and cannot for this reason simply be explained away as a "defense." In its positive aspect, Eliot's profound attachment, whatever the potential contradictions, to religious belief reflects his recognition that the project of secularization has been, in one important respect at least, a failure. The secular mind's continued attachment to the absolute, however impersonalized (Deism), or egoized (Romanticism), or psychologized (the unconscious), reflects a failure to define a new, uniquely secular end for the self and society, a conception of human success that does not originate in and tie us to a divinity-haunted past.

As for the generally defensive nature of Eliot's formalism, Hartman points out: "The corpses that sprout and speak in

The Waste Land are carefully reduced to voices moving sym-
phonically through a poem that acts as their requiem" (*CW*,
55). The poem exists as much to segregate and mute the
power of the dead voices as to preserve it. Hartman goes on
to observe, I think with great penetration, that "Eliot does
not deny our intellectual and spiritual burdens, but he would
like critics and poets to meet them as problems of craft, translation, and verbal digestion" (*CW*, 58) and, further, that

> Eliot is not concerned with intellectual revolution or a medium-
> istic profaning of the dead, but with purifying the language,
> with enabling it to digest—if it must—a "heavy fund of histori-
> cal and scientific knowledge." One result of this conservatism is
> a distrust of "ideas," that is, excess baggage of a spiritual or
> intellectual kind. Allegory that tends to overload language either
> by pictorializing the newest science (e.g., Newtonianism in the
> eighteenth century) or reconciling an archaic with a more re-
> fined form of belief (Christian typology, Spenser's "dark con-
> ceit")—allegory as free-form science or free-form theology—is
> subdued to a poetics of the image. Eliot's conservative Modern-
> ism identifies the poet's critical or intellectual ability mainly
> with that of purification, the filtering out of "mere ideas" or
> technical terms not yet polished into poetic diction.
>
> (*CW*, 57)

Eliot's poetics of the image presents itself as the "purification" of an "overloaded" language, defending poetry against
infection by "pseudoscience" and resisting attempts at an easy
reconciliation of archaic and refined forms of belief. But "purification" might as well be replaced by "segregation" since the
concern with a language proper to poetry can result and, to a
substantial degree, has resulted in literature systematically
stripping itself of concerns that preserved its intellectual importance for centuries and surrendering them to social science. As a consequence, literature becomes the ghetto in
which ideas and beliefs cast off as archaic in the march of
secular humanism are segregated. A poetry that refuses the
"oversimplification" of archaic belief or knowledge finally

presents itself as the means by which the Moderns gain the upper hand over the Ancients by standing between the past and present and segregating them in the name of purity.

Eliot's remark, "The dead writers are remote from us because we know so much more than they did," is in itself a capsule summary of the eighteenth-century humanist's belief, fearful or gleeful, that the social importance of poetry—its historical role and power—was being superseded by the role of knowledge and the power of secular reason. In the context of this disturbing echo of the Enlightenment, Eliot's addition—"and they are what we know"—seems less obviously an "unexpressed theology of communion or psychology of incorporation" (*CW*, 55). Or perhaps we may say that critic and poet alike are being incorporated into the realm in which the archaic elements of the humanistic mind are segregated. Yet the archaic can only be segregated, not destroyed, for, as I have suggested, our conceptions of human success, the very form of our desire, remain archaic as well. Hence, in a society that eschews superstition and exalts reason, nothing is more socially acceptable than a superstitious awe of culture. This superstitious awe is the exact opposite of a calm assurance that the metaphor of history continues to work, which I believe the statement strives to express.

Ideally, we could see in this statement assurance that the metaphor of history offers us knowledge against the dead as it offers resurrection to the dead through our knowledge of them. But such a view is at odds with the entire project of purification, which bespeaks a futile desire both to be reconciled with the past as a source of authority and to defend against it as a distant reality with insistent claims on the present.

In dramatic contrast, Hartman points out, Bloom makes an attempt to reject both Eliot and what the French call the "Sciences of Man," and, as a result:

The entire enterprise of criticism becomes unreal: no longer a distinct, well fenced activity, delimiting mine and thine. The critic does not pretend to forget himself in the work of art, as the artist had presumably done in creating it: the consciousness of tradition produces something quite different from the "extinction" of personality Eliot sought as his ideal. It makes every strong literary personality of the past into Hamlet's father's ghost, a revenant and a "questionable shape."

(*CW*, 58–59)

In other words, the critic is plunged back into history, deprived of the illusion that history stops just short of the present in order to present itself for objective contemplation—an illusion that takes the form of a conviction that the modern or contemporary is always more unlike the past as a whole than any two moments in the past were unlike each other. So now even the claim that the integrity of the past must be protected by guarding against its too-easy assimilation reveals at its base the more fundamental fear that the present really will prove to be at one with the past, and that the analytic vantage point, the perspective of distance or difference from which the modern views history, will be lost.

When the unique status of modernity is called into question and history comes flooding back in, "a ghostly and tricky dimension enters which plays havoc with the established rituals of criticism" (*CW*, 58). But the established rituals of criticism are revealing themselves to be a mirror that reflects on both sides: from within the field of literature as it has come to be understood, it reflects archaism back at archaism; from outside the field of literature, it reflects modernity back at modernity. From within literature the threat is that the mirror will be shattered and that modernity, in the form of the extrapoetic, the impure, will come plunging through. From without, the threat is that archaism, religion, or something much worse will engulf a "rational" modernity. Transmission from one realm to another occurs only through the ambivalence of the critical commentator: the disciplinary goal of purifying literature of the extraliterary (that is, whatever would link it with some other, modern discipline) commits him to the archaic, where he finds confirmation of his activity's value; on the other hand, the stance in relation to history, the alienation that makes the whole program of purification possible, is, in its turn, dependent on the critic's personal status as a Modern with everything that that implies ideologically.

For Hartman, Bloom is engaged in "accusing poetry in order to save it":

> Or, to use a related figure, he engages on a Faustian wager against poetry, one that seeks to break the illusions of art by subjecting them to the extremest, the most reductive aspects of Freudian and Nietzschean analysis. He will not believe that art is consolation, or that poetry can endure as an abiding force unless it survives a greater degree of probing than the New Critics, even with their criterion of toughness, applied.
>
> (*CW*, 61)

In doing so, Hartman continues, Bloom uncovers the "offensiveness" of poetry and acknowledges "that its greatness has not been integrated into our lives" (*CW*, 61). All this may be so, but we can go even farther to say that Bloom confronts the professional critic with the suggestion that he does not *want* the difficult greatness of poetry integrated into our lives—that, like his colleagues in other disciplines, he wants it confined to Literature where it "belongs."

Through his notion of misreading, Bloom demystifies reading and writing in a single stroke, exposing at once the archaism lurking in the modernist critical stance and the antiliterary modernism lurking in the superstitious inflation of literary values. As a result, archaist and modern are both plunged back into the universal solvent of history—a fate that they embrace no more enthusiastically than the Hebrews of the Old Testament greeted the prophets' declarations that history was not yet over and their fate not yet decided.

When Hartman casts Bloom as a kind of ascetic, whose de-idealizing scourgings represent a way of "accusing poetry in order to save it" (*CW*, 61), we may suspect Hartman of some idealizing of his own since he ignores the fact that Bloom has no apparent confidence in poetry's salvation. In ignoring this rather dark difficulty, Hartman seeks to evade the archaism that he has exposed and emphasized—the same archaism that Bloom embraces and in which other critics are unwittingly trapped by their illusions. Hartman retains a residual commitment to the Enlightenment notion of salvation through progressive refinements in self-consciousness— a hope he shares with those he criticizes most sharply and which prevents him from following Bloom onto his own archaic ground.

In the context of Hartman's own revisionism (even more so in the case of Bloom's) such a faith seems more of a defense against hopelessness than a vision of some possible future, and Hartman's maneuverings to put a positive face on Bloom's apparent pessimism about the prospects of poetry serve only to emphasize how small a claim literary knowledge, as it is currently understood, actually makes on the future. No less than more conventional critics, revisionists tend to define themselves in terms of the author/critic's relation to the past, presenting criticism as a purely retrospective mode of knowing.

In *Criticism in the Wilderness,* Hartman and, through him, Bloom present several alternatives to the idealizing Longinian model of our relationship to the literary past, which has dominated critical orthodoxy since the eighteenth century. Bloom's by now quite familiar model is that of Freudian defense, notably the repression that never quite succeeds and thus opens itself up to the return of the repressed. Since Bloom denies the reality of the Freudian second chance or successful sublimation, there is no way for the poet to convert a retrospective knowing of his precursor into a prospective knowing of a possible future of his own. When Bloom argues that the precursor comes into being only in the misreading of the ephebe, he is admitting that the closest the revisionist can come to envisioning a future is to represent himself as someone else's future, the fulfillment of a past prophecy.

To Bloom's model of psychic defense Hartman adds those of ritual propitiation and asceticism. If, as was suggested earlier, literary history is to be seen as a series of sacrifices, these two modes of sacrifice have rather different implications. If the poet's self-curtailment is a ritual propitiation, then misreading is a straightforward defense against the burden of influence. Yet the element of self-wounding, which goes well beyond simply offering up something of value, a ritual substitute, is far more similar to the stance of the extreme ascetic who accepts no ritual substitutions.

The ascetic wills against desire in order to defend it from a catastrophic disappointment. In the case of literature this may involve defending a desire to see it as something self-renewing and of permanent value by positing its inevitable decline. From such an ascetic perspective, the anxiety of influence and the entropic literary history it implies are a defense of creative aspiration in the present—a notion explored by John Guillory in his splendid, as yet unpublished essay, "Figurations of Minority."[2]

As the primary means of creative freedom's defense, the death of literature receives extraordinary valorization, almost as if, in the absence of a vision of the future of literature based on a convincing account of its social role and value,

2. Parts of this essay have appeared in *Critical Inquiry* 10 (1983), 173–98.

the pain occasioned by the thought of its death is the sole guarantee of its worth. Requiring that we will what we do not desire, asceticism tends to be marked by the alienation of desire from itself, by an inauthenticity that calls desire into question. In this connection, it is interesting to note that when Hartman defends against Bloom's apparent pessimism by arguing that Bloom is testing what he loves in order to establish its greatness, Hartman in effect defends him by saying that he doesn't mean it—an alienation of intention from intention, of desire from desire, of language from language that strikes to the heart of critical revisionism as that which embraces this alienation in order to defend against it. And all of these lurking inauthenticities point back in the direction of our earlier observations about secularization, suggesting perhaps that revisionism, contrary to what Hartman maintains, defends secularization against itself.

So now we are in a position to see that, among other things, revisionism may be the ultimate defense of a beleaguered tradition's authority against our excessive demands upon it. This is certainly true of the Kabbalah as a revision of the orthodox rabbinical tradition, as we will see. And we should remember that Bloom's literary history actually strengthens the distinction between a "modern" present and a fundamentally different "archaic" past on which many of the pretensions of a rational, disciplinary criticism are based. Similarly, Bloom dissolves the myth of a clear criticism/literature distinction because it is a less effective basis for critical authority and literary value than the equally mythical archaic/modern distinction.

If, as Hartman insists, criticism is ritual propitiation with profanation built in, it is highly conservative profanation whose effect is to renew the need for that which it profanes. Revisionism can then be seen as tradition's last and strongest line of defense, in which a privileged qualitative distinction between then and now becomes not a loss but a liberating difference taking criticism as its form.

THE NATURE AND LIMITS OF REVISIONISM: ASCETICISM, THE KABBALAH, AND GNOSIS

It should be clear by now that Bloom's revisionism is more extreme, and more extremely conservative, than Hartman's. In order to investigate more thoroughly the implications of this revisionism, I want to return to the topic of asceticism to examine it more deeply both as a historical phenomenon and as the topic of some of Bloom's most interesting remarks in *Kabbalah and Criticism*.

By the fourth century, the ascetic movement, largely precipitated by the very success of the church, came to pose a fundamental threat to the institutional authority of the Christian bishops. The decline of persecution and the rapid spread of Christianity greatly increased the diversity of the congregations, especially after the growing wealth and power of the bishops had made conversion advantageous for reasons of patronage (*EC*, 174–77). What they perceived as the secularization and corruption of the church prompted many of its most militant members to withdraw in order to pursue their spiritual goals undistracted. Henry Chadwick tells us that theirs

> was a theology dominated by the ideal of the martyr who hoped for nothing in this world but sought for union with the Lord in his passion. Just as the cross was God's triumph over the powers of evil, so the martyr shared in his triumph in his own death. The ascetics continued this spirit after the persecutions were past. They strove to achieve the same self-sacrificing detachment from the world. The evangelical demand for sacrifice, however, was fused with attitudes toward frugality and simplicity inherited from the classical past. The Monastic movement had room not only for simple folk but for men educated in the tradition of Plato and his ideal martyr, Socrates, in the cynic principle of

self-sufficiency, and in the stoic doctrine that happiness consists in suppressing the desire for anything one cannot both get and keep, and therefore demands the suppression of the passions for a life of right reason.

(*EC,* 177)

In addition, the ascetic sense that the presence of others hinders the soul's movement toward God, which, according to Chadwick, is based on such Neoplatonic ideals as "the flight of the alone to the alone" (*EC,* 177), encouraged not just the renunciation of fleshly indulgence but of society as well.

Generally, the ascetic identification with the martyrs did not involve the actual embrace of death but the endurance of lesser sufferings in symbolic substitution. They suppressed lesser desires in the hope of fulfilling a greater desire. Dangerously, they thus created a rupture in desire itself, such that it was the path at once to eternal truth and to catastrophic error. Beyond this they put themselves in the position of desiring what, in the cases of the original martyrs, was valuable because endured against all desire. Desiring to re-create an *agon* or struggle that was the result of circumstances belonging to another time, they drastically reduced the experience of the martyrs to its most literal and accessible aspect—agony—which became perversely valuable apart from the real necessity that gave it meaning.

Such a mentality must be driven to even greater negativities by a need to defend against the sense of inauthenticity engendered by the difference between wounds endured and wounds self-inflicted. In its relation to history, asceticism clearly involves an effort to create the kind of continuity that, despite its best efforts, reveals rather than hides a still deeper conviction that there really is an absolute difference between then and now. Thus, asceticism defends the value of Christian martyrdom only at the cost of confirming its irrevocable unavailability in the present. This, of course, is not unlike defending literature by prophecying its end or insisting that we should value great books because, in the immediacy of our possibilities, we are permanently cut off from that greatness.

The resemblance between the asceticism flowing out of the success of Christianity and the critical tradition growing out of secular humanism is not coincidental. Both are revisionisms seeking to guarantee the continuity of tradition, or, at least, of its "essential" aspects, in the face of their own oppressive sense of the present as a hostile, if not totally alien, environment. In the case of asceticism, as Chadwick points out, classical elements actually running counter to the essential spirit and doctrines of the new religion find a place, first, in Christian consciousness, then in Christian institutions, as the church grudgingly and suspiciously accepts monasticism. The coexistence of such an incoherent combination of conflicting values not only introduces a kind of permanent instability into the church but, in consequence, also drives it into an increasingly extreme series of revisionisms, culminating in the Reformation.

The countervailing source of stability upon which the very possibility of the church is based is the canonical Bible. Also a revisionism, canonization is distinguished from asceticism's personal, internalized conception of value by its focus on an externalized, institutionalized basis for valuing. It is most instructive to recognize that, from one point of view, the ascetics subverted canonical authority by taking it too literally, by seeking to recover in literal form the closeness to God, spiritual urgency and catharsis in suffering, and even the prophetic inspiration associated with the apostolic and classical era of Christianity, from which subsequent Christians had been permanently cut off when the canon put an end to authoritative prophecy and established a metaphorical distance/similarity relationship between the Christian past and present. The church and all its living members resided in this metaphoricity, which sustained and was sustained by their community. It was precisely this community, based on the orthodoxy defining the relationship between an idealized past and its metaphorical transformation in the visible institutions of the historical present, that was threatened by ascetic literalism. This asceticism, rather than being a mode of participation in the Christian community, was a mode of differentiation, isolating each ascetic within his own asceticism and involving the transformation of salvation into a personal rather than a communal/historical event and the rejection of the metaphor of history by means of which the Christian community achieved its collective identity.

In this context, we might venture to suggest that "Bible" signifies a certain paradigmatic symbiotic relationship between canonical text and community. In *The Elements of Semiology,*[3] Roland Barthes clarifies his notion of "writing" by arguing that it corresponds with a view of "idiolect" as a community of individuals interpreting linguistic statements in the same way. If "writing" then signifies a common mode of interpreting—a community of interpreters—then canon or canonical text can be taken to signify not a collection of discrete texts or a text so much as the object of interpretation as it is defined in order to sustain a community of interpreters.

If the Bible is the paradigm of the text in our culture and history, the distinctions between objective and interpretive conceptions of the Bible, between institution and community, ramify through all subsequent representations of the text. The objective, discrete conception of the text is fundamentally institutional in nature and in our Anglo-American, New Critical tradition finds its justification in pedagogy—the institutional, conventional form of knowledge (that is,

3. Trans. Annette Lavers and Colin Smith (New York: Hill and Wang, 1978), p. 21.

mass education demands that culture be available despite cultural ignorance). The difficulty with such a discrete, institutional conception of the text is in the ease with which it renders interpretation not only irrelevant but incomprehensible to the community it purports to sustain. We will skip over the too easy example of pointless and numberless (not to mention devastatingly predictable) New Critical readings to consider the more urgent example of writing instruction, ostensibly taught as an indispensable element of participation in our cultural community. Yet so artificial is the standard of quality in such classes, so exclusively relevant to the institution of the university classroom, that as many times as not, the effect is paradoxically to enhance the alienation of institution from community and of individual from both.

The alternative is a more diffuse conception of the text as something that exists only in the interpretive communities it sustains. Bloom begins from such a conception but rapidly narrows it in his notion of misreading so that the text exists only in and through subsequent texts that are necessarily misreadings—that is, confirmations that no community is possible. Thus, Bloom defends against an institutional hardening of the possibilities of the text by an even more extreme ascetic denial of possible community.

In *Kabbalah and Criticism,* Bloom discusses in some detail Nietzsche's argument in *The Genealogy of Morals* that the ascetic ideal was the only means man had ever found to give meaning to suffering:

> The ascetic ideal had kept man from nihilism, saving the will but at the expense of guilt, a guilt involving hatred of common humanity (with all natural pleasure). For the ascetic ideal is an interpretation, one that in turn inspires a change in the process of willing. This change signifies "a will to nothingness, a revulsion from life," yet still a purposefulness. Life thus uses asceticism in a struggle against death. Nietzsche, magnificently contrapuntal, attains a triumph in antithetical thought by declaring

that to be ascetic is thus to be life-affirming. The artist in particular transforms the ascetic ideal by incarnating "the wish to be different, to be elsewhere." . . . To be different, to be elsewhere is a superb definition of the motive for metaphor, for the life affirming deep motive of all poetry.

(*KC,* 51–52)

In the Nietzschean view, the ascetic's revulsion from life, based on his interpretation of it as a spectacle of suffering and death, ultimately poses the purposiveness of its own withdrawal against the nihilism connected with the negating power of death. In effect, asceticism poses the death instinct against itself in a kind of spiritual jujitsu. Everyone suffers and dies, but by willing his own suffering and thus embracing death, the ascetic thinks to make these the signs of his election, the validation of his spiritual integrity. Because this act of will involves assuming a stance antithetical to the community, the act that denies that the suffering and death of the individual ascetic are a punishment necessarily implies just that for everyone else, effectively negating what, for orthodoxy, is the redeeming aspect of the myths of the Fall and of Original Sin: a delicate ambiguity, emphasizing now one, now the other, over whether suffering and death are conditions of our historical being for which we cannot be held responsible or experiences which we have personally failed to redeem in the inadequacy of our willing.

In his poem *Milton,* William Blake, English literature's greatest student of the ethics of redemption, takes that great poet to task for believing that he can achieve his personal redemption through his disgust with and renunciation of the temporal community and makes the ascetic/solipsistic artist renounce his heaven-for-one in order to return and bend his magnificent will to the task of collective redemption. Blake displays a profound understanding of the kind of danger represented by the ascetic emphasis on the individual will. As an interpretation that reduces the ethically significant dimension of human behavior to the willful embrace of suffering and even death, it grants these realities a special status as absolute measures of value, which replaces with death the New Testament's emphasis on the moral imperative to love as the basis for all valuing. Thus, an ethic is created in which suffering is always seen as more substantial, less illusory than joy, and a kind of balance is tipped away from mere mourning over the objective losses of existence toward a melancholy or perhaps even a melancholia, in which life itself becomes our narcissistic wound, the hated/loved object of our ambivalence.

At one point, Bloom refers to "the fundamental human problem at the heart of all influence anxiety, which is the deep, hidden identity between all psychic defense and the fear of dying" (*KC,* 84). Asceticism, interestingly, is anxious not about poetic influence but about reality influence, almost as if by avoiding the community, one could avoid the common fate of human beings.

The importance of asceticism for *Kabbalah and Criticism* and for Bloom's theories in general hinges on his connection between the ascetic impulse and the impulse to metaphor. As I have already suggested, the impulse to be elsewhere is not necessarily ascetic or life-affirming, raising the question of why such a connection is an integral part of his argument, introducing as it does the central section of his book.

Bloom's concept of metaphor, like his concept of Jewishness, is diasporic—an infinitely mobile, errant one, in which meaning wanders from trope to trope by a continuous process of rhetorical substitution. Death is the most literal, the most irreducible, level of meaning, and thus trope, with its seemingly infinite possibilities for substitution, defends against that literality (*KC,* 90). For meaning to reside within poems instead of between them is thus to arrest the play of tropes and make of every act of literary interpretation either the death of the text it interprets (by substituting itself successfully) or a failure by definition (by its failure to substitute itself successfully).

Superficially, then, it may appear that the survival of literature depends on the failure of interpretation, the inevitability of misreading. Similarly, it might be argued that the triumph of interpretation necessarily involves the death of literature. Thus, Bloom's "misreading" and the eighteenth-century conviction that the progress of reason is the death of poetry are sides of the same coin.

Bloom's model for the defensive substitution of trope for trope, or of reading for original, is that of psychic defense. Unfortunately, like all psychic defenses, tropes against literality are invariably incomplete, serving to emphasize the presence of what they intend to defend against. The errancy of meaning and, hence, of knowledge may indeed defend against the reduction of all knowledge to the knowledge of death, yet by virtue of its very incessant movement from the Kabbalah, to psychoanalysis, to philosophy, to history, to literature, and so on, Bloom's interpretation nevertheless has the effect of reappropriating all knowledge that falls within its purview to the knowledge that we must die.

The failure of substitution at the rhetorical or interpretive level is good because it allows the play of tropes that defends against the literality of death to continue and thus allows literature to go on. It is dangerous for two reasons: (1) every substitution is a risk, holding out the possibility of a catastrophic failure if it succeeds too well; and (2) it leads us to embrace our own failure as the price of survival. Put bluntly, one must continuously foresee the end of literature as the price of its survival.

If literal meaning brings the play of interpretation to an end and presents the stasis of death as the measure of meaning, it is by no means apparent that reducing meaning to that which resists the reduction of meaning to the knowledge of death is the solution to the problem. If the complex ethics of asceticism suggest anything, it is that such an extreme defensive reaction threatens to make itself a reflection of what it seeks to avoid and a parody of what it most values. In Bloom's case, he articulates a theory of poetic defense that puts the fear of death at the center of literary and interpretive awareness. Yet it must also be said that no critic is more aware than Bloom of the formidable spur and block to the development of an adequate ethic that is represented by our continual hunger for compensation, made even more powerful by our reluctance to acknowledge what we wish to be compensated for.

Nevertheless, as a critic, Bloom appears to be in the almost impossible position of wishing the falseness of his own theories, or of insisting in some way on their inauthenticity, if not in the making then in the reception. After all, if they are flatly and accurately descriptive, they fulfill the catastrophe they prophecy. This is not, I must emphasize, the function of any perversity on Bloom's part but of the perverse position of interpretation in post-Enlightenment letters. We turn now to a closer examination of *Kabbalah and Criticism* and *Agon* in order to see how Bloom seeks to cope with this perversity.

At the center of *Kabbalah and Criticism* is a distinction between the Kabbalah and Gnosticism—a distinction that Bloom has a great deal of difficulty maintaining for complex and difficult reasons. The distinction is based on the fact that mainstream Kabbalists "sought *knowledge,* but unlike the Gnostics they sought knowledge in the Book" (*KC,* 47)—they were Bible-centered. For these orthodox Kabbalists, it remained a mode of intellectual speculation and not a means of access to a godlike knowledge indistinguishable from power or, perhaps, to God himself:

> By centering on the Bible, Kabbalah made of itself, at its best, a
> critical tradition, though distinguished by more invention than

critical traditions generally display. In its degeneracy, Kabbalah has sought vainly for a magical power over nature, but in its glory it sought, and found, a power of the mind over the universe of death.

(*KC*, 47)

As "at its best, a critical tradition," Kabbalism appears to receive Bloom's endorsement for accepting a principle of limitation that Gnosticism does not. Certainly we are encouraged to see in the Kabbalistic division between a Book-centered orthodoxy and more radical, gnosticizing tendencies the analogue of a deeply divided modern secular tradition, equally trapped if not so obviously in the Book, then in books, and also vainly trying to extend its power into the extraliterary realm (or defensively rejecting such efforts as if heretical) in order to conceive how, now that the Bible is no longer everything, mastery in and over books can be mastery over anything else. For modern criticism, the implicit goal is not magical power but the influence, social legitimacy, and claim on the future of social science.

If we accept Bloom's implicit analogy between the Kabbalistic and the modern critical traditions, it is clear that the limitation he appears to endorse in the Kabbalah is experienced as a frustration by at least some modern critics, including Bloom himself. This impression is borne out by the fact that, from the very first, Bloom is developing within his exposition of the orthodox Kabbalah a revisionistic, Gnostic Kabbalah that answers more clearly to the plight of the modern revisionist critic—a radicalizing revisionism within a revisionism.

Initially, Bloom characterizes the Kabbalah as "a struggle between Gnostic and Neoplatonic tendencies, fought out on the quite alien ground of Judaism, which in its central development was to reject both modes of speculation" (*KC*, 15–16). Just a few pages later, Bloom refers to Gnosticism and Neoplatonism as "the starting points for the more comprehensive vision of Kabbalah" (*KC,* 18). Yet the rhetoric of the Kabbalah is, for the purposes of Bloom's argument, never substitutable for that of Gnosticism. Again and again, it is by recourse to what is most Gnostic in the Kabbalah that the connection is made with revisionary poetics until, in his apologia for the esotericism of his method, Bloom is led to state explicitly that a Kabbalistic model "is ultimately a Gnostic model" (*KC,* 87).

Bloom's frankest and most important revisions of the mainstream Kabbalah occur, first, when he differs from the broader historical and philosophical emphasis of his major source, Gerschom Scholem, and stresses the Gnostic-like *Sefirot* and, second, when he chooses Issac Luria as his arch-Kabbalist. Although the *Sefirot* or divine emanations of Moses de Leon, as modified by Moses Cordovero, provide Bloom with the structural and functional analogues of his famous revisionary ratios (*KC,* 55, 62–63), it is Luria, at once the "archetype of all Revisionists . . . for all kinds of belated creativity that came after him, from the Italian Renaissance to the present" (*KC,* 93) and an "even more Gnosticizing Kabbalist than Cordovero" (*KC,* 58), who provides Bloom not only with an image of his own gnosticizing but also with an account of the necessity and ultimate significance of Kabbalism for his own critical project. Certainly Luria's transformation of the unidirectional continuity of creation into a discontinuity in which creation flows back on itself and is transformed is a tempting analogue of the way in which Bloom's clear historical distinction between Gnosticism and Kabbalism is overwhelmed by a gnosticizing tendency ultimately traceable to Bloom's own predicament as a modern, secular critic of literature. Given all of this, what is the reason for the ambiguity in Bloom's use of the Kabbalistic model, and, more importantly, why *Kabbalah and Criticism* and not *Gnosticism and Criticism?*

Our answer lies, I think, in Bloom's statement that the

origin of the Kabbalah is in the plight of diasporic Jews and arises from the question:

> How does one accommodate a fresh and vital new religious impulse, in a precarious and even catastrophic time of troubles, when one inherits a religious tradition already so rich and coherent that it allows very little room for fresh revelations or even speculations? The Kabbalists were in no position to formulate or even reformulate much of anything in their religion. Given to them already was not only a massive and completed Scripture, but an even more massive and intellectually finished structure of every kind of commentary and interpretation. . . . Their achievement was not just to restore Gnosis and mythology to a Judaism which had purged itself of such elements, but more crucially to provide the masses of suffering Jewry with a more immediate and experiential personal faith than the strength of orthodox tradition might have allowed.
>
> (*KC*, 33–34)

As Bloom describes it, the crisis resulted from the disparity between the strength of the orthodox tradition and the weakness of its recipients—victims of "a new and intensified Exile, following the expulsion of the Jews from Spain in 1492" (*KC*, 32). The implication here is that the closed canon and the interpretation that defended that closure lacked the means of acknowledging the reality of the Jews' new suffering; in its very strength, it seemed closed to their weakness. The greater danger, against which Kabbalistic revisionism sought to defend, lay in the temptation simply to reject the tradition and blame God for their suffering.

The connection between rejecting the tradition and blaming God is an important one, for if the closed canon of Scripture represents the manifest presence and authority of God, the accompanying body of interpretation represents the independent capacity for good or ill, which is the foundation for a history distinct from God's willing. Without such mediation and such a history, everything including evil must be traced directly to God. In short, then, the Kabbalists hoped to save the possibility of belief and their own integrity as believers by means of the revisionary expedient of asserting simultaneously the incompleteness of existing interpretation and the continued integrity of the canon.

The genius of the Kabbalistic strategy is in the way it uses the very temptation to accuse in the defense of the tradition. If it stands in danger of being rejected, the tradition is not so invulnerable after all, and a shared vulnerability becomes the basis of its continuing relevance. In this way, it becomes possible to "open God to the sufferings of his own creatures and of his own creation" (*KC*, 77) without accusing him.

The plight of fifteenth- and sixteenth-century Jews with regard to their tradition invites (I think intentionally) comparison with that of the eighteenth-century poets and humanists discussed by Bate in *The Burden of the Past and the English Poet* (discussed in some detail in Chapter 2 and which Bloom cites in *The Anxiety of Influence* as one of his own major sources [*AI*, 8]) and suggests that, in both cases, crises of authority and possibility are first and foremost crises in interpretation. Indeed, it may be that interpretation has relatively little to tell us about the real state of letters at any time and can only speak of its own condition as an indication of the state of our relationship with our own demiurgic free will and the history it sustains. If this is so, then the secular literary tradition is distinguished from the sacred tradition by the fact that to accuse it leads not to a revulsion from God but from ourselves as the makers of what we survey. Thus, for the modern interpreter, the Kabbalah, staying as it does within the Book and its tradition, represents the possibility of attributing our suffering to a contingent inadequacy in our interpreting rather than to any disorder inherent in our processes of desiring or to a permanent incommensurability of desire and history.

A critic cannot speak fretfully about the plight of modern letters, nor can he predict the coming apocalyptic end of the literary tradition except as a hyperbolic expression of the extremity of his own position as the recipient of a two-thousand-year-old exegetical tradition that seems hopelessly at odds with his historical situation. In this context, the suspicion arises that a clear-cut distinction between literature and interpretation allows critics to project the precariousness of the present uneasy critical alliance of the belletristic essay and the Germanic footnote as a misfortune befalling traditional literary genres in a hostile modern social environment. Such defensively rigid generic thinking makes it impossible to conclude that literature is merely changing and not being destroyed. Secular interpretation as we understand it, as a retrospective knowing, seems most vulnerable in its difficulty in envisioning change positively. From within literary criticism, for instance, a fundamental transformation of the discipline into something more active and effectual would surely be seen as the end of interpretation and maybe even of literature—perhaps this is the real problem Bloom addresses in his fascination with catastrophe creations like that of Gnosticism.

But we are still some distance from an adequate explanation of Bloom's apparent endorsement of the Kabbalistic solution, in part because, as we have already seen, he finds it impossible to reside there. If the Kabbalah avoids the ultimate self-accusation directed at desire itself, in *Agon,* when Bloom comes to embrace gnosis openly, he makes this accusation more explicitly than ever before.

However, clinging to the Kabbalah with its self-limiting willingness to be "merely" critical, dependent for its authority on the Book rather than some extratextual truth or power, also preserves Bloom's identity as a critic, an interpreter of texts, rather than a theologian and believer. It is only this willingness at least to bow in the direction of text centeredness that keeps Bloom recognizably within the post-Enlightenment literary/interpretive tradition. Thus, if we return for a moment to Hartman's argument that Bloom accuses poetry in order to save it, the Kabbalah represents the fine distinction between that and *really* accusing poetry.

Finally, we must go back to Bloom's difficult distinction between a "magical power over nature" and a "power of the mind over the universe of death" (*KC,* 47). Where, we must wonder, is the mind's place if not in the created world, and what is the nature of the power it exercises there? From the perspective of the mainstream Kabbalah, the mind's place is ultimately the Book, and the mind's power is a power in and for the Book. The decision not to seek a "magical power over nature" is essentially a decision not to risk mixing mind and nature by going outside the Book. Bloom's distinction seems almost to assume that the limits of the Book as a context for interpretation stand in surety for the distinctiveness of an intellectual essence— mind—or a spiritual essence—soul.

To go beyond that limit even in the quest for power is to risk the loss of that distinctiveness and that element of inviolability that it assumes in each of us. By contrast, the Gnostics refuse the limits of the Book and take the incredibly bold step of reducing the entire created world to the fact of death, giving up even the comforts of mind and soul to the demiurge, in order to conceive their proper place and the domain of their powers in another creation entirely. In this way, death and the nature it infests become negative tropes for the true God—a God not of limitation but of desire. Ultimately then, the Gnostic differs from the Kabbalist in that the latter balks at the extreme sacrifice of giving up the Book and its God, along with the idealized God within, to demiurgic status, perhaps realizing the dangers of conceiving desire ascetically, as a negative act of will and not as an embrace. For Bloom, Kabbalism in its more orthodox aspect represents revisionism as the defense of tradition; in its more radical, Gnostic aspect, the Kabbalah represents an attempt to move beyond the tradition to envision something new, something elsewhere.

As a revisionism refusing to accept the limits of this world or its creator, Gnosticism stretches the notion of revision to its very limits, perhaps beyond. Yet the Gnostic dependence on a relentlessly negative perspectivizing of the orthodox tradition creates a dependence that ties gnosis to orthodoxy as the very ground of its antithetical being. Thus, gnosis is perpetually faced with the danger of being reincorporated into the demiurgic tradition as mere parody. The traditional Gnostic defense against this eventuality is the rejection of writing, available to anyone who can read, in favor of the direct oral transmission of sacred knowledge from master to initiate. As soon as written statements of Gnostic doctrines (either by the Gnostics themselves or by orthodox churchmen) became available, there began a simultaneous process of condemnation and absorption. Bloom's own stance reflects this situation in his repeated insistence that he seeks no disciples or any wide acceptance of his arguments as "true." He further postpones the inevitable reduction and absorption of his ideas, their domestication into the institutionalized critical tradition, by the dizzying speed and virtuosity of his publication, which gives him a flexibility and capacity for constant self-revision approximating that of orality.

The frequently heard criticism that Bloom publishes too much too quickly and that his statements are imperfectly consistent with one another clearly amounts to an accusation that he is violating the proper imbalance between the authority of the tradition and the imaginative desire of the individual writer, which the limits of a written tradition and the further difficulties of the institution of publication are intended to enforce.

The adoption of an institutional canon gave form and authority to a distinct tradition of Christian orthodoxy, preventing its reabsorption into Judaism. By defining all other writings as secondary or "merely" interpretive, the canon, despite its role as the basis for accusations of heresy, paradoxically makes it once again safe to write. Before the formation of the canon, every new doctrinal speculation, every new version of the life of Christ or the acts of the apostles, was potentially a sweeping revision of Christian belief. The unrestrained production of such writings threatened to turn the nascent religion into another theosophy among many. For modern secular critics, the corresponding threat is to the disciplinary status of interpretation, without which writing would once again become a truly temerarious act, justified only by its appeal to large numbers of readers or great brilliance and imaginative power—a crushing burden of responsibility.

For Bloom, the modern interpreter's most profound link with the Kabbalists is a shared suffering, a vulnerability to disillusionment. He tells us:

> The great lesson that Kabbalah can teach contemporary interpretation is that meaning in belated texts is always wandering meaning, even as the belated Jews were a wandering people. Meaning wanders, like human tribulation, or like error, from text to text, and within a text, from figure to figure.
>
> (*KC*, 82)

This comparison of interpretive suffering with historical suffering suggests a deep identity between the use we make of our capacity to interpret and our relationship to history; it also gives point and pathos to Bloom's remark: "As a theory of meaning, Kabbalah tells us that meaning *is* the hurt that meaning itself is hurtful" (*KC*, 80)—meaning is exile.

The exile that makes meaning possible manifests itself as belatedness, and the form of that belatedness, partially described by the revisionary ratios, is Bloom's own procedure of rhetorical substitution—his endless wandering from the language of religion, to psychology, to philosophy, to rhetoric—which rehearses a similar homelessness, since no rhetoric ever actually subsumes and becomes entirely sufficient to the purposes of any other. Being cut off from the substance, the literal, is the price paid for meaning. But this suffering is also the freedom to trope and thus to be elsewhere—our defense against the literality of death. At least Bloom in his asceticism would have us believe that suffering can be turned against death in this way—that interpretation or "misreading," by keeping open the wound of meaning, preserves the freedom to evade the literality of death by troping.

Bloom's most radical moment in *Kabbalah and Criticism* comes during his discussion of *Zimzum,* the second of Luria's revisions of the *Sefirot,* or divine emanations. *Zimzum,* according to Bloom, "became the ultimate trope of Exile, or the ultimate psychic defense of Exiled Jewry" by explaining suffering as the result of God's necessary contraction or withdrawal in order to clear space for creation. Thus, we are told, God defended himself from "responsibility for unmerited evil, and for the suffering of his people" (*KC,* 83). But we are not really talking about God's defense; we are talking about Kabbalism as man's defense against his own impulse to an accusation so hurtful, a reduction so complete, that it cannot be acknowledged, only defended against. For Kabbalists, it was important to avoid the Gnostic alternative of making God a demiurge, for the essence of the demiurgic is to make God a mere trope of himself, and a negative trope at that.

Zimzum intervened between the equally demiurgic alternatives of God's indifference or his direct responsibility for suffering, but only "at the price of deconstructing an overdetermined tradition" (*KC,* 83). Yet, in this context, the deconstruction is Bloom's, not Luria's, and the overdetermined tradition is not that of the Talmud but of divine transcendence in the Jewish, Christian, and Christian/humanist traditions. At this point, Bloom goes very much against the Kabbalistic tradition and suggests that *Zimzum* is "God's anxiety"—a bold trope: "God had breathing trouble [an anxiety attack?] and this trouble created the world" (*KC*, 83). The idea that the world was created not out of strength but out of anxiety represents a devastating reduction of God's status—a reduction explainable only in terms of the compensation it promises to make possible.

Immediately after suggesting that the world originates in God's anxiety attack, Bloom quotes Freud on the fundamental link between anxiety and the fear of death, and goes on to conclude: "The Kabbalistic model here illuminates the fundamental problem at the heart of all influence anxiety, which is the deep, hidden identity between all psychic defense and the fear of dying" (*KC*, 84). If we add to this Bloom's argument from *The Anxiety of Influence* that the poet suffers more greatly from the anxiety of influence in proportion to his greater outrage that he must die (*AI*, 10), we can see that Bloom's revision not only exposes God to death anxiety but influence anxiety as well. What can this mean?

If we do not conclude that God is literally afraid to die, then the anxiety of influence and the human fear of death upon which it is based must be tropes for whatever God might conceivably be anxious about. Similarly, if the human fear of death is compared with a divine anxiety that cannot, by definition, be literal, then in the context of interpretation this too must be a trope. God represents the possibility of an anxiety that is *not* death anxiety, transforming fear of death into a trope rather than a sufficient definition of anxiety. In effect, the only ascetic sacrifice adequate to hold the literality of death at bay is the offering up of God's divinity to anxiety, to the demiurge.

By contrast, the Kabbalists fought to maintain the distinction between the divine and the human by preserving the mediating function of the Bible and its tradition. For them, it was important to insulate God from his creation because his absolute and unknowable difference constituted the firmest basis for a hope that something actually exists beyond the death decreed by nature. For those Romantics, most particularly Wordsworth, who sought to translate this tradition into a secular context, God's unknowable and therefore untainted goodness was easily translated into a fundamental, preconscious, preadult, instinctual goodness, which was also the surest source of our compensation.

The Gnostic/ascetic alternative also found its Romantic translation in the refusals of Blake and Shelley to accept Wordsworth's sublimations—a strain of Romanticism that issues in Nietzsche's deconstructions of the orthodox moral tradition and, later, in Freud's own rather tortured investigations of the possibility that our most fundamental instincts are not life-affirming at all but seek to betray us to death.

It is to this point that Bloom brings us in *Agon*. When modern revisionism attacks the instincts, it attacks one of secularity's most cherished myths. If the instincts can be trusted to direct man if not toward the good, then at least toward his own self-interest, Original Sin is no longer necessary to provide the bedrock commonality upon which a universal ethic (and implicit anthropology) can be based. But if the instincts lead us toward destruction, and our survival and prosperity depend on antithetical and artificial creations of mind and imagination like religion, philosophy, or literature, then the literality and self-sufficiency of the text, which is based on the notion that what appears first is most fundamental and most true, is called into question and the theological roots of interpretation are once more central to an ethically aware criticism.

But before we pass on to Bloom's argument in *Agon*, so closely related to *Kabbalah and Criticism*, we must briefly consider the intriguing question of what God might conceivably be anxious about. In Bloom's account, the Kabbalah originates in the suffering of diasporic Jews and, through the mediation of the interpreter's own suffering, succeeds in opening up the tradition to that suffering. In the course of this argument, Bloom, the secular critic, comes very close indeed to presenting the influence anxiety of the creator/interpreter as the analogue of God's anxiety. About what influence can God be anxious if not that of his own creation? After all, the whole point of the Kabbalah as a defense is that God is in danger of being defined by the evils of his creation.

Interestingly, it is in Wordworth's *Prelude* that we find one of Romantic literature's clearest articulations of the problem for the secular artist, and the crisis comes precisely at the moment when Wordsworth succeeds in putting Milton and the tradition he represents in a position of inferiority. For about six hundred lines in the "London" section of *The Prelude* (Book VII), Wordsworth succeeds in maintaining a defensive distance between himself and the masses of humanity inhabiting the city. But on the one occasion, when he unexpectedly finds himself "lost / Amid the moving pageant," he is vouchsafed this vision:

> Of a blind Beggar, who, with upright face,
> Stood, propped against a wall, upon his chest
> Wearing a written paper to explain
> His story, whence he came, and who he was.
> Caught by the spectacle my mind turned round
> As with the might of waters; an apt type
> This label seemed of the utmost we can know,
> Both of ourselves and of the universe;
> And, on the shape of that unmoving man,
> His steadfast face and sightless eyes, I gazed,
> As if admonished from another world.
> (lines 639–49)

In his fine essay, "The Notion of Blockage in the Literature of the Sublime," Neil Hertz remarks brilliantly, if somewhat enigmatically, of this episode that it keeps Words-worth "from tumbling into his text" (NBLS, 84). To do so would presumably be to suffer the same devastating reduc-tion-to-text as the blind beggar. Just as the visual spectacle of the London crowd threatens to overwhelm Wordsworth's distinct selfhood, the self-representing text, written for all to see, strikes directly at his imaginative freedom. As a fixed and public utterance, now as available to any reader as to its own author, the achieved text threatens to define and there-fore limit the imagination of its creator. The fall into the text is the fall into the community over which the author has no control. The text is at once the means by which imagination and creative identity are manifested and by which the author is appropriated to the community and the tradition, largely on their terms.

The revelation of this dilemma occurs as Wordsworth is also granted the illusion of superiority over the greatest of his precursors, Milton, which is also the illusion that he has stepped outside the anxiety of influence. The figure of the blind beggar is a devastating reduction of Milton, who made a virtue of blindness by claiming that it enhanced the anti-thetical and spiritually superior quality of insight. Unlike Wordsworth, whose sight ties him to the external world with which he still seeks to be reconciled, the beggar is protected from the danger of being imaginatively over-whelmed. However, in rejecting the external world, he falls prey to the text as the necessary form of the poetic self's manifestation and its tie to demiurgic creation.

In this moment of triumph over Milton, Wordsworth is also faced with the realization that his own poetic ambition and his residual fear of the external world threaten to betray him to the same fate. The episode implies that, however painful, the anxiety of influence is the secular revisionist's best defense against the far more intractably internal prob-lem of our inability to bless and believe in what we create—

to define a relationship to our own productions not tainted from the first by a sense of our own unworthiness, of self-hatred. Such self-hatred is, in literature, the inevitable consequence of staking the poetic imagination against death, refusing the mediating comforts represented by the second chance of Freudian sublimation. Under such circumstances, the only alternative to self-hatred is to blame poetry, resulting in a profound ambivalence in which it is at once the means of achieving creative desire and the demiurgic constraint preventing that achievement.

Just as the Romantic poet is, at least insofar as he is like Wordsworth, torn between the will to imaginative power and guilt, the modern critic at once assumes the power to interpret as he sees fit and compensates with a contradictory self-abasement before literature as shibboleth. In this context, the difficulty with revisionism, at least as practiced in this country today, is that it has still not moved beyond the problematic formulated for us by the Romantics.

Bloom is, of course, well aware of this—an awareness reflected in his remarks on literary history: "When you know both precursor and ephebe, you know poetic history, but your knowing is as critical an event in that history as was the ephebe's knowing of the precursor" (*KC*, 62–63). Bloom admits that revisionism does not begin history anew, that it is a continuity at least of discontinuities, and reveals the pathos of a desire for more. He addresses himself to the nature of this "more" in *Agon*, where he tries to move away from the idealizing/sublimating tradition of English Romanticism, with its dark underside and potential for catastrophic disillusionment, toward the American pragmatism of Emerson.

Agon proceeds from a distinction between historical Gnosticism and its essence, gnosis:

> a timeless knowing, as available now as it was then, and available alike to those Christians, to those Jews and to those secular

intellectuals who are not persuaded by orthodox and normative accounts or versions of religion, and who rightly scorn the many mindless, soft pseudotranscendentalisms now swarming, but who know themselves as questers for God.

(*A*, 4)

This way of knowing yields a knowledge more than rational, with a transformative effect on both the knower and the known (*A*, 4–5), speaking a language of desire and possession (*A*, 14). In short, gnosis is like if not equivalent to poetic knowledge (*A*, 4), and both are more like each other than any kind of philosophy (*A*, 11). Thus, Bloom presents gnosis as the true analogue of what we seek in poetry, rejecting the more traditional or, at least, orthodox choices of philosophy and theology. Indeed, Bloom adds a new twist to Hartman's attack on M. H. Abrams's account[4] of "natural supernaturalism" or secularized religious belief by arguing that far from being a "saving remnant" of lost religious belief that elevates poetry, it is the poetry residing at the heart of theology from the very beginning that has always given theology its power (*A*, 151–52). In all of this, Bloom regards himself as the heir of a third (after the Wordsworthian and the Shelleyan), distinctively American, strain of Romanticism, that of Emerson's "Self-Reliance," pragmatically stressing not truth but usefulness as a goal and measure of value.

In essentializing Gnosticism as gnosis, Bloom reaches toward an intensely personal articulation of his visionary hope, the "more" than history that poetry-as-gnosis has to offer. It is very difficult for Bloom to be more specific since his gnosis carries him to the very border of interpretation as a form of institutionalized public utterance; indeed, he is carried to the very border of our present understanding of what is meant by poetry by his insistence on breaking down the

---

4. See *Natural Supernaturalism* (New York: Norton, 1971).

distinction between religion and secularity, which is so constitutive of our sense of ourselves and our activities. Bloom's treatment also reveals one of the great dangers of taking gnosis out of history and creating an antithesis between gnosis and Gnosticism: having forsaken history, how can the desire that gnosis embodies ever be translated into a hopeful vision of the future? Bloom's must remain a vision out of time.

It is the Gnostic way, despairing of the future (indeed, denying the importance of such a historical question to begin with), to substitute the "elsewhere" or the "other" for the "about to be." In practice, this involves Bloom in an alienation, perhaps more ideological than real, from the critical community. At the outset, Bloom tells us that he is writing in order to "explore and develop a personal Gnosis" which may only *possibly* issue in a Gnosticism, which may only *perhaps* be available to others (*A*, 4).

At a later point in the argument, Bloom emphasizes his Gnostic alienation and expresses his frustration at the critical community to which he remains tied by raging against consensus as if consensus and community were necessarily the same:

> I hope I have made clear, by now, that in expounding my own critical theory and practice, I neither want nor urge any "method" of criticism. It is no concern of mine whether anybody else ever comes to share, or doesn't, my own vocabularies of revisionary ratios, of crossings, of whatever. What Richard Rorty cheerfully dismisses as "the comfort of consensus" I too am very glad to live without, because I don't want to privilege any vocabularies, my own included. Autonomy and novelty are the goals of strong reading as they are of strong writing, so that I am charmed when I observe Frank Lentricchia ending his recent book *After the New Criticism* by saying that my desire to be an original theorist is what is most retrograde and anti-intellectual in contemporary criticism. "Intellectual" seems to mean "consensus" in that view, a view held in

common by traditionalist academics and by post-Heideggeri-
ans. They want agreement, as though an MLA election or a
Deconstructive banquet would suffice either to arrive at a common meaning or a decision that meaning can't be decided.

(A, 38–39)

True, the intellectual (and spiritual) value of consensus
seems rather limited, especially when hostile. However, in
his willingness to embrace a Gnostic isolation, Bloom rather
ignores his own practice in writing books assuming an audience, a community that, if unwilling to agree on answers to
the problem of textual meaning, can at least agree on the
importance of the question. When Bloom insists that the
critic has no privileged perspective external to the literary
history he surveys, that the critic's knowing immediately
becomes part of the historical being of what is known, he
presumes both a community and a history since there can be
no history (as opposed to biography or chronicle) without
community, and history is *the* communizing metaphor of
Western culture.

Gnostics have never succeeded in avoiding history or
community. In rejecting these things, they have only
granted orthodoxy the power to write their history and to
define their community for them. Such a stance made it
possible for orthodoxy to isolate Gnosticism as a heresy
and to represent it as a peripheral phenomenon. In accepting such a characterization, however, gnosis paradoxically
succeeds in entering the orthodox, historical community on
its own terms, as the return of the repressed daemon.
Thus, the relationship between Gnostic isolation and orthodox consensus is not mutually exclusive but symbiotic
within the community defined by a history that neither can
entirely control or evade.

For all the radical appearance of his stance, Bloom seems
reluctant to give up the trappings of demiurgic, rational,
pseudophilosophical criticism. He stops well short of taking

recourse to imagery or terminology so esoteric as to make his work incomprehensible in the context of traditional conservative forms of criticism. Or perhaps the possibility of Gnostic radicalism is already delimited by criticism itself, an activity recognizable as such largely in the context of an Enlightenment rationalism and philosocentrism (to parody Derrida) profoundly at odds with the Gnostic impulse. A thoroughgoing gnosis might no longer be recognizable as a criticism at all, which emphasizes that for a gnosis to be a rhetoric of freedom and of desire, as Bloom wishes to see it, it must reside within a community even as it insists on its alienation.

This necessary ambivalence of the Gnostic stance seems closely related to a complaint frequently heard about Bloom's criticism—that it is difficult to tell whether he is describing what "is" (offering a true, if revisionary, account of the nature and history of poetry) or arguing for poetic and critical revisionism as what should be, something to be desired and pursued. The evasiveness of such a distinction is perhaps built into the historical relationship between gnosis and orthodoxy in our Western interpretive community.

Perhaps we can further contextualize Bloom's remarks by suggesting that revisionism *is* the ambiguous interdependence of gnosis and orthodoxy in an interpretive community based less on shared beliefs than on shared institutions. Originally, the formation of the institutionalized canon and of the church proceeds from a revisionary reading of the Old Testament. To put it another way, the revisionism and the orthodoxy it seeks to revise come into being simultaneously, as reflections of one another. Because of this special relationship, revisionism becomes both a vehicle of change and a means of defending the continuity of institutions. This is, of course, a more historicized, more benign version of Bloom's notion of misreading, but it has the virtue of helping us to understand his continuing attachment to institutional criti-

cism, at least in practice, as well as his difficulty in envisioning a future for letters once he has rejected the validity of
that institutional criticism.

The primary basis of Bloom's insistence on the identity
between poetic knowledge and gnosis is presented in two
closely argued chapters on "Freud and the Sublime" and
"Freud's Concepts of Defense and the Poetic Will." Despite
the fact that early in his argument Bloom maintains that "the
peculiar rigors of transference and counter-transference and
the waywardness of the unconscious combine to prevent
psychoanalysis from becoming a Gnosis" (A, 8), in these
chapters he finds in the post-1914 writings evidence of a
Freudian gnosis tied to the developing theory of the drives
and the related idea of an anxiety preceding all occasion.

According to Bloom, Freud's later work is haunted by the
possibility "that a monistic vision of human aggression
would crowd out the dualistic vision of human sexuality"
(A, 126)—a fear to which the theory of the drives both gives
voice and seeks to defend against. Everywhere implicit in
Bloom's discussion, and in Freud as Bloom understands
him, is a sense that the defense is a failure and that the theory
of the drives is a much more effective vehicle for the articulation of anxiety than for desire, that perhaps anxiety itself is
more real than desire.

If, Bloom asks, "the later Freud teaches us that our instinctual life is agonistic and ultimately self-destructive and
that our most authentic moments tend to be those of negation, contraction and repression," then "is it so unlikely that
our creative drives are deeply contaminated by our instinctual origins?" (A, 98). In making this connection, Bloom
ranges himself not only against idealizing accounts of creativity but also against the entire tradition identifying drives
or instincts with a life-enhancing natural being—a tradition
fundamental to secularity's pretensions to being able to do
without a religion-based ethic. In Bloom's account, the tra-

ditional connection of creativity with the essential self forges an alliance not with Eros but with Thanatos. In art, as in life, anxiety overpowers desire.

Yet Bloom also offers poetry or figuration as a defense, just as he offers the theory of the drives as a defense against the danger it articulates. The contamination of the instinctual, of the natural within us, by a drive to death contaminates "is" itself, and literal meaning comes to be identified with death in the coda to *Beyond the Pleasure Principle,* as Bloom points out (*A,* 136). To accept literal meaning then as authority, a standard of reference in determining truth, is to elevate Thanatos over Eros, anxiety over desire.

In this case, the artificial language of the merely figurative, of the self-consciously fictional, becomes the language of Eros, life's defense against the death instinct. Not only then is the notion of defense a trope, but trope is the most effective defense (*A,* 124). Freud, Bloom argues, defends against the fear that life itself is a kind of catastrophic fall out of an ideal equilibrium into a vexing and constant excitation that only death can heal by posing against the death drive an urge to immortality, which Bloom identifies with the urge to the sublime of the poetic will. This defense is the greatest of tropes, intending to make of death itself a trope (*A,* 124, 144).

This is achieved through what Bloom terms a "supermimesis," a form of negation pioneered by the Gnostics, for whom the material and historical catastrophes of earthly existence were reduced to mere tropes of the much greater catastrophe of creation itself. "Of course," Bloom adds, no amount of supermimesis can actually reverse these demiurgic catastrophes (*A,* 90). From a certain entirely human point of view, that is a damnable "of course," setting the price of Gnostic negation at the acceptance of defeat in this world. Such a gnosis makes us free only if we assume that we have nothing left to lose.

Psychoanalytically, Thanatos itself may be seen as a supermimetic defense against the death that, according to Bloom, the creative mind rebels against more strongly and insistently than others. Just as catastrophe troped upon is still catastrophe, death troped as Thanatos is still death. Yet from a sufficiently Gnostic perspective, a perspective willing to give up the created world and equate it completely with Thanatos as the universe of death, catastrophe creation and Thanatos alike are superb defenses against that greatest of dangers, acceptance—the conclusion that what is, this demi-urgic creation, is anything but a falling away. Indeed, this is the lesson of Eros and Thanatos alike, for, as Bloom points out, why should there be drives of any kind intended to restore an innate condition unless there has been a fall from it? (*A*, 137–38).

This shift in perspective dramatizes the difficulty, if not impossibility, of carrying on some sort of direct dialogue between Gnostic and orthodox across the gulf separating their respective presuppositions. The Gnostic position par-ticularly is designed to negate, rather than interact with, orthodoxy, denying its appeal to such "givens" as love of this life, desirability of historical success, and so on. This raises some interesting questions about the status of Bloom's reading of Freud.

For instance, when Bloom claims (*A*, 130) to see at work in the late Freud a reaction formation designed to defend against the return of Freud's repressed literality or scientism, we must wonder whether insofar as Bloom's argument is a gnosticizing one and is consistent with his own statements, it can specify such a defense as *internal* to Freud's text. That is not to say that no reaction formation is there but only that it is the business of demiurgic, descriptive criticism to privi-lege the literal being. A gnosis, on the other hand, would be able to make statements about the relationship governing the interpreter's desires and anxieties with the text, not about relationships internal to the text itself. Thus, what Bloom-as-Gnostic says about Freud can only apply to Bloom's relationship to Freudian texts.

Of course, Bloom's criticism is not pure gnosis, as he obviously does purport to make descriptive statements that are neither fantastic nor offensive (as are Gnostic readings of Genesis and other orthodox texts) to conventional criticism. His is a mixed mode, highly effective in some ways, severely limited by its own gnosis in others. Most notable is a consequence of the Gnostic's denial of any communizing history upon which an exchange can be based. On the one hand, the Gnostic Bloom rejects such a history; on the other, the academic Bloom constantly refers to such a history by virtue of which he writes what is still recognizably literary criticism. However, there is still no means by which these two Blooms can become sufficiently aware of each other to avoid a serious split in Bloom's argument. The anxious Bloom never engages or is reconciled with the hopeful Bloom; the historical Bloom and the ahistorical Bloom seem unaware of each other; the Gnostic Bloom seems oblivious to the freight of orthodoxy he carries, and so on. It is almost as if the text itself provides the space in which a perpetually self-revising community, including Gnostic and orthodox, can be manifested, yet still without any mutual recognition.

The negating, nonparticipatory nature of Gnosticism also accounts for what is at once its greatest strength and its most glaring weakness: by definition, it cannot fail. Bloom notes:

> It is a familiar formula to say that failed prophecy becomes apocalyptic; and that failed apocalyptic becomes Gnosticism. If we are to ask: "What does failed Gnosticism become?" we would have to answer that Gnosticism never fails, which is both its strength (through intensity) and its weakness (through incompleteness). A vision whose fulfillment, by definition, must always be *beyond* the cosmos, cannot in its own terms be said to fail *within* our cosmos.
>
> (*A*, 67)

The cost of this invulnerability is high, however, for in rejecting this creation and its history, the Gnostic renounces, as we have seen, any vision of a hopeful future in this world. As a result, Bloom finds himself in the unusual position of insisting on the prospective value of an Emersonian, pragmatic gnosis, even as he lacks any optimism about the future of letters.

In addition, we must wonder if Bloom is right in saying that Gnosticism cannot, by definition, fail. For the Gnostic initiate, whose faith in that other creation was absolute, the knowledge of the true God—a knowledge necessarily and absolutely alienated within knowledge—and the subsequent reduction of the other aspects of human existence was not too high a price to pay. But in order to support such a faith, even the Gnostics required a division between redeeming transcendence and suffering creation so absolute as to require two gods and a compensation so great as to raise the initiate to the level of virtual divinity. But what if this faith failed in the face of the overwhelming burden of being in this world? Structured so that from within failure is logically impossible, Gnosticism would have nothing to say about its possible fate under such circumstances. Perhaps at this point it is time to venture a guess that the closest analogue, if not the direct historical product, of failed Gnosticism *is* secularization as we have come to understand it. It is against our secularity as a perpetually self-detecting Gnosticism that Bloom must strive in order to constitute his gnosis.

This suggestion is not as wild as it sounds once we recognize how strong the Gnostic impulse has been even in the most conservative critics in the post-Enlightenment tradition—critics who want to see literature as a world elsewhere, on a completely different moral and spiritual plane from other disciplines and from the rest of society; critics who desire a disciplinary, rational criticism, addressed to what is uniquely and essentially literary in texts and who want to see poetry itself purified of extraliterary ideas and language. The result is a literature so alienated in modern life and institutions that its destruction seems prophesied in everything around it, leaving the critic/author under enormous pressure to commit the ultimate Gnostic apostasy of acceptance.

For post-Enlightenment criticism, the question of futurity seems most vexing. We must wonder if, in this century, correcting the excesses of the Romantics and Victorians, criticism has not more or less given the future over to social science (which has promptly reduced hope to predictability and, failing that, further debased it into the power to manipulate) and applied science (with its endless gimmicky tomorrowlands). Criticism has chosen to define itself either retrospectively, as a purely historical activity with little or nothing to say about the present (which for this kind of critic stretches back at least twenty-five years) or in terms of an ideal "elsewhere" (the Gnostic alternative)—both equally distant from a genuine futurity or from a language for re-involving literature in the key debates of modern society.

The attempts of Bloom and Hartman to call our attention to the religious origins of interpretation aim at opening up a drastically narrowed sense of critical horizons. Their extensive use of psychoanalysis, philosophy, and other "extraliterary" ideas and vocabularies has also created a new sense of the literariness at the heart of other disciplines to replace the old "literature and . . ." rubric, in which, like zookeepers, critics place literary and some other language in a cage and hope they'll mate (like pandas, they seem to have forgotten how). Despite their apparent radicalism, these revisionists seem to have restored much of its history to criticism and with it, the middle ground from which it is possible to make literature once again a central concern of other disciplines.

But in returning to critical consciousness so much that was repressed in the name of disciplinary pretensions, the revisionism of Bloom and Hartman has also brought criticism face to face with problems it may not be able to solve while it remains in anything like its present form. The revisionists' own limited hopefulness about the future may well be based on a truly unenviable position: recognizing the failure of secularization and being aware of the degree to which our critical practice is embedded in the eighteenth century, their choice seems to be between keeping up the charade of a clearly inadequate, platitudinizing critical rationale or abandoning entirely criticism as presently understood, which means giving up an assured institutional audience and attempting to form a new one. This is a truly terrifying prospect, revealing that if there is such a thing as a critical or literary community, it is based not on agreement but on a common need for an institutionalized audience, a professional readership.

True to his own account of the repressive structure of all revisionism, Bloom's own revisionism uses the powerful critical myth of the anxiety of influence to repress the more fundamental and intractable problem of the post-Enlightenment mind's guilt and self-hatred. At the same time, Bloom's emphasis on the poet's rebellion against his own death directs us back to this repressed difficulty by suggesting that the failure of secularization, repeated over and over again in the failure of "misreading," originates in the secular mind's inability to accept its own death without the hedging of transcendences substituted for the traditional Christian compensation of eternal life or for the traditional classical compensation of fame, redefined as an "immortal freemasonry."

Bloom's dualistic literary history, with its sharp distinction between Miltonic and post-Miltonic, ultimately argues that earlier poets were more accepting of their own deaths. Perhaps this was because poetry, regarded as a more public, less personal form of utterance, made more effective claims on posterity, making the prospect of fame more meaningful; perhaps it was because poetry itself was seen as a more adequate embodiment of the immortality within. What is apparent is that when the poetic is internalized and essentialized as an attribute of the self, the poet becomes alienated from poetry as an inadequate expression of an inner absolute. The result, in Bloom's account, is that the poet's personal outrage invades, perhaps even becomes the central concern of, his poetry. Bloom's literary history is, in this regard, a potential critique of the familiar modern tendency to make imaginative and even institutional creations expressions of personal outrage. The most familiar extraliterary example of this is the modern bureaucracy structured to express an almost hysterical suspicion of bureaucracies. As a result, administration is so loaded down with Byzantine checks and balances that its consequent ineffectuality can only confirm our sense of bureaucracy's inadequacy as an expression of public will or as the guardian of public well-being.

The Emerson of "Self-Reliance" combines a Gnostic thrust beyond institutional and traditional constraints with a pragmatic suspicion of the tendency to universalize and therefore depersonalize ideals. In this way, Bloom suggests, Emerson's pragmatism prevents him from becoming the victim of his own idealizations; he is never so driven to alienation or outrage that he loses faith that the available means, however tainted by the demiurgic, are sufficient to construct his gnosis. Thus, Emerson represents the limitation that Bloom must impose on his drive toward a visionary absolute. Without this restraint (already identified in our discussion of the Kabbalah) Bloom would become so alienated from the resources of his own tradition that his gnosis would be that about which it is impossible to write or speak, marked only by silence.

The Emersonian pragmatism that Bloom argues for in

Agon, like the philosophical pragmatism of Richard Rorty,[5] by whom Bloom is influenced, represents an attempt to separate the desire and outrage of the self in quest of the absolute from the means of imaginative and institutional creation as a way of maintaining a sense of hope and a faith in available instruments of expression. Both Bloom and Rorty recognize in the Romantic idealizing of literature and in the Kantian idealizing of philosophy futile attempts to obscure the real nature of the Western tradition, which is to build systems on historical contingencies. In this broader context, it is the historical role of revisionism to allow this productive but dangerous contradiction to go on by providing a perpetually failed idealism with a past catastrophe, a fall, as a defense against despair and self-hatred in the present.

5. See *The Consequences of Pragmatism* (Minneapolis: University of Minnesota Press, 1982).

2

CANON AND CRITICISM

In Chapter 1, we succeeded in establishing by means of a close examination of the revisionisms of Bloom and Hartman the importance of certain concepts—gnosis, asceticism, and secularization—for modern criticism. These concepts seem particularly important not just because their continuing relevance hints at a much greater coherence and unity of concern in our tradition than contemporary critics are often prepared to grant, but also because they are accessible to a process of wider historical contextualization that promises to clarify the problematic of interpretation by expanding the frequently over-narrow compass of what is comprehended in more conventional notions of "literary criticism." In fact, it sometimes seems that we could only half-facetiously define literary criticism as a discipline conceiving of itself in such narrow terms that it can answer none of the questions it raises.

To offer a historical exposition at this point may seem a bit belated, but the procedure does have the advantage of allowing us to focus an account, which must be by its very nature highly selective, on the particular questions and hypotheses already developed out of current critical debates. To this end, I propose here to return to Bloom's primary source on Gnosticism and to trace a slightly different history out of it—a history giving pride of place to the influence, somewhat slighted by Bloom, of the notion of the canon in the unfolding of the sacred and secular traditions of letters.

Since I have neither the space nor the learning for an exhaustive history of canonicity in the West, I necessarily confine myself to what I regard as the three crises of the canon: (1) the background and establishment of the original Christian canon and its impact; (2) the accession to authority of the secular canon in the eighteenth century and its consequences for poetry and criticism; and (3) contemporary challenges to the effectiveness of the canon as a vehicle of a humanist ideology and as a means of organizing knowledge and establishing values.

In this way, I hope to provide a firmer historical background for some of the speculations of the previous chapter and lay the groundwork for a more detailed historical/interpretive study of the Sensibility and Romantic poets in Chapter 3.

TOWARD A CHRISTIAN CANON: GNOSIS, PROPHECY, APOCALYPTIC, AND HISTORY

Bloom's essentializing and ahistorical distinction between gnosis and Gnosticism in *Agon* is lent historical credibility by the bias of his primary source on the nature and history of Gnosticism, Hans Jonas's *The Gnostic Religion,* which argues powerfully for a Gnostic essence that can be characterized apart from the bewildering variety of Gnosticisms. Indeed, for Jonas, this essence is all but synonymous with what is common to the religions of the Mediterranean at about the time of Christ. This strategy is for Jonas a necessary part of completing the process begun by his great predecessor, Adolf von Harnack, of moving the study of Gnosticism away from its traditional characterization as a Christian heresy.

Jonas begins his study by reconsidering the famous remark of Harnack that Gnosticism represents "the acute Hellenization of Christianity." Since Harnack's time, the availability of new manuscript sources has shifted the emphasis away from the Hellenic to the Oriental and Judaic origins of Gnosticism. According to Jonas, Gnosticism has increasingly been revealed in the course of these studies as characteristic of the culture of the entire eastern Mediterranean area—a culture whose pervasive feature was syncretism (*GR,* xvi). He goes on to argue that, despite the disparate nature of Gnostic sources and the fragmented nature of the movement itself, a single Gnostic spirit or essence can be discerned. It is particularly important, he feels, to attempt a definition of this essence because Gnosticism represents one of man's most radical answers to his burdened condition and, as such, provides insights that other modes of understanding cannot (*GR,* xvii).

Jonas's approach to this essential Gnosticism begins with an account of the spread of Greek culture during and after the time of Alexander and of the rise of a Hellenistic culture encompassing the whole of the eastern Mediterranean. There were two basic stages in this process. In the first, Greek culture imposed its language and institutions on the East, transforming it in its own image. In the second stage, coinciding roughly with the time of Christ and the efflorescence of the great Gnostic movements, the eastern equivalent of Greek cosmopolitanism, religious syncretism, came to have a heavy influence on Hellenic culture. This religious syncretism expressed itself primarily in theocracy, the mixing of gods. The appeal of these theocratic tendencies accounts for the transition from an initial period, in which influence flows from Greece to the East, to a second period, in which the current of influence flows from the East to the West (*GR,* 18–20).

"The theocracy," Jonas tells us, "expressed itself in myth as well as in cult, and one of its most important logical tools was allegory, of which philosophy had already been making use in its relation to religion and myth" (*GR*, 20). It was by means of allegory as a mode of abstraction that Greek culture was disengaged from the conditions peculiar to the city-state and rendered transmittable to the alien environment of the East. The Logos, or power of conceptualization, was Greece's great gift to the East—a gift that enabled it to render its own primarily mythological modes of thought into a transmittable and, hence, influential form (*GR*, 21). So Jonas's two stages in the course of Hellenistic culture can be understood as the conceptualization of myth and the remythologization of concept.

All the religious movements that develop during this period of Eastern domination are characterized by a concern with salvation, by a transcendent conception of God, and by a radical dualism in the realm of being—between God and world, spirit and matter, light and dark, good and evil. Thus, "the general religion of the period is a dualistic transcendent religion of salvation" (*GR*, 31–32).

Gnosis is, of course, the Greek word for knowledge, and at the heart of Gnosticism is a radical conception of the nature and power of knowledge. Jonas tells us that

> in the more radical systems like the Valentinian the "knowledge" is not only an instrument of salvation but itself the very form in which the goal of salvation, i.e., ultimate perfection, is possessed. In these cases knowledge and the attainment of the known by the soul are claimed to coincide—the claim of all true mysticism.
>
> (*GR*, 35)

Such a radical conception of knowledge reveals that logical, rational knowledge is instrumental in nature, abstracted and alienated from being. Gnosticism attempts to restore knowledge to being, claiming that knowledge is being's ultimate form. This contrast between Gnostic and more familiar, instrumental conceptions of knowledge suggests that there is a relationship between contemporary attempts to restore the status of literature to critical writing and the traditional anxiety about the status of poetic knowledge, especially about its efficacy outside the poem itself. If knowledge of literature is extraliterary, then literature is incomprehensible as a form of knowledge or mode of knowing; it is conceivable only as an act, a gesture, or, perhaps, a ritual. Similarly, if criticism is not a form of literature, then it can be (and is) a form of almost anything but literature, and its relationship to the literature it considers is no more privileged or less problematical than that of psychology, history, economics, or sociology—all of which make claims to instrumentality, which, though less obviously vulnerable than those of criticism, are nonetheless ripe for deconstruction.

The Gnostic conception offers the most radical conceivable answer to the question of the instrumentality of knowledge, of its relation to being—an answer that embraces the alienation implicit in "knowledge of . . ." as the metaphysical basis of a cosmology. Similarly, to insist that criticism is literature is to argue that the alienation implicit in "interpretation of . . ." is not external to but endemic in all literary objects. It calls into question all claims that the essence of the literary work is unity or wholeness.

Jonas goes on to add a further "Abstract of Main Gnostic Tenets" (*GR*, 42–47), defining the single myth informing the variety of myths devised by leading Gnostic thinkers. In theology, he tells us, there is a radical dualism between an absolutely transmundane God and this world, an antithetical creation not His own. Because of this antithetical relationship, God cannot be known in or through the world. Such knowledge "requires supranatural revelation and illumination and even then can hardly be expressed otherwise than in negative terms" (*GR*, 42–43).

In the Gnostic cosmology, the universe is the domain of

the archons and their leader, the demiurge, who created and rule it in ignorance of the true God's existence. For the Gnostics, the vastness of creation serves only to emphasize man's alienation, his distance from God (*GR,* 43–44). The Gnostic anthropology regards body and soul alike as under the influence of the archons. Imprisoned within the soul is the pneuma, or divine spark—the only remnant of a precreation unity of being—ignorant of itself and only to be awakened through knowledge (*GR,* 44). Eschatologically, radical dualism determines the nature of Gnostic salvation, the goal of which is to release the inner, pneumatic man from the bonds of the world and return him to the realm of light. This requires a knowledge of the transmundane God's existence, of the initiate's own divine origin, and of the true nature of the world determining his present situation. All of this knowledge is withheld from him by the ignorance that is the "essence of mundane existence," and, therefore, revelation is a necessity.

The bearer of this revelation

is a messenger from the world of light who penetrates the barriers of the spheres, outwits the Archons, awakens the spirit from its earthly slumber, and imparts to it the saving knowledge "from without. . . ." The knowledge thus revealed . . . comprises the whole content of the gnostic myth, with everything it has to teach about God, man, and world; that is, it contains the elements of a theoretical system. On the practical side, however, it is more particularly "knowledge of the way," namely, of the soul's way out of the world, comprising the sacramental and magical preparations for its future ascent and the secret names and formulas that force the passage through each sphere. Equipped with this *gnosis,* the soul after death travels upwards, leaving at each sphere the psychical "vestment" contributed by it: thus the spirit stripped of all foreign accretions reaches the God beyond the world and becomes reunited with the divine substance. On the scale of the total divine drama, this process is part of the restoration of the deity's own wholeness, which in pre-cosmic times has become impaired by the loss of portions of the divine substance.

(GR, 45)

Finally, in the realm of morality, Gnostic thought rami-fies in two quite different directions on the basis of the same general rejection of mundane or demiurgic prohibitions. On the one hand, possession of the gnosis encourages an ascetic separation from the tainted things of this world. On the other hand, this rejection of mundane prohibition can also lead to libertinism. Indeed, by thwarting the design of the archons, the libertine's "immorality" contributes to the work of salvation and may be seen as a positive duty (GR, 46). At an ethical level, asceticism and libertinism are clearly inconsistent. Their coexistence in gnostic practice indicates that the relevant context is not ethical but metaphysical and makes it clear that the character of Gnostic thought derives from a constant metaphysical reference.

In the context of a metaphysic, Gnosticism reunites knowledge not only with being but with being in its ulti-mate form. But if we imagine a Gnosticism divorced from metaphysics, we are confronted by an alienation subversive of all values capable of supporting a community. In this sense, those who attack critics who, like Bloom, insist on the unity of literature and criticism are suggesting that we are being offered a Gnosticism without the saving meta-physic. This is certainly the case if we regard Gnosticism (or criticism) in purely conceptual terms. But is this accurate?

Jonas concludes his abstract of Gnostic tenets with this caveat:

> Even the reader unfamiliar with the subject will realize from the foregoing abstract that, whatever heights of conceptualization gnostic theory attained to in individual thinkers, there is an indissoluble mythological core to gnostic thought as such. Far

remote from the rarefied atmosphere of philosophical reasoning,
it moves in the denser medium of imagery and personification.
(*GR*, 46–47)

So if we strip the conceptual elements away from Gnosticism, those that can be subsumed under some more familiar
category of knowledge—theological, cosmological, etc.—
what remains is the myth or fiction. Similarly, if we strip
literature of reference to concepts claimed by other fields of
knowledge, what is left but the fact and quality of fictionality? From a certain worldly, secular point of view, the Gnostics' radicalism lay in attributing the fictional exclusively to
God, the factual or "real" exclusively to the demiurge. If
this does not mean that fictionality must be the alienated
metaphysic of a secular culture, it does at least suggest that
God and fiction are the two great historical avenues by
which knowledge has been reunited with being.

For Jonas, the relationship between concept and myth in
Gnosticism is governed by a particular concept of allegory—
a concept that departs from its Greek sources and suggests a
fundamental reordering of the Hellenistic episteme. He tells
us:

> Allegory, probably an invention of the philosophers, was
> widely used in Greek literature as a means of making the tales
> and figures of mythical lore conform to enlightened thought. By
> taking the concrete entities and episodes of classical myth as
> symbolic expressions of abstract ideas, such time-honored ele-
> ments of tradition and popular belief could be so conceptualized
> that a general consensus of truth seemed to unite the most ad-
> vanced intellectual insight with the wisdom of the past.
>
> (*GR*, 91)

The tendency of such allegory is toward a harmonization,
essentially respectful of tradition and never contradicting the
myth or its valuations.

On the other hand:

Gnostic allegory, though often of this conventional type, is in its most telling instances of a very different nature. Instead of taking over the value system of the traditional myth, it proves the deeper "knowledge" by reversing the roles of good and evil, sublime and base, blest and accursed, found in the original. It tries, not to demonstrate agreement, but to shock by blatantly subverting the meaning of the most firmly established, and preferably also the most revered, elements of the tradition. The rebellious tone of this type of allegory cannot be missed, and it therefore is one of the expressions of the revolutionary position which Gnosticism occupies in the late Classical culture.

(GR, 91–92)

Such allegorization, Jonas points out, might as well be regarded not as exegesis but as a tendentious rewriting of the original text:

Indeed, the Gnostics in such cases hardly *claimed* to bring out the correct meaning of the original, if by "correct" is meant the meaning *intended* by the author—seeing that the author, directly or indirectly, was their great adversary, the benighted creator-god. Their unspoken claim was rather that the blind author had unwittingly embodied something of the truth in his partisan version of things, and that this truth can be brought out by turning the intended meaning upside down.

(GR, 95)

Yet this rejection of traditional history is not a rejection of history or of traditional texts, for it is through the secret or hidden meanings that they contain that the true history is revealed—a history necessary to preserve the tenuous link between the pneuma and its cosmic origin.

In the final section of his book, Jonas argues that the true importance of Gnosticism (and here he disagrees most strongly with Harnack) is most apparent not in relation to the Christianity with which it is usually linked, but in relation to the Greek worldview to which it is most directly opposed. He begins with a discussion of the nature of the cosmos, which, for the Greeks, was not only a term denoting the totality of creation but, because *cosmos* is a term denoting order, it was also one of praise or admiration (*GR*, 241). As Cicero says, writing in this tradition in *De natura deorum,* man himself was born to contemplate the cosmos and to imitate it; he is far from perfect, but (through his participation in the cosmic order) he is a little part of the perfect (*GR*, 245). Such a view establishes the clearest relationship between cosmology and ethics, based on a faith that "this world is the ALL, and there is nothing beside it; it is perfect, and there is nothing equalling it in perfection" (*GR*, 245–46). Nothing, of course, could be farther from the Gnostic view.

In his monumental *History of Dogma,* the great New Testament scholar and historian of the early church, Adolf von Harnack, discusses pre-Christian Gnosticism as a rather loose, uneasy amalgam of Jewish apocalyptic, Babylonian, Persian and other Eastern "mysteries," and ideas borrowed from Greek philosophy, all applied to the Old Testament under the overarching influence of Hellenic philosophizing and spiritualizing (read, conceptualizing) tendencies. As Harnack notes: "This spiritualizing was the result of a philosophic view of religion, and this philosophic view was the outcome of a lasting influence of Greek philosophy and of the Greek spirit generally on Judaism" (*HD*, I, 224).

As a result, by the time Christians came to confront the problems of developing their own reading of the Old Testament:

> From the simple narratives of the Old Testament had already developed a theosophy, in which the most abstract ideas had acquired reality, and from which sounded forth the Hellenic canticle of the power of the Spirit over matter and sensuality, and of the true home of the soul. Whatever in this great adaptation still remained obscure and unnoticed, was not lighted up by the history of Jesus, his birth, his life, his sufferings and triumph. The view of the Old Testament as a document of the

deepest wisdom, transmitted to those who knew how to read it as such, unfettered the intellectual interest which would not rest until it had entirely transformed the new religion from the world of feelings, actions and hopes, into the world of Hellenic conceptions, and transformed it into a metaphysic.

(*HD*, I, 225)

The orthodox Talmudists had a powerful defense against the Gnostic conceptualization of the Old Testament—a defense not available to Christian readers. As Bloom points out: "The Talmudists took the Scriptures as true text, and kept the line clear between text and commentary" (*KC*, 53). Christians never had the luxury of beginning from a simple acceptance of the Old Testament; from the very beginning, their Old Testament had to be an interpreted Old Testament. Harnack writes that as soon as Christianity

wished to give account of itself, or to turn to advantage the documents of revelation which were in its possession, it had to adopt the methods of that fantastic [Gnostic] syncretism. We have seen above that those writers who made a diligent use of the Old Testament had no hesitation in making use of the allegorical method. That was required not only by the inability to understand the verbal sense of the Old Testament, presenting divergent moral and religious opinions, but, above all, by the conviction that on every page of that book Christ and the Christian Church must be found.

(*HD*, I, 224)

But, as we have already seen, the current of influence did not flow in only one direction, for the gnosticizing tendencies held somewhat in check by the Talmudic adherence to the text of Scripture found fertile ground in the emerging Christian religion. The figure of Christ, his coming, death, and resurrection, seen as the culmination "of those mighty spiritual powers whose conflict is delineated in the Old Testament" (*HD*, I, 226), provided the ideal vantage point from which a revisionary and systematic conceptual mythologization of humanity's place in creation and in the divine order could be carried out. In addition, the relative diversity and doctrinal disorganization of early Christianity offered an interpretive freedom not available in an already overdetermined Jewish tradition. Finally, and not the least important, the simplicity, even asceticism, the emphasis on moral living, and the spiritual enthusiasm of early Christian communities held a powerful appeal for those heavily influenced by Hellenistic philosophy's traditional dichotomy of spirit and flesh. From a Gnostic point of view, Harnack tells us, the philosophic life was already there in Christian communities; it remained only to formulate the philosophic doctrine "and after what other model could the latent doctrine be reproduced than that of Greek religious philosophy?" (*HD*, I, 236). The traditional identification of Gnosticism with Christianity is then at least partly based on the enthusiasm with which Gnosticism attached itself to the new religion.

The two points toward which Harnack is driving throughout his discussion of Gnosticism are these: (1) that Scripture and interpretation of Scripture never were clearly separable in emergent Christianity; and (2) that gnosticizing tendencies were, from the beginning, central to Christianity and that the notion of a clear separation between a heretical Gnosticism and an orthodox Christianity is a belated revision of its own origins by a triumphant orthodoxy. Let us turn now to examine this second point more closely.

Harnack points out that the Catholic church was afterward willing to acknowledge only those writers of the first century who were content to confine speculation to the allegorization of the Old Testament. All those who undertook in this period to "furnish Christian practice with the foundation of a complete systematic knowledge, she declared false Christians, Christians only in name" (*HD*, I, 227). In reality, no such clear-cut distinction existed at the time. At the practical level, many Gnostics made no attempt to separate themselves from orthodox Christian communities; they professed the Articles of Faith, either holding secret reservations or regarding their Gnostic beliefs as "in addition to" those of their uninitiated Christian fellows; and Gnostic tendencies not infrequently appeared among the bishops, deacons, and presbyters who were supposed to be the bulwarks of orthodoxy and catholicity.

Harnack characterizes the true historical relationship between Gnostic and orthodox as essentially consisting "in the fact that the Gnostic systems represent the acute secularizing or hellenizing of Christianity, with the rejection of the Old Testament; while the Catholic system, on the other hand, represents a gradual process of the same kind with the conservation of the Old Testament" (*HD*, I, 227–28). The Gnostics' eventual rejection of the Old Testament and the God of creation marked them off most decisively from orthodox Christians. Yet, as Harnack suggests, the Gnostic style of speculation, their philosophizing and systematizing tendencies, play a key role in the emergence of the Catholic system and the development of a doctrine to support and distinguish it from other religions, especially Judaism. In this sense, it is quite accurate to say that, condemned as heresy, Gnosticism gains half a victory in the growth of the Catholic church itself. Harnack goes so far as to say that in terms of their position in the history of dogma, the Gnostics were *the* Christian theologians of the first century. They were the first to work up the tradition systematically, and they undertook to establish Christianity as an absolute religion, distinct from Judaism (*HD*, I, 228). Originally, heresy was not at the borders of the new religion; it was at the very heart.

For the Gnostics, the easiest and most logical way to establish Christianity's independence from Judaism was to reject the Old Testament altogether, on the grounds that the wrathful God of the Jews, creator of a suffering world, could not possibly be the redeeming God of Christ. Yet without the Old Testament and the historical, traditional element it brought to Christianity (not to mention the formidable block to conceptual reduction represented by the New Testament/Old Testament tensions and by the internal contradictions of the Old Testament itself), the infant religion might well, under the pressure of Hellenic ideas, have been quickly transformed from a religion into still another philosophy of religion (*HD*, I, 228–29).

Harnack too provides a brief survey of the key elements of Gnosticism, which he discusses under the headings of the speculative and philosophical, the mystic element connected with worship, and the practical or ascetic. He agrees with Jonas about the representative quality of Gnosticism, arguing:

> The close connection in which these three elements appear, the total transformation of all ethical into cosmological problems, the upbuilding of a philosophy of God and the world on the basis of a combination of popular mythologies, physical observations belonging to the Oriental (Babylonian) religious philosophy, and historical events, as well as the idea that the history of religion is the last act in the drama-like history of the Cosmos—all this is not peculiar to Gnosticism, but rather corresponds to a definite stage of the general development. It may, however, be asserted that Gnosticism anticipated the general development, and that not only with regard to Catholicism, but also with regard to Neoplatonism, which represents the last stage in the inner history of Hellenism.
>
> (*HD*, I, 231–32)

The words "inner history" seem especially significant for the more Harnack talks about it, the more elusive the distinctiveness of Gnosticism becomes. Not exactly a philosophy of religion, not exactly a religion, Gnosticism seems increasingly to represent, especially where Christianity is concerned, the alienated inwardness of a community increasingly concerned with the external dimension of its existence in this world. It is as if the Gnostics' self-imposed role as the mysterious, inner dimension of the Christian community could somehow guarantee the existence of a transcendent, invisible realm, while presenting itself merely as an earthly reflection of a cosmic dualism.

The staggering boldness of Gnostic interpretation was clearly linked to this sense of representing an inner dimension to the world of appearances (apparent authority, apparent history, apparent community)—an absolute knowledge transforming faith in the literality of the revealed word into a knowledge of God, nature, and history. Gnosticism, which had provided the interpretive and conceptual instruments needed to establish a Christian orthodoxy, remained, because of its insistence on secrecy and the absolute privilege of the initiate, a powerful source of instability in the church, made even more subversive by the fact that Gnostic initiates and defenders of orthodoxy shared so many of the same interpretive and conceptual tools. Despite these similarities, however, a clear divergence between Gnostic and orthodox exists over the fundamental question of whether interpretation is to be conceived as the quest for absolute truth or for a truth valued for its usefulness in sustaining an inclusive religious community in this world.

At the heart of Gnostic interpretation, Harnack tells us, is a "mythology of ideas," created by the conversion of concrete forms, often drawn from the sensuous (as opposed to conceptual) mythology of Oriental religion, "into speculative and moral ideas, such as 'Abyss,' 'Silence,' 'Logos,' 'Wisdom,' 'Life,' while the mutual relation and number of these abstract ideas were determined by the data supplied by the corresponding concretes" (*HD,* I, 232). The result is

> a philosophic dramatic poem similar to the Platonic, but much more complicated and therefore more fantastic, in which mighty powers, the spiritual and good, appear in an unholy union with the material and wicked, but from which the spiritual is finally

delivered by the aid of those kindred powers which are too exhalted to be ever drawn down into the common. The good and heavenly which has been drawn down into the material, and therefore really non-existing, is the human spirit, and the exhalted power who delivers it is Christ. The Evangelic history as handed down is not the history of Christ, but a collection of allegoric representations of the great history of God and the world. Christ has really no history. His appearance in this world of mixture and confusion is his deed, and the enlightenment of the spirit about itself is the result which springs out of the deed.

(*HD*, I, 232)

Clearly this "mythology of ideas" of Gnostic interpretation stands somewhere between the sensuous but nonetheless literary/interpretive mythology of the Greeks and the more highly rationalized conceptual mythologization of the literary text characteristic of our modern literary interpretation. Indeed, this Gnostic allegory of ideas, with its irreducible dramatic, fictive element may well be the closest analogue to what secular criticism actually does, lending substantial support to Bloom's insistence on the importance of gnosis.

To the accounts of Jonas and Harnack, Elaine Pagels adds a valuable discussion of the differences between Gnostic and orthodox Christian diagnoses of the human condition and its origin, as well as an interesting assessment of the lessons to be learned from Gnosticism. She argues in *The Gnostic Gospels,* her highly appreciative study of the Nag Hammadi manuscripts, that, for the orthodox Christian, sin separates humanity from God—we suffer because we fail to achieve the moral goals that he has set for us. For the Gnostics, however, it is ignorance that determines our suffering by allowing us to be driven by forces we do not understand (*GG,* 123–24). The Valentinian creation myth (Bloom seems particularly attached to Valentinus) finds the origin of all things in the terror, pain, and confusion born of ignorance;

humanity begins with the anticipation of death and destruction (*GG,* 144). This is at least superficially similar to the Freudian view that the potential for neurotic conflict is inherent in the child's near-total ignorance of its own origins and hence of the conditions of its continued being.

Because it was through the body that humanity came to know pain and the fear of death, the Gnostics tended to distrust it (*GG,* 144). By contrast, orthodox Christianity affirmed the natural order, including the flesh, as essentially good except where we have tainted it by our sins. Thus, the orthodox Christ exists less to lead us out of this world to enlightenment than to bring the fullness of God down to sacramentalize earthly experience (*GG,* 146).

As is suggested by the popular success of Pagels's book and the ease with which Bloom's Gnostic Kabbalah is appropriated by his Freudianism (and vice versa), many elements of Gnostic belief are readily accommodated to the psychology that provides the basis for our own modern, anthropocentric view of knowledge. If Foucault is right in *Mental Illness and Psychology* and in *The Order of Things,* and it is only within the last two or three hundred years that we have constituted ourselves as a privileged and distinct object of knowledge, then it is only recently that we have become metaphors for ourselves, and we must be careful to recognize that the essential difference between Gnostic and orthodox Christianity is not between a psychological and a nonpsychological view, but between a view that links metaphorically the inner life of the individual with an immutable and transcendent reality and a view linking metaphorically in history the fate of the individual and his community with the working out of God's progressive design. For the Gnostic, psychology is merely an aspect or fragment of a transcendent reality; for the orthodox Christian, it is an aspect of the salvation history that is the only ground of community between God and man.

Perhaps most decisive of all in the long run is the fact that so much of what the Gnostics believed to be essential remained unwritten. After all, anyone can read what is written down, even those who are not "mature." Thus, Gnostic teachers usually reserved their sacred instruction, sharing it only verbally (GG, 140). This is, of course, in dramatic contrast to the orthodox insistence that all essential knowledge is contained in a canon of Scripture equally available to all who would listen or read.

At the beginning of her discussion, Pagels writes a bit wistfully, perhaps even bitterly:

> It is the winners who write history—their way. No wonder then that the viewpoint of the successful majority has dominated all traditional accounts of the origin of Christianity. Ecclesiastical Christians first defined the terms (naming themselves "orthodox" and their opponents "heretics"); then proceeded to demonstrate—at least to their own satisfaction—that their triumph was historically inevitable, or, in religious terms, "guided by the Holy Spirit."
>
> (GG, 142)

She notes that the Christian tradition owed its survival to the organizational and theological structure developed by the emerging church, almost as if this fact was extraneous to the whole question of what should or should not be included in history (GG, 142). The historical triumph of Christian orthodoxy had less to do with its absolute success in repressing competing tendencies—the church has always had its influential heretics—than with the fact that orthodox Christianity conceived of itself as a historical entity and worked hard to achieve the combination of literal and interpretive community that could sustain such an entity. Naively, Pagels writes as if the activity of writing history were self-explanatory when, in a real sense, each side in the controversy got what it most valued: orthodoxy achieved dominance over the Christian community and its temporal course, and Gnosticism's attachment to secrecy and silence was institutionalized and its asceticism confirmed in persecution as heresy. If, as Pagels implies, the church needed heretics in order to define its own orthodoxy, it is also the case that the Gnostics required a certain amount of persecution in order to confirm their alienation from the demiurgic order of this world. Historical victory depends on adopting the tools of historical existence, on making oneself accessible to history—this the Gnostics did not do.

When Pagels complains that historians, tending to be intellectuals, interpret in terms of history of ideas as if ideas themselves were the mainsprings of human action, perhaps she should emphasize not their preoccupation with ideas but their assumption that history is the thing. The Gnostics would probably not have regarded with such a sense of lost possibility their historical role as the repressed underside of orthodoxy; history was simply not as important to them as to orthodox Christians or, for that matter, to Elaine Pagels.

Nowhere is the contrast between Gnostic and orthodox attitudes toward history more clearly drawn than in the dispute, crucial at the time and crucial for the future of Christianity, over the relevance of the Old Testament. The key figure in this dispute and one of the great geniuses of the early church was Marcion. Although not a Gnostic in his theology, Marcion rejected the Old Testament and the figurative/allegorical mode of interpretation that forged the link between its history and Christian gospel, arguing that the advent of Jesus's God of love marked an absolute break in the history dominated by the Old Testament God of wrath and retribution. To him, it was inconceivable that the Gods of Moses and Jesus could be one and the same (*EC*, 29). It was in order to lay the groundwork for a new, Christian history that Marcion formulated the first canon of New Testament writings and established some of the earliest doctrinally distinct Christian communities (*EC*, 40). And it was, in part, in order to put the Marcionites outside the pale of the church that the biblical canon as we know it was formed.

The church's dispute with Marcion raises fruitfully the question, troubling to Christians then and now, of why the inclusion in the canon of the Old Testament should be so important, despite the disturbing contradiction between the old law and the new gospel. Marcion's formulation of the problem suggests that it is the question of history itself—or perhaps, of whether history is to be the master trope of Christian awareness—that is at stake in the formation of the canon. Another way to put this is to say that Marcion and the bishops disagreed over whether the canon should reflect the problematic nature of history as it was actually being experienced by Christian communities or provide an alternative to the complexity of that problematic existence.

In his *History of Dogma*, Harnack provides a more detailed account of the Marcionite heresy and its significance. The law/love antithesis between the Old and New Testaments is translated into a flesh/spirit antithesis that is at the root of Marcion's asceticism (*HD*, I, 273–74). So strong is this asceticism that Marcion denies that Christ was born or subjected to any process of human development—he simply came down from heaven. Despite this rejection of material origins, however, Marcion does follow Paul in emphasizing the redemptive significance of the death on the cross (*HD*, I, 277).

Marcion used the Pauline Epistles to argue that the apostles did not understand Christ and that, therefore, Christ inspired Paul lest the gospel of grace be lost. But, Marcion argued, even Paul had been largely misunderstood. Marcion never claimed a new revelation for himself, nor did he claim for himself the status of prophet. A true revisionist, he claimed only that he was purging Paul of interpolations and restoring the true text of the gospels. He used the notion of canon in order to select from among the wealth of traditional materials available to him (*HD*, I, 279–81).

But in severing Christianity from the Old Testament, Marcion also sacrificed what Harnack calls "Christianity's dearest possession"—the belief that the God of redemption and the God of creation are one and the same. Harnack then says:

> The antinomianism of Marcion was ultimately based on the strength of his religious feeling, on his personal religion as contrasted with all statutory religion. That was also its basis in the case of the prophets and of Paul, only the statutory religion, which was felt to be a burden and a fetter, was different in each case. As regards the prophets, it was the outer sacrificial worship, and the deliverance was the idea of Jehovah's righteousness. In the case of Paul, it was the pharisaic treatment of the law, and the deliverance was righteousness by faith. To Marcion, it was the sum of all that the past had described as a revelation of God: only what Christ had given was of real value to him.
>
> (HD, I, 282)

Above all, Marcion's attempt illustrates the importance of the Old Testament to early Christianity as the only means of defending a Christian monotheism that was by no means firmly established (HD, I, 285). The orthodox rejection of Marcion's vision of two Gods, two histories, and two communities reflects a similar determination to find in a single, unified canon the master trope for a single history, encompassing all created time, shared by one God with one community.

The continuing significance of the Marcionite stance is suggested by some striking similarities between his attempt to divide the Old from the New Testament and Freud's attempt in the very late (1939), bizarre book Moses and Monotheism[1] to show, on the basis of a combination of mythological, historical, and psychoanalytic inference, that the Moses of the Old Testament, the great father figure of Judaism was, in fact, two distinct individuals: Moses, the Egyptian, who led the Jews out of Egypt and sought to impose

1. The Complete Psychological Works of Freud, ed. and trans. James Strachey (London: Hogarth Press, 1964), XIII, 7–137.

on them the highly idealistic religion of an invisible God, and against whose tyrannical fatherhood they revolted by killing him; and a second, later Moses, who fused collective memories of and guilt over the earlier Moses and his invisible God with the ceremonies of Middle Eastern mystery worship and led them into the promised land. Thus, Freud accounts for the continuing conflict in the Old Testament between a temple worship dominated by the priests and the prophets' emphasis on an invisible God who cannot be identified with or confined within any set of rituals. The ultimate origin of tensions in the Jewish kingdoms of the Old Testament was, Freud argues, an original Oedipal conflict obscured in the revisionary history of the Old Testament.

Freud's attempt to substitute the Oedipal anthropology of *Totem and Taboo* for Old Testament history represents another attempt at reorigination. He argues, in effect, that psychoanalysis constitutes a fundamental break in the metaphorical continuity of our experience of history from the Bible to the present—not only must history begin again, but we must reinterpret origins in terms of that new beginning.

Like Marcion, Freud reveals that monotheism is a trope for the continuity of history, a continuity allowing history to take the place of nature as the mastertrope of man's conception of his own existence, the stage upon which human destiny·is worked out. Conversely, antinomianism is a trope for the discontinuity of history, arguing that history is a metaphor too weak to subsume the extremes of existence, expressed by Freud in the form of Oedipal conflict. Unlike Marcion, however, Freud avoids any attack on divine unity, confining his attack to the identity of Moses, the temporal, human father of our historical tradition. Nonetheless, Marcion had already demonstrated that the kind of logic that Freud directs at Moses could as easily be directed at the Bible as a whole, or at God himself (themselves?). So why the restraint?

The answer lies, I think, in the Enlightenment origins of Freud's own particular brand of scientific rationalism. Consider, for example, that Deism differs decisively from earlier forms of nature worship in the assumption that the divine text of nature can be mastered. In this context, we can see that, from a Deistic perspective, the monotheism that replaces the polytheism or pantheism of earlier attempts to identify divinity with nature is no longer a metaphor for the unity of history; it is primarily a reflection of a monolithic human intention to master the natural and historical environments.

For reasons having to do with his own intellectual heritage, Freud can question Old Testament history but not the one God to whom that history ultimately attests. Thus, Freud comes to grief in *Moses and Monotheism* because, not content with presenting psychoanalysis as the origin of future history, he attempts to revise the past as well, submitting his argument to a retrospective struggle for authority that it cannot win. Implicitly accepting that the authority of the new "science" depends upon its ability to function as an antimyth, Freud concedes to the past the authority he seeks to usurp. Psychoanalysis, or any other mode of interpretation, becomes senseless if it seeks to substitute itself for the outward, historical dimension of its own existence. A psychoanalysis makes as little sense apart from the history that makes it possible and gives it value as the notion of the unconscious without the context of consciousness.

At stake both in Marcion's attack on the Old Testament and in Freud's attack on the identity of Moses is the question of whether any later writing can fulfill, subsume, or replace any earlier one, hence rendering it unnecessary. In *A Map of Misreading* and *Poetry and Repression,* Bloom approaches this question through his discussion of metalepsis or transumption, "the revisionist trope proper and the ultimate poetic resource of belatedness" (*Map,* 101). Metalepsis is a "trope-reversing trope, a figure of a figure" (*Map,* 102), and the tropes or figures being reversed are, in his account, of earliness and lateness. Bloom tells us:

> In a metalepsis, a word is substituted metonymically for a word in a previous trope, so that a metalepsis can be called, maddeningly but accurately, a metonymy of a metonymy. . . . The metalepsis leaps over the heads of other tropes and becomes a representation set against time, sacrificing the present to an idealized past or hoped for future. As a figure of a figure, it ceases to be a reduction or limitation and becomes instead a peculiar representation, either proleptic or "preposterous" in the root sense of making the later into the earlier.
>
> (*Map,* 102–3)

Bloom's prime examples of the transumptive power of metalepsis are drawn from Milton, in whose work "the merging of metalepsis with allusion produces the language's most powerful instances of a poet subsuming all his precursors and making of the subsuming process much of the program and meaning of his work" (*Map,* 103). It is, of course, the consistent failure of later poets, especially the great Romantics, to equal Milton's subsumptive/transumptive success that puts the anxiety of influence at the center of Bloom's post-Miltonic literary history and fuels his apparent pessimism about the poetic future.

In order to clarify the nature of Milton's achievement, Bloom offers the famous "Optic Glass" passage from *Paradise Lost* (I, 283–313). Samuel Johnson, Bloom points out, complained that Milton's "adventitious" image of Galileo and his telescope as a part of a comparison of Satan's shield with the orb of the moon "crowds the imagination with the discovery of the telescope, and all the wonders which the telescope discovers" (*Map,* 130)—in other words, it is an anachronistic extraneity threatening to usurp the entire passage, a passage heavy with allusions to Homer, Virgil, Ovid, Dante, Tasso, Spenser, and the Bible.

102 · Literary Revisionism

Bloom cleverly leaps on Johnson's observation and characteristically turns it to his own purpose. It is there, he says,

> because the expansion of the apparently extrinsic image crowds the reader's imagination, by giving Milton the true priority of *interpretation,* the power of reading that insists on its own uniqueness and its own accuracy. Troping upon his forerunners' tropes, Milton compels us to read as he reads, and to accept his stance and vision as our origin, his time as true time. His allusiveness introjects the past, and projects the future, but at the paradoxical cost of the present, which is not voided but is yielded up to an experiential darkness, as we will see, to a mingling of wonder (discovery) and woe (the fallen Church's imprisonment of the discoverer).
>
> (*Map,* 132)

As is the case here, Milton's transumptive allusions involve a wrenching reorientation of perspective, which, by its imaginative power, utter rightness, and unavailability to precursor poets, imposes a new stance on an entire tradition of allusion and implies the positive advantage of lateness.

The obvious question at this point is, Why were none of the poets after Milton able to equal or surpass his success in employing this transumptive allusiveness? They certainly tried to do so, for, as Bloom points out, the metaleptic reversal of Milton "dominates the imagery of the closing lines of many major Romantic and Post-Romantic poems" (*Map,* 103).

Part of the explanation lies in the peculiar nature of Milton's greatness. Bloom argues:

> Milton, who would not sunder spirit from matter, would not let himself be a receiver, object to a subject's influencings. His stance against dualism and influence alike is related to his exaltation of unfallen *pleasure,* his appeal not so much to the reader's senses as to his reader's yearning for the expanded senses of Eden. Precisely here is the center of Milton's own influence upon the Romantics, and here also is why he surpassed them in greatness, since what he could do for himself was the cause of

their becoming unable to do the same for themselves. His achievement became at once their starting point, their inspiration, yet also their goad, their torment.

(Map, 126–27)

This is affecting but also somewhat evasive since it manages to beg the question of why what Milton could do for himself should necessarily be the cause of the Romantics' becoming unable to do the same for themselves. Even if we answer with Bloom that it was because they could no longer be first, we are left wondering why priority should be so much more important after Milton than before.

Clearly, Milton's success in turning lateness to advantage seems closely related to his accepting attitude toward history. The theme of our expulsion from Eden becomes in *Paradise Lost* an attempt to define a productive attitude toward the often disastrous history initiated by the Fall. Here, the relevant contrast is not between Satan and Christ but between Satan and Adam and Eve and, behind them, between Satan and Milton—a contrast emphasizing Milton's own strongly prospective view of human history and the absolute necessity of imagining so as to avoid the sundering of history from desire. Such an absolute distinction between history and desire is fundamental to Bloom's insistence that any post-Miltonic notion of a fortunate lateness is a lie against time and must surely imply that, for sensibilities less powerful (by definition) than Milton's, suffering is somehow inherently more real than joy.

Bloom provides a partial explanation of how this division comes about when he comments:

> Internalization of the precursor is the ratio I have called *apophrades,* and in psychoanalysis it is hardly distinguishable from introjection. To trope upon a trope is to internalize it, so that aesthetic internalization seems very close to the kind of allusiveness that Milton perfected, the Romantics inherited, and Joyce brought to a new perfection in our own century. Yet conflicts

can be internalized also, and the Freudian theory of the superego seems dependent upon the notion that a father's authority can be internalized by the superego. Romantic internalization, as I have shown in another study, "The Internalization of Quest Romance," takes place primarily in intra-subjective terms, the conflict being between opposing principles *within the ego*. Further internalization, then, may aid in freeing a poet from super-ego anxieties (the constraints perhaps of religious or moral tradition) or from ambivalence towards himself, but it is not of any use as a defense against precursors or id-anxieties, though it does enter into the final phase of the influence-struggle.

(*Map*, 152–53)

From Bloom's Freudian perspective, Romantic internalization evades traditional religious and social restraints, making possible at one level a revolutionary poetry. However, it also internalizes in Oedipal form the conflict with the poetic precursor, which becomes a struggle within the ego, inseparable from poetic identity. In this sense, the poetic that so liberates with reference to religion and society confines with reference to the precursor. Bloom's account rather strongly implies that history itself must be escaped in order to lift the burden of the religious/moral superego, the result being the internalization of the conflict between history and desire in the more personal form of a debilitating conflict within the ego itself—a conflict manifested in Bloom's own work, as he would be the first to insist.

Yet once again Bloom seems a bit evasive in his remark that Milton's allusiveness "seems very close" to the aesthetic internalization of the Romantics, sidestepping the question of why Milton is not similarly affected. Bloom seems to be suggesting, without explaining how it is possible, that Milton is able to achieve the appearance and benefits of internalization without actually internalizing—at least not any way accessible to Bloom's Freudian vocabulary.

A number of not necessarily exclusive historical arguments can be offered in explanation of Milton's privileged position. For instance, it could be argued that he was in a position to use transumptive allusion on precursors whose own work does not anticipate such a trope. In addition, it is hard to imagine that the protestant radicalism of the seventeenth century in general and Milton's own religious radicalism, pushing him farther and farther to the left in his own lifetime, could lead anywhere except to religious quietism (as a reaction) or to secularism (as an extension). Bloom's very evasiveness implies an awareness of the availability of such an argument—an argument for the primacy of historical circumstance in making it possible for us to see Milton as the first secular, internal poet without knowing it.

Given this recognition of Milton's peculiar status as a great believer whose radicalism could not be contained in the conventions of belief, we can also see that Milton's exploitation of what Bloom terms "interpretive priority" is based on the canonical priority of the Bible and of biblical interpretation for Protestant Christians—a priority of interpretation that Milton seizes upon just before it begins to be turned against the Bible itself, in a historical moment in which interpretation still points back to belief but is also being turned on belief in a revisionary fashion. Milton's is a confidence in interpretive priority, which, it could be argued, is simply not available in a secular age that knows itself as such.

In the final analysis, however, Bloom's understanding of Milton seems to be observed retrospectively from the vantage point provided by Romantic secularism. Significantly, the "almost" internalization of Milton becomes internalization as we understand it only when Wordsworth's *Prelude* makes internalization and secularization virtually synonymous, and it is only after Wordsworth that poetic internalization becomes fully accessible to Bloom's Freudian analysis. If, as Bloom points out, allusion is, properly speaking, covert reference and Miltonic allusion is very like internalization, we arrive at the conclusion that secularization is for the Romantics essentially a system of covert reference—to the matter of divinity, one assumes. This helps not only to clarify the nature of secularization and the role of allusion in creating a properly secular poetic; it also clarifies how the implicit historical underpinning of Bloom's argument is a kind of demonic parody of the conventional, Abramsian view of secularization as sublimation.

Finally, where the psychological question of internalization intersects the historical question of secularization, we find ourselves returned to the difference that, in Bloom's view, makes Miltonic allusion almost but not quite Romantic internalization—a difference that, based on our analysis so far, can only be the degree of self-hatred and the inability to believe wholeheartedly in anything self-created, to which we referred in Chapter 1.

Returning now to Freud and Marcion, we can see that in granting so much importance to the task of revising the Moses story, Freud fails to convince us that it has been subsumed and is now irrelevant. Not only is he defeated by the covert analogue between the project of monotheism and that of a monolithic human rationality; he is also thwarted by his dependence on a definition of interpretation rooted in the very history he seeks to supersede. The notion that interpretation functions by acting as if writing were merely a formalized reading and uses reading as a form of (re)writing is founded for us in the anomalous relationship between the Old and New Testaments. Similarly, the interpretability of speech and behavior in psychoanalysis is founded on the relationship of conscious and unconscious, which is in form like this interchangeability of reading and writing.

Marcion, on the other hand, seems to evade entirely this kind of inconsistency by simply rejecting the Old Testament out of hand. For the early churchmen, however, this meant the loss of monotheism through the loss of a unified history. In addition, the surrender of history in favor of this final revelation surrenders the domain of human error (and free-dom) distinct from God's will. It is difficult not to feel that the adoption of Marcion's view would have altered consid-erably the quality of our secular history. For instance, the same history that insulates God from blame by sustaining a distinction between the domain of human error and God's will also sustains for an idealizing humanism a distinction between an errant, mundane humanity and an ineffable, es-sential, and inviolable self.

Bloom's position is very instructive when compared with Marcion's. In *Poetry and Repression* (*PR,* 87–89), Bloom argues the inadequacy of figural interpretation in sustaining the claim that the New Testament "fulfills" the Old. Like Marcion, Bloom rejects this definition of the relationship be-tween the two Testaments as an unconvincing failure. Unlike Marcion, however, he does assume that it is natural that the New Testament define itself with reference to the Old and try to subsume it. For Bloom, the New Testament fails just as Freud fails, because of the inseparability of reading from writ-ing. No late text can entirely supersede an earlier one because the very identity of the later project originates in its relation-ship with what it seeks to replace. No late text can fulfill any earlier one because the interpretive ("misprising") nature of reading/writing means that what is fulfilled is always some-thing distinct from the original.

Bloom's alternative to figural fulfillment and to superses-sion is transumption, which shares characteristics with each but nonetheless manages to avoid their failures. Transump-tion is a form of "covert" allusion, with powerful reorient-ing effects, which is covert precisely in order to avoid con-ceding a determining authority to what it seeks to surpass. Thus, Freud's psychoanalysis is transumptive insofar as its existence makes the traditional vocabulary of Mosaic Law seem tangential or unnecessary; it fails to be transumptive when it seeks to make itself into an open, subsumptive allusion to Moses. In this view, the covert nature of transumptive allusion represents an effort to use interpretation against itself—to exploit the interchangeability of reading and writing without submitting to the element of historical determination that it represents. Historically, the development of transumptive allusion, clearly there if not fully developed (Bloom tells us) in Dante, culminates with Milton and seems largely to coincide with the process by which biblical interpretation is slowly forged into an instrument to be turned against the Bible in the name of reason. Also, historically, the effectiveness of transumptive allusion appears to depend on a tension, which, in the English tradition after Milton, can only be contrived in ways that infect the interpretive process of reading/writing with that nagging sense of the ingenuine, which lurks in Bloom's term *misprision,* no matter how hard he tries to make it descriptive and nonevaluative.

In short, as "covert" allusion, transumption is Bloom's trope for the activities of secular humanism itself, and revisionism is its characteristic stance. When this humanism detaches itself from Christianity and the question of belief, it becomes a revision of a revision, and the revisionist stance ceases to revise, becoming a kind of system of retrospective allusions to its own earlier incarnations. As a result, revisionism is no longer able to articulate a genuinely critical position, capable of resisting immediate reabsorption into the social and cultural status quo. What passes for such a critical position is a purely retrospective attachment (a complex nostalgia, really) for more efficacious but now impossible revisionisms. This is Bloom's sense of the fate of the orthodox defense, which is, it should by now be clear, no nearer to some nonrevisionary origin than Bloom is; the relevant distinction is not between the original and its revision but between two revisions in a long line of revisionings.

It is also interesting to note that, if we accept Bloom's contention that no later work fulfills any other, it is but a short step to the conclusion that no work, however great, fulfills and uses up any imaginative possibility—it fulfills only the possibility it creates, not some entity outside itself that can no longer be used. Thus, literature could not, at least theoretically, use up its possibilities and complete the closure of literary history; instead, it merely accumulates works ad infinitum, many of which are immediately forgotten as new ones are appearing. Out of this accumulation, open at both ends, certain works are chosen to construct a past, which is the necessary basis for a sense of community in the present. Significantly, it is against this implication of Bloom's rejection of fulfillment that his notion of a now-impossible transumption, pointing to the winding down of literature to its inevitable and seemingly imminent end, is designed to defend. Literature must end, not renew itself ceaselessly; it must work out and complete its own inner logic, the equivalent of a salvation history, rather than undergoing continual random transformations. Only then can the ascetic self-denial of the writer be transformed into the unfallen enjoyment of the text, freed from the burden of history.

As I have already suggested, in Bloom's stance can be seen a kind of demonic parody of the conventional critic's insistence that literature is a privileged domain in matters of humane value. Bloom's is a negative version of this humanist theology, and his notion of transumption at once discredits naive accounts of the relationship between literature and values and reimposes on his deconstruction of fulfillment the limitations of the literary history it sustains—the closed literary history that confirms the privileged relationship between literature and value in the ultimate conjunction of their mutual decline in this world. Bloom, of course, would argue that since the eighteenth century, literature has largely defined its end negatively and hence that his own negative humanist theology is infinitely more appropriate.

This bias toward the assumption that the essence of literature resides in its special relationship (negative or positive) to values is especially apparent in Bloom's remark: "The Old Testament is far too strong, as poetry, to be fulfilled by its revisionary descendant, the self-proclaimed New Testament. . . . Unless one believes in Revelation, then there is no doubt whatsoever which is the stronger text" (PR, 88–89).

What, we may ask, is the point of talking about such texts apart from belief, as if we could in some way arbitrate with authority between their claims? The texts that Bloom judges here seem only to exist in the judgment itself, and "poetry," in the name of which the Old Testament is too strong, is a synecdoche for that privileged vantage point from which beliefs are depersonalized into humanistic values, arbitrated between and judged, and from which our historical heterocosm is recast as a homocosm. In capsule form, this passage re-creates the way in which literary humanism covertly draws on the resources of religion in order to enforce the primacy of humanistic "values" over religious beliefs and to separate value from belief and attach it to reason.

These observations bring us back to Marcion's rejection of Old Testament history and to the question of why the orthodox church fought so hard to retain it and the monotheism it sustained. The answer, I think, lies in the relationship between God, man, and history articulated in the works of the prophets and acted out in their disputes with the secular authority of kings and the institutional worship of the temple.

Over and over again in the Old Testament the authority of history is confirmed in the attempt to swerve from it, in attempts to assert that the problematic of salvation history and of God's nature (as opposed to his history) has somehow been resolved. But the establishment of the Jewish kingdoms does not signal the coming end of the salvation history any more than the codification of the laws, building of the temple, and regularization of worship signal that God's ways are now definitively known—that covenant has become contract.

In his splendid book, *The Prophets,* Abraham Heschel argues on the basis of a detailed review of the prophetic books that what the prophets emphasize is not knowledge of God, of his ethos, through historical event, but participation in his pathos. The prophet, speaking of what will happen, speaks not of what is happening to man but of what is happening to God. Theirs is the problem of expressing their experience, through history, of God's inwardness in terms of the human and the external (*P,* II, 24).

According to Heschel, an important element of Isaiah's message is that it is the powers of history, not the elements of nature, that carry out the design of God. Historic events reflect divine situations—God's anger, his weariness, his affection (*P,* II, 82). In Isaiah 6, the Lord tells the prophet that he will speak *in order* not to be understood; he will be a prophet in order to contradict the apparent purpose of prophecy (*P,* II, 89). Similarly, when Jonah delivered at the Lord's behest a detailed prophecy of the coming destruction of Ninevah, the people repented and God changed his mind, leaving the prophet looking at best like a fool and, at worst, in danger of his life (*P,* II, 286–87).

There are many places in the Old Testament where the Lord sets a man up as a prophet only to contradict his prophecies and undercut his authority. Significantly, these failures and contradictions have no effect on the status of the prophet as prophet. The essential characteristic of the prophet is not a self-aggrandizing authority based on a foreknowledge of the future but insight into the present pathos of God reflected in prophecies of what should happen if the people do not mend their ways or if God does not show mercy. The prophetic emphasis is on a relationship with God based not on contract but on covenant—not a legal relationship binding on both parties but an intensely personal relationship (*P*, II, 230–31). Heschel remarks at one point:

> Understanding of God is contingent upon the distinction between being and expression. Its quality depends upon one's relationship with the divine. Since the time of Descartes it has been asserted that the understanding of other selves takes place through analogy. While it is true that we do not experience a person independently of his bodily actions or expressions, yet through, and in connection with, these expressions, other selves are experienced with the same immediacy with which we experience our own selves. Our conviction as to their existence is based on directly experienced fellowship, not upon inference. To the prophet, knowledge of God was fellowship with Him, not attained by syllogism, but by living together.
>
> (*P*, II, 223)

As post-Cartesians, we tend to comprehend the world (or comprehend ourselves comprehending the world) by extending outward from ourselves through analogy (thus limiting the world in our own images). But for the prophets, Heschel argues, the experience of God is not only immediate; the immediacy of his otherness coincides with the deepest, most profound self-understanding. Priority is given not to self-experience but to the experience of fellowship with the other.

It is important to understand that pathos is, in this context, not an attribute but a situation; it is not a psychological state but the mode of God's involvement in history and the means by which his presence may be known. It must also be recognized that prophetic history has a double aspect, for God's power in history does not reside in historical processes but in interventions. History per se is where God is defied and justice suffers defeats (*P*, II, 226). History becomes then a complex interaction of continuities and interventions, in which man and God are involved in a dialogue between what man does as an expression of his own reason, fears, and desires and what God does as a manifestation of his pathos. Thus, prophetic history is not so much a psychology of God, certainly not a psychology of man, as it is a kind of psychology of divine creation, which must be differentiated from what we mean by "psychology" because it measures and defines inwardness by the quality and range of its outward engagement rather than making our inwardness the measure of all things.

It is easy to see how this emphasis on God's pathos was, for later Christians, a powerful block against philosophical reductionism; it is also easy to see how the link between pathos and history, locating the focus of our experience of our own being in the experience of the other, countered a Gnostic emphasis on personal psychology that so threatened orthodoxy, with its institutional, community bias. Yet there is a problem here since, on the face of it, the orthodox church's attachment to the visible community and institutions of worship would seem to be more closely related to the worship of the priests and temples than to that of the prophets, or at least this is how it seemed to Gnostics and other heretics, early and late.

Such a view, however, leaves out one essential fact: the eventual failure in the sixth century B.C. of prophecy to sustain its hold on the Jewish imagination. In his essay, "Apocalyptic and History," S. B. Frost argues that prophecy came to grief over the difficulty of recognizing God's will in contemporary events.[2] While some could see in the early years of exile God's judgment on the sins of his people, when exile was followed by long years of Persian, Greek, and Roman domination, the credulity of reasonable men and

2. S. B. Frost, "Apocalyptic and History," in *The Bible and Modern Scholarship,* ed. J. Philip Hyatt (New York: Abingdon Press, 1965), pp. 98–113.

women was stretched to the limit. Surely the "punishment" was out of all proportion to the crime.

The prophetic notion that history could serve as a revelation of the divine mind faced its severest test with the Babylonian assault on Judaea in the sixth century B.C.—an event that engendered violent conflicts of interpretation (everywhere apparent, for example, in Jeremiah) among would-be prophets. As events developed, such conflicts could only worsen until, eventually, the mainstream of Jewish thought came to feel that prophecy places an impossible burden on history to confirm desire and fully embody the true complexity of the relationship between God and his people. As a result, history was largely abandoned as the focus of religious concern and future expectation in favor of law or apocalyptic.

At this time, law replaced the prophet's personal, historical God with an eternalized, largely static deity, confined within the very network of prohibitions he had handed down (Heschel's contrast between covenant and contract). This sense that, through law, God is somehow limited and rendered predictable is the familiar object of repeated attacks by the great Old Testament prophets, who continue to insist in the face of priestly and secular authority that history remains the only means of knowing God as he is *now*.

The apocalyptists, important forerunners of the Gnostics in many regards, recognizing that the religion of the prophets demanded more from history than it could provide,[3] sought by the third or fourth century B.C. to place God beyond the arena of history and looked forward to the day when man would follow. Prophecy takes what Frost calls a "teleological" stance, envisioning the culmination of God's intent in history. In contrast, apocalyptic heavily mythologizes history in order to envision the culmination of God's

3. James L. Crenshaw, *Prophetic Conflict* (New York: Walter de Gruyter, 1971), p. 104.

intent in the end of history itself—a stance Frost calls "eschatological."[4] In order to achieve this, the apocalyptists envisioned another, eternal creation—a kingdom of God—parallel to our own and with which our world would at some future point intersect, thus bringing mundane history to an end. To defend God against responsibility for the evils of this world, they even posited the existence of angels to whom the rule of this world had been entrusted for the duration of historical time and whose misrule was responsible for our suffering.

Yet if history is no longer the text manifesting divine intentionality and this other, eternal creation is the true focus of religious concern, then temporal events become meaningless and the entire expanse of mundane history stretches before us as a kind of wasteland, divorced from God's redeeming intentionality.[5] For the true apocalyptist, expecting the end at any moment, this is not a problem. But Jewish apocalyptic, like later Christian apocalyptic, comes to grief over history's resolute refusal to end.

In addition, Frost's account of how apocalyptic results from demanding too much from history should also cause uneasy stirrings in the mind of the modern critic. Can it be that the uneasy intimations of the decline and apocalyptic end of literature that have haunted the imagination with special intensity since the Enlightenment are simply the consequence of demanding too much from literature? Is it actually the case that the response to the work, which criticism seeks to articulate, is more complex than the original and that our sense of the inferiority of criticism signifies not the greater richness of the original but our frustration at criticism's inability to signify the full measure of our demand? If we can bring ourselves to accept that literature is so much less than

4. "Apocalyptic and History," p. 109.
5. Ibid.

we want it to be, can it become (once again) more than it is? It seems that this would require no less than a third (or is it the fourth?) great redefinition of humanism.

In his book, *Prophetic Conflict,* James Crenshaw examines extensively the tensions between prophet and prophet and prophet and people in the Old Testament, concluding that prophetic conflict derives from the uneasy relationship between the reception of the Word in a divine mystery and its articulation to men in a nuanced and cogent way. Because of this gap between reception and transmission, no valid criteria could ever be developed for distinguishing true from false prophecy.[6] This sounds disturbingly like the secular critic's difficulty in answering the question, How do you know that your interpretation is what the author intended?—a gap between reception and transmission threatening both the authority of the individual interpretation and the legitimacy of the activity itself.

At least the modern critic can reply that what the author intended is only one, and not necessarily the most interesting or useful, criterion for validating an interpretation. This position was hardly available to those who saw themselves as dealing with God's Word; His "real" intention was everything. And perhaps this analogy between the difficulty of validation in prophetic and critical interpretation makes even clearer the ultimately theological roots of the primacy of authorial intention and of text over commentary in the work of many modern critics. Authorial intentionality lends authority to the activities of the critic and provides a common focus upon which an interpretive consensus can be formed and critical practice institutionalized—at least in theory.

Yet there is a glaring difficulty with this deceptively clear, practical choice of a locus of interpretive authority: it must

6. *Prophetic Conflict*, p. 110.

inevitably be violated by the very interpretive act it is supposed to authorize. An interpretation, any interpretation, adds its words to the text, words not originally intended or authorized. Generally, this difficulty is gotten around by defining it out of existence. In secular interpretation, an absolute distinction between literary language and interpretive language is created, which, in effect, frees the interpreter to do pretty much as he pleases as long as he loudly proclaims his subservience to the author of the original (all the while keeping his fingers crossed). In practice, it is a virtual certainty that the critic will go considerably beyond authorial intentionality strictly defined because, quite simply, what we can all agree to be the author's original intention is in the great majority of cases interesting to the professional critic only as the starting point he quickly moves beyond.

This is the difficulty with E. D. Hirsch's promethean efforts to find in intentionality the epistemological basis for valid interpretation[7]—by the time he has, with the requisite rigor, segregated meaning (what can be agreed upon with reference to intentionality) from significance (that which is of interest but, by its very nature, beyond consensus), there is virtually nothing left in the former category to engage the sophisticated intellect. Granted, a requisite attention to authorial intention is necessary to the pedagogical role of the teacher of English literature, but it is extremely important that we not mistake the demands of pedagogy for the limits of critical thinking.

Bloomian misreading is the result of combining the "misreading" of authorial intentionality inherent in every interpretive addition, the historical consequences of Enlightenment melancholy and Romantic ambivalence, and the results

7. See E. D. Hirsch, *Validity in Interpretation* (New Haven: Yale University Press, 1967) and *The Aims of Interpretation* (Chicago: University of Chicago Press, 1976).

of modern Anglo-American criticism's obsession with authorial intentionality and the epistemological basis of criticism. Recognizing the intimate relationship of adherence to
authorial intentionality and the literature/criticism distinction with the futile dream of a single epistemological ground
of criticism, Bloom refuses the question as posed, rejects the
intellectual primacy of consensus, and embraces a personal,
pragmatic gnosis based on his conviction that being right is
critically of little value if the point is of interest merely as a
part of a misconceived and futile project. In this context, we
can see that it is ultimately difficult to tell whether Bloom
has actually rejected the problematic of authorial intention or
simply taken its adherents at their word and followed its
implications out to their conclusion, daring them to uncross
their fingers and follow.

For the Christian, the violation of authorial intention inherent in interpretation (and specifically warned against at
the end of the New Testament) is defined away by means of
the notion of the biblical canon. The notion that the Bible is
the Word of God instantly elevates it to a status rendering all
other utterance interpretive. In this sense, all postcanonical
writings are commentaries. Every book is subject to the
closest scrutiny for what it may imply about the Book, even
as writing is freed to address itself to other matters. This
freedom is primarily based on the conflation of interpretation and writing after the canon, a conflation that makes it
possible to see whatever is created as something interpretable
and to affect interpretation by creating new objects to be
interpreted.

We are familiar with this process in the way much modern literature, especially poetry and criticism, increasingly
aware of the presence of a sophisticated professional audience, has grown toward that audience and away from the
reading public as a whole. However, lacking the common
reference point of the canonical Bible, this high culture is

without the means of relating itself back to the larger society except in terms of a steadily reiterated awareness of its own alienation.

To return now to our historical discussion, the vulnerability of prophecy and apocalyptic to contradiction by history limited their effectiveness as vehicles for the expression of human desire and paved the way for the new Christian message. The hiatus between the heyday of prophecy and the rise of the church allowed Christianity to regard itself as completing the prophetic attempt at the redemption of history or, perhaps more accurately, since Christian revisionists necessarily regarded this earlier attempt as a failure, as completing the historical redemption of prophecy. Interpreting Old Testament prophecy as a sign of the alienation of desire from history, Christianity offered itself as a reuniting of history and desire by means of Christ, whose incarnation reconfirms God's immanence in his creation and its history. In order to be fully manifest, this vision required that Old Testament prophecy be a part of the Bible and that the Old Testament as a whole be included as the history being redeemed in the new revelation. Without this background, much of the significance of the new religion would have been obscured. The means of achieving all this was the canon, to which we now turn in detail.

THE CANON: SACRED AND SECULAR

In the conclusion of his history of the early church, Henry Chadwick remarks:

> The central question of the apostolic age turned on the continuity or discontinuity of the Church with Israel. Those who wanted to assert the continuing validity of the Mosaic Law, and Gentiles who, at the opposite extreme, urged the abandonment of the Old Testament were alike rejected. The accepted way became St. Paul's *via media*. The Old Testament retained a permanent place in the Christian Bible as the history of a divine

education of the race, a tutor to bring men to Christ, and a book to be interpreted in light of Christ. In consequence the Church may never have felt completely at home with the Old Testament, but it has never been able to do without it.

(*EC,* 285)

With the coming of the subapostolic age (A.D. 70–140), the deaths of those who could speak with direct knowledge of the teachings of Christ, or even of the teachings of one or more of the original apostles, created a crisis of authority threatening the very existence of a distinct Christianity. Chadwick tells us:

> The second century was accordingly the age when the basic pattern of Christian doctrine began to be tersely summarized in embryonic creeds, when the ministry achieved its universal threefold shape of bishop, presbyter, and deacon, and when finally the canon of the New Testament came to be formed. Order and unity were urgently needed, especially because of the centrifugal tendency of Gnostic syncretism. The conquest of Gnosticism may be counted the hardest and most decisive battle in church history.
>
> (*EC,* 286)

Thus, by the end of the apostolic age, Christianity faced a threefold challenge: (1) to distinguish itself from Judaism, into which (without the immediate and counterbalancing authority of the apostles) it was in danger of being reabsorbed as long as its gospel remained an allegorical extension of the Old Testament; (2) to prevent its reduction into a philosophy of religion at the hands of a wide variety of metaphysical Platonizers; and (3) to prevent its further reduction into a myriad of fragmented and enclosed mysteries at the hands of the Gnostics.

In response, the second-century church developed the three cornerstones of a specifically Christian orthodoxy: (1) the apostolic Articles of Faith, marking the generally accepted fundamentals of Christian belief; (2) the apostolic succession of bishops within the church, establishing a link between the present authority of the church and that of the original apostles; and (3) the New Testament canon of apostolic writings. In each case, the measure of authority becomes apostolicity—an authority based in a precarious but fertile relationship of presence, absence, and anticipation. Clearly, this authority is still present in the persons and actions of the bishops, yet it is not fully present because the authority of the original, apostolic Christianity can be (and frequently was) turned against that of the bishops. Finally, though lost in its original form for the present, this untainted apostolicity can still be anticipated as a part of a millenial "return" of ideal Christianity. In modern, secular letters, the commanding cultural authority of literary greatness is much more exclusively based on the conviction that it is no longer possible—a conviction depending on an entropic literary history very different from the sense of history giving apostolic authority its prospective thrust. As we conceive it, literary greatness refuses the mediate incarnation, as in the authority of the bishops, which would maintain it as an intimate part of our lives. It remains much more a possession of the past than something that can be anticipated in the future, a reproach rather than a hope. It is part of our purpose here to account for this difference.

By and large, secular literature, especially criticism, has failed to fully confront the problem of hope, which is the very heart of its inheritance from the sacred literature and commentary that has shaped it in so many other, more apparent ways. On the basis of what we have done so far, we can suggest two possible factors contributing to this difference. First, we have failed to achieve our secular equivalent of incorporating the Old Testament into the canon. As we have seen in our discussion of the notion of secularization, our engagement with our own history confirms us in the role of disinterested observers, not participants. Trumpeting most loudly the virtues of the past, we simultaneously announce its irrelevance. When the balance of identity/difference tips so far in favor of difference, we inevitably become alienated from the only store of images, ideas, and experiences available to us for the construction of an image of the hoped for.

Second, intimacy is precisely what the idealizing of greatness tries to prevent. Cutting us off from weakness and failure, it also cuts us off from possibility, from the whole problematic of desire. It is this kind of intimacy that Bloom seeks to restore, with his frequently unpretty attribution to poets and poetry of all the Oedipal conflicts and evasions that we are accustomed to identify in our own lives. To my mind, it is an extraordinary circumstance, crying out for examination, that it should be regarded as an outrage to attribute to the dead, however great, the weaknesses and conflicts we accept with such equanimity as explanations of ourselves. That Bloom's own intimacy with the poetry of the past carries him so far from hope is a measure of the degree to which he too is enmeshed in the ways of thinking he seeks to deplore.

Although it would hardly do to slight the importance to the church of the Articles of Faith or of an institutionalized hierarchy of authority, we can gain a clearer sense of the tremendous impact of Christianity's new dependence on the notion of the canon from Harnack's extensive catalogue of its effects in his *Origin of the New Testament*.

First, the canonical New Testament immediately emancipated itself from the conditions of its origin in order to become simply the gift of God and Christianity's last court of appeal (*ONT*, 116). In other words, the canon is thoroughly revisionary, both internally, in relation to the Old Testament, and externally or historically, in relation to its own origins—it effects a radical displacement of history into the realm of the ideal. Through the medium of the canon, history is transformed into a salvation history, answering to desire. As Harnack puts it: "The New Testament has added to the Revelation in history a second written proclamation of this Revelation, and has given it a position of superior authority" (*ONT*, 121) so that Revelation and canon become one: "All that happened, happened only that it might be taken up into the book, and that in the book and working from the book it might first effect that for which it was intended" (*ONT*, 122).

Taking its place beside the facts for which it vouches, the New Testament canon transforms the facts in its own image—into words, a written text—and as Christians approach the inevitable conclusion that "history required this literary revelation at least as a complement," the words "what was written was written for our learning" come to be understood as if they meant "what happened for our learning must be written" (*ONT*, 122–23); that is, what is written must have happened for our learning by virtue not of its having happened, but of having been written.

An extreme example is provided by Origen (184–254), who argued that God reveals Himself in two great parallel creations, the Bible and the cosmos. The latter is the outcome of divine thoughts; the former is the system of divine thought itself. If Christianity is the religion of the book of divine ideas, "then it necessarily followed that the Revelation in historic fact, including the historic Christ, of which the Book gives the narrative, must fall into the background when compared with the Revelation in writing and must become something symbolic. It is necessarily 'mythos,' while in the Book the 'Logos' bears sway" (*ONT*, 123).

From such a perspective, canon becomes the subsuming antithesis of the mundane, literal history of mere events. In terms more familiar to secular criticism, since the Book subsumes into itself its own origins, there is no longer any external, prior intentionality to which it refers—the Book is the Revelation, it does not merely express it as the secular work is frequently treated as an expression of its author's intention. Significantly, even Christians who rejected such speculative theories as Origen's were freed to adopt in practice a position not so very different by their dependence on the notion of the canon as written revelation. But it is not enough to say that by substituting the literality of its own written being for the literality of historical event, the Bible encourages the abstraction of its ostensibly historical narrative "mythus." In the fullness of its written being the canon bestows on all it contains a kind of equality of importance. As Harnack puts it:

> Because the Bible of the two Testaments contained an enormous wealth of material of every possible variety, all this belonged to Religion, indeed was Religion. Religion is just so much knowledge concerning what happened on the second day of Creation as it is knowledge of the loving kindness of God, of the journeys of the Apostle Paul as of the Coming of the Saviour.
>
> (*ONT,* 124–25)

Thus, if the canon made possible the idealization of history, it also prevented that idealization from becoming a philosophy of religion capable of substituting itself for Scripture. Thus, the canon makes of Christian orthodoxy the subsuming antithesis of both mundane historical literality and philosophical abstraction.

Second, without the New Testament, the temptation was always there to establish the independence of the new religion from Judaism by rejecting the Old Testament altogether. The inclusion of the Old Testament in the Christian Bible in a role subordinate to that of the New and the resulting tension between the predominantly historical Old Testament and the gospel teachings of the New Testament prevented Christianity from becoming simply and literally a religion of the Book (*ONT,* 126, 130) and introduced into the canon a productive element of relativity. "The inconsistency and inconvenience of having in the sacred Oracles of God elements of graduated, indeed sometimes antiquated value" (*ONT*, 130) were, Harnack argues, certainly compensated for by the way in which this relativity—encouraging such notions as that of Irenaeus that the Old Testament belongs to the childhood of humanity, the New Testament to our maturity (*ONT*, 127)—gives Christianity a permanent vested interest in a historical as well as an ideal vision of truth.

Chadwick tells us that, for Irenaeus:

> The history of salvation is a progressive education, in which God has gradually brought man forward step by step in a long process culminating in the incarnation of the divine Word with a universal gospel diffused throughout the world by the church.
> (*EC*, 80–81)

This dynamic, progressive, relativistic principle internal to the canon makes it the means by which Christianity stands in a continuously subsumptive relation to historical event and prevents the hopefulness of Christian history from being fatally damaged by the repeated disappointment of millenarian and apocalyptic expectations. It is no mere coincidence that the decline of such immediate expectations and the formation of the canon are so intimately related in the history of the early church.

More immediately, this development finally made it possible for the Pauline conception that the Law is abolished through its fulfillment in Christ to assume a central place. Without this historical, developmental aspect of the canon, such a conception had seemed in practice to support Gnostic reductions of Christian salvation, in which arcane knowledge of the "true" significance of revelation replaced the literal word with a personal, privileged key to salvation.

Superficially at least, Irenaeus's view of the Old Testament as an account of our progressive education toward the

Christianity by which it is to be rendered, if not obsolete, then much less important, resembles that eighteenth-century view of poetry as something necessary and proper to earlier stages of civilization, rendered peripheral by the progress toward perfection of modern society. But for Irenaeus, the shape of history is fully revealed in the canon, and all future events are fully subsumable under the overarching authority of its salvation history. Irenaeus's history is not entropic because its progress does not depend on nor is it measured by the increasing irrelevance of the past; it is prospective without negating the past because the Old Testament is a permanent part of the canon's written revelation, indispensable to Christian knowledge.

By contrast, the eighteenth-century progressivism, which measures the advances of society by the decline of "archaic" activities like poetry, is less a prospective vision of the future and ends of society than a defense against the past. No longer sure of its end or direction, such progress can only define itself as a moving away from the things of the past, requiring the devaluation of what has been and of what is.

Third, the New Testament preserved the most valuable literature of primitive Christianity, while delivering the rest to oblivion and limiting the transmission of later works (ONT, 131). Without such a principle of limitation the church and Christianity itself, as a coherent form of religious belief, might well have fallen victim to a flood of apocryphal writings (ONT, 136–37). On the face of it, however, we might expect the formation of an authoritative canon to choke off the development of a legitimate Christian literature once and for all. This did not happen because, even though the New Testament marked the boundaries of Christian orthodoxy by ending the production of potentially canonical writings, it also cleared the way for ordinary Christian literary activity (ONT, 138). With the formation of the canon it was no longer necessary to assume that every Christian writing was inspired by the Holy Spirit, nor to assess it in terms of a potentially transforming effect on Christian belief. Taking up the pen as a Christian was no longer in and of itself an act of presumption, risking transgression, as prophetic speech must necessarily be. By suppressing literary creation at its own level and by denying the equivalence between Christian writing and prophetic speech, the canon redefined all subsequent prophecy as interpretation and opened up a potentially infinite secondary space in which literature could flourish.

> The way was now opened even for a light literature with religious coloring; for the idea of literature was no longer objectionable, and one could make use of it in every direction so long as one paid due homage to the Holy Scriptures.
>
> (*ONT,* 140)

Indeed, "if the Bible was a cosmos, like the universe, it needed for its interpretation every form of science" (*ONT,* 139). From this perspective, all forms of knowledge and all forms of writing stand in an interpretive relation to the Bible. Such an encompassing and various view of Christian knowledge proved more than a match for the more narrowly conceived Gnostic conception of religious knowledge and drove it from the field (*ONT,* 140).

Fourth, it should be recognized that if the New Testament obscured the true origin and historical significance of its contents by creating an eternal and idealized simultaneity among its diverse elements, by impelling men to study it in order to reconcile this diversity, it brought into existence conditions favorable to the critical treatment of its own contents (*ONT,* 140). As Harnack points out, because of its inconsistencies "the inspired canonical document itself imposes the empirical and allegorical method of interpretation" (*ONT,* 142), inviting an interpretation that substitutes itself for the original sense of the text. At the same time, the diversity and inconsistency of the canon also called into being critical and historical methods of treatment culminating in a "science of interpretation" (*ONT*, 144).

Initially these must seem rather odd observations, looking back from our modern vantage point, in what is elsewhere a catalogue of the canon's benefits for Christianity. Certainly, writing in Germany near the turn of this century, Harnack was aware that the "critical" treatment of the Bible, the "empirical and allegorical method of interpretation," and the new "science of interpretation," while useful tools for formulating, defending, and applying Christian dogma, could be, indeed had already been, turned against the Bible in the name of secular reason with devastating effect. Yet, on further consideration, we can see in Harnack's remarks his sense of the Bible's ultimate victory over precanonical and modern secular detractors alike. Subsuming into itself earlier interpretive instruments and imposing itself on the form and development of interpretation as it came to be understood and practiced in the West, the Bible and its canonicity achieved a centrality in matters of interpretation and competing value that is as much a function of the nature of thought and its instruments in our culture as it is of belief.

Fifth, Harnack continues, the New Testament "checked the creation of new events in the scheme of salvation," but it also "called forth and encouraged the intellectual creation of facts in the sphere of Theology and of a Theological Mythology" (*ONT*, 144). In speaking of a "Theological Mythology," Harnack refers to the way in which certain assumptions about the canon—perfection, absolute unanimity, the validity of allegorical interpretation, and so on—construct new facts not in the realm of biblical history but in that of ideas about the nature of God and of Christ by combining, comparing, and recombining at will the various elements constituting the simultaneity of the canon. Still, if the formation of the canon made possible the seemingly infinite multiplication of interpretive facts, it also provided a barrier minimizing their effect on the basic shape of Christian belief sustained by the gospel story.

It is, I think, fairly obvious that the notion of a secular canon of works enjoying a status above and distinct from that of even the most brilliant interpretation of them operates both to perpetuate our involvement through the act of interpretation and to stabilize a cultural self-image and continuity that the freedom of interpretation might well shatter beyond repair. But the defenses erected by the biblical canon against the destabilizing potential of the very interpretation it makes possible and that aids in perpetuating its authority are intended to protect the unique and unchanging identity of God and the promise of collective redemption he represents. To anticipate my argument somewhat, the sanctity of the secular canon does not defend a specific vision of redemption so much as a loosely defined set of values, personality traits really, like tolerance, rationality, and a capacity for idealization, which are thought to promote in some way the future perfection of the individual and society. This particular humanism is embarrassingly open to the contradictions of history; as we all know, great books all too seldom make great people. So behind this cultural self-image of secular humanism is the real object whose integrity is guaranteed by the integrity of the secular canon—an inviolable individual selfhood, a "true" or essential being, in which the possibility of individual transcendence and, perhaps, collective perfectability dwells, safe from the destructiveness of history and our collective existence.

Sixth, the New Testament marks the limit of the period of Christian revelation, giving Christians of later times a belated, somewhat inferior status. On the other hand, not only does it preserve a knowledge of the ideals and claims of primitive Christianity (*ONT,* 146), it also comforts the Christians to follow by making it unnecessary to apply to themselves in their own times the desperately high standards necessary for the early, heroic Christians (*ONT,* 148). Bringing to an end the classical age of Christianity, the Book defines the era in which the ideals it expresses are given free play even as it perpetuates them as the basis of an orthodoxy scaled down to more attainable, human dimensions. It is crucial to recognize that with the formation of the canon, Christianity stands fully revealed, and the belatedness of future generations of Christians does *not* imply a greater distance from redemption.

This is in sharp contrast to the situation for the secular artist as portrayed by Bate and Bloom. Because the secular canon is never fixed and the "religion" of humanism never fully revealed, salvation or the achievement of poetic desire remains a salvation for one in which the poets are in a direct and intensely personal competition—the achievement of one detracts from all the others, and the higher the canon elevates the greats of the past, the greater the burden on the poetic future. The concentrating and distilling effects of canonization, enhanced by the efforts of professional critics, make the canon and its tradition the enemy of present creation.

Seventh, the formation of the New Testament completes the identification of the Word of the Lord with the teachings of the apostles. Because it is apostolic and canonical, every utterance, however trivial, is given tremendous importance. On the one hand, Pauline Christianity very nearly threatened to push aside Christ himself; on the other hand, Paul was in turn replaced by a canonical ideal of him (*ONT,* 150–51). As Harnack remarks:

> Men's minds were ever haunted by the spectre of the Canon. Either they laid violent hands on the man, robbed him of a part of his soul, and modelled him into a figure of strictly logical consistency—for was he not Paul of the New Testament? and even if he was that no longer, still he must be a type—or they were disgusted with him, heaped upon him complaints and re-

proaches which they would never have made if they had not received him out of the New Testament. Still this martyrdom of the Apostle continues; still critics who are elsewhere impartial will not allow a man's right to be more and also less than his own type and his own ideal.

(*ONT,* 152)

But, Harnack goes on to point out, whatever distortions the man may have undergone by virtue of his inclusion in the canon, that position made it possible to include certain of Paul's doctrines, such as the centrality of salvation by faith alone, at the center of Christian belief (*ONT,* 153–54).

Harnack's description reminds us of the tremendous demand that the idealizings of canonization place on human reality and of their tendency to purchase stability and consistency by narrowing conception to exclude very real and urgent aspects of our lives. This is even more true of secular canonizers, for whom the real concerns of poets, critics, and readers often seem too threatening and who defensively distort the figures with which they deal to much less profit than church canonizers have distorted Paul.

Finally, the canon gave the church the weapon it needed to ward off heresy. Indeed, without it, it would have been difficult if not impossible to develop, much less enforce, any notion of heresy at all. At the same time, the canon, especially the New Testament, constituted the court of control before which the church itself could be (and, oh, how frequently) called to account (*ONT,* 154).

To summarize, with the formation of the biblical canon, prophecy comes to an end and heresy becomes possible, as prophetic participation in God's changeable pathos—at once a threat and a promise of imminent millennium—gives way to the eternal present of the Book, in which interpretation becomes our primary mode of participation. The canon involves at one level an injunction to silence, even as at another level it initiates and commands a vast activity of commentary and interpretation. Under these conditions writing is more closely akin to a mode of falling silent, pregnant with significance, than to prophetic speech, and the author is closer to audience than actor. When an author writes, he removes himself from the realm of speech, of normal existence, into a space defined by the distance between text and text, text and world, text and interpretation and, ultimately, between the mundane history continuous and contiguous with present reality, and the privileged, prelapsarian, precanonical period, which, being both anterior and perpetually yet to be, brackets, fixes, and defines the present in terms of its own abstract, ideal history.

Bloom's discussion of the closure of the biblical canon in *Kabbalah and Criticism* begins with his observation that it is only by the authority of institutional Judaism and Christianity that the Bible is complete (*KC*, 98). Although we may well take exception with Bloom's implied denigration here, the point itself is well taken, emphasizing the intimate relationship between the nature and possible ends of interpretation and the institutions that sustain it, promote it, and help or fail to help define its ends. The same, of course, may be said for literary activity in general.

The closure of the biblical canon and the possibility of sustaining it by means of interpretation was a function of the nature of Christian institutions, most especially of the church. The relative disorganization of the secular canon and the perpetual confusion over the ends of interpretation are functions of modern secular institutions, deeply divided in their very foundations. The sociology of academic and literary institutions is beyond the scope of this study, although one cannot help but speculate that the reluctance of interpreters to regard such questions as well within the scope of their discipline is a defense against a knowledge of how deep this institutional confusion really is.

Bloom goes on to compare the closing passages of the

Old and New Testaments. The Old ends with Malachi's prophecy:

> Behold, I will send you Elijah the prophet before the coming of the great and dreadful day of the LORD:
> And he shall turn the heart of the fathers to the children, and the heart of the children to their fathers, lest I come and smite the earth with a curse.
>
> (Malachi 4:5)

The theme of father/son relations is central throughout the Old Testament, in which instances of paternal cruelty or filial disloyalty are metaphors for the people's disloyalty to God and their defiance of his ways. Similarly, disruptions of primogenitor emphasize the qualitative rather than genealogical or natural character of God's ways and dramatize the disruptive effects of his interventions in a human order not equipped to receive him. In the more traditional view then, Malachi's prophecy foresees a reconciliation of God and his sons, between the divine order and the order of man. In effect, it promises that every man will have a personal knowledge of God and be personally known by him, that every man will be, in Heschel's sense, a prophet.

When Bloom interprets this to mean that the "Oedipal anxieties are to be overcome" (*KC,* 99), he expresses his sense of the fundamental identity between the burden of history and the challenges posed by the family in the life of the individual. To be released from one is to be released from the other, Bloom suggests, and it is the recognition of their connection that is prophetic. In effect, the prophecy promises an intensely personal, yet collective, reconciliation with history—a reconciliation that it implies will be the end of prophecy and of "writing" as the Old Testament understands it.

Of course, it is the claim of the New Testament that it is the fulfillment of this promise, the end of prophecy and of canonical writing. In keeping with this claim, the New Testament aims at a much more decisive and explicit closure in this passage from Revelation:

> For I testify unto every man that heareth the words of prophecy of this book, If any man shall add unto these things, God shall add unto him the plagues that are written in this book:
> And if any man shall take away from the words of the book of this prophecy, God shall take away his part out of the book of life, and out of the holy city, and from the things which are written in this book.
> He which testifieth these things saith, Surely and come quickly: Amen. Even so, come, Lord Jesus.
> The grace of our Lord Jesus Christ be with you all. Amen.
> (Revelation 22:18–21)

Remarkably, this passage threatens those who would change the Book with . . . changes in the Book! For if the Bible articulates and imitates that history which potentially includes the participation and redemption of all, then any change in the text risks an exclusionary change in history. The prophet admonishes whoever would change the Book to better suit desire that what he desires is already there, waiting to be read aright. Thus, the imperative is not to write but to interpret, and all postcanonical Christian writing, however powerful, is subsumed under the category of reading.

With the closing of the Christian canon, the comprehensive representation of sinfulness—that for which one can be stricken from the book of life—becomes misinterpretation or the violation of a text. Thus, the focus of our struggle for reconciliation with God and against evil shifts from prophecy or canonical writing to interpretation. An offense against God's authority necessarily involves a text-violating misinterpretation because now there is no authority without a text. And this in turn points to the great mission assigned interpretation by the closing of the canon: to re-present experience in textual form, which, after all, every interpretation must do in order to interpret, for not to be a text (that is, interpretable) is now to be dead to God.

This combination of circumstances, announced at the end of the Christian canon, offers itself rather forcefully as the historical origin of Bloom's linked convictions that all writing can be considered a form of reading and that all reading, insofar as it is a form of writing (and here any new writing added to the Book is a mistake) is misreading. Naturally enough, Bloom strongly resists his reabsorption into the tradition he seeks to de-idealize. Here is his comment:

> St. John the Divine declares the Bible closed with a palpable anxiety as to how this declaration is to be enforced. The issue is *authority*, as it always is in all questions of canon-formation, and it is worth noting that both Malachi and St. John base their authority on the supposedly immediate future, on a First or Second coming of a reality that they seek to introject. Proleptic representation is the inevitable rhetorical resource of all canonizing discourse, which means that all canonizing must be done at the expense of the presence of the present moment. When you declare a contemporary work a permanent, classic achievement, you make it suffer an astonishing, apparent, immediate loss in meaning. Of its lateness, you have made an earliness, but only by breaking the illusion of modernity, which is the illusion that literature can be made free of literature. All canonizing of literary texts is a self-contradictory process, for by canonizing a text you are troping upon it, which means that you are misreading it. Canonization is the most extreme example of what Nietzsche called Interpretation, or the Will-to-Power *over* texts. I am stating the thesis that canonization is the final or transumptive form of literary revisionism.
>
> (*KC*, 100)

In light of what we have already seen, three observations come to mind immediately. First, Bloom ignores the distinction, both historical and theoretical, between St. John's ending to his apocalypse and the actual closure of the canon. The church's answer to his anxiety is the *relationship* between the idea of the canon and the institution of the church, which makes closure possible—a closure which has for the most part and despite St. John's fears been remarkably successful in protecting the integrity of the canon.

Bloom's reluctance to acknowledge this distinction reflects his desire to see closure as an event internal to the text, as indeed he wishes to see canon formation itself—a desire also reflected in his discussion of proleptic representation. Here, then, is our second point: proleptic representation (the technique of bestowing on lateness the authority of origins) is, properly speaking, necessary to all prophetic or apocalyptic rhetoric, which is what Malachi's and St. John's writings are, regarded apart from their somewhat distinct functions in aiding canonical closure. But given the fact that canonical closure brings prophecy to an end and makes possible the almost infinite delay of apocalypse, it seems rather to use proleptic representation to establish itself antithetically as a third and different way of defining humanity's relationship to God and history.

Third, we must wonder if canonization, or interpretation itself for that matter, really is a will-to-power over *texts*. Bloom's whole analysis of the relationship among canonization, misprision, and fear of death seems to suggest instead that interpretation is a will-to-power over reality through the mediation of the text, in which the mastery of the text is really aimed at the reality whose nature is captured and represented in our culturally and historically determined conception of what constitutes a text. In this regard, what Bloom characterizes as a will to power over texts is actually the purchase of a (possibly illusory) power over reality through submission to the text.

As the transumptive trope of trope in literary revisionism, canon is both a trope and not a trope, just as the Bible is both a book and, as the Book, not a book. When a work is canonized, a fundamental change does occur in the quality of its meaningfulness, yet no substitution of one discourse for another occurs as in other tropes. (Another way to say the same thing is that all discourses together become by means of interpretation substitutable for the canon.) The point of salient interest here is that canonization substitutes the text for itself in order, as in the case of St. John, to change its ultimate significance. Even if this is not always true in literal fact, it is true by definition since any discourse substitutable for the canon must be for that very reason canonical.

Thus, not only does canonization mark the limit of Bloom's revisionary play of rhetorical substitutions, his tropology; it is also the final *transumptive* trope of revisionism—both the border of and outside revisionism. Historically, the explanation is simple enough. Interpretive revisionism originates in canonization and is sustained only in relation to canonical authority. The formation of the biblical canon represents the point at which the prophetic/apocalyptic urge in all revisionists becomes internal to the canon and is recast in conservative form as revisionism.

Working backward from here, we can see that the illusion of modernity, which Bloom calls "the illusion that literature can be made free of literature," is the illusion of a decisive, absolute discontinuity in history, a fundamental change in direction. If revisionism and the perpetual sense of modernity it characterizes originate in the canon, then the cherished illusion of revisionism is that something other than reabsorption into the canonical tradition is possible. No less than the rigidly orthodox, however, the revisionist can end only in either failure or canonization.

If the biblical canon internalizes prophecy and apocalyptic as revisionism, the prophet or apocalyptist in every revisionist can only express himself in the wish for/fear of the end of literature and the canon that defines it. The coming end of poetry or literature is the revisionist's equivalent of "Surely and come quickly. . . . Even so, come, Lord, Jesus."

The reason for Bloom's concern, noted earlier, with keeping canonical closure internal to the text is clarified by canonization's ambiguous position as the transumptive trope of revisionism. If canonical closure is external to the text, as Bloom seemed earlier to recognize, the very notion of a completion determined by conditions internal to the text, in the absence of the kind of external authority represented by God or the church, opens up the specter of texts held perpetually open to interpretation by the impossibility of declaring them closed and of a literature perpetually open-ended, lacking the authority to culminate, transform, or close. This sounds rather like the status quo in secular letters, and Bloom's reluctance to embrace it can only be understood if we recognize that something without such closure can never end, only change, and no prophetic or apocalyptic desire can be fulfilled or sustained there.

For the Bloom of *Kabbalah and Criticism,* secular canon formation represents "a question of sad importance: 'which poet shall live?' " (*KC,* 96). Even as we read this defensive formulation, we know that Bloom's real concern is with the corollary question, Which poet shall die? Yet this question too seeks to postpone the melancholy, all-too-obvious answer, All poets must die. For Bloom, the tradition is largely an idealizing/daemonizing defense against this knowledge, although we are justified in wondering if Bloom's demythologizing of the tradition is not just as firmly based as traditional idealizing in a reluctance or inability to distinguish the fate of the poet from the fate of the poetry. For the traditionalist, the permanence of poetry is in some sense seen as a kind of immortality for the poet; for Bloom the fact of the poet's death is a narcissistic wound from which he does not expect poetry as a whole to recover. And all this defensiveness and ambivalence is understandable enough when we realize that what the idea of a great tradition holds out to the poet is a demand that he strive so that what he creates may live on without him. This situation of course brings Bloom back to the subject of psychic defense, as he speculates:

> If tradition is, as Freud surmised, the equivalent in culture of repressed material in the mind of the individual, then rhetorically considered tradition is always an hyperbole, and the images used to describe tradition will tend to be those of height and depth. There is then something uncanny (unheimlich) about tradition, and tradition used by Eliot, say, as a hedge against the daemonic, is itself, however orthodox or societal, deeply contaminated by the daemonic. The largest characteristic of tradition, on this view, is that tradition becomes an image of the heights by being driven down to the depths, or of the depths by being raised to the heights. Tradition is itself then without a referential aspect, like the Romantic Imagination or like God, Tradition is a daemonic term.
> What the *EinSof* or Infinite Godhead was to the Kabbalists, or the Imagination was to the Romantic poets, tradition is now to us, the one literary sign that is not a sign, because there is no other sign to which it can refer.
>
> (*KC,* 97–98)

Bloom does not comment further on tradition-as-hyperbole for the very obvious reason that he is perilously close here to deconstructing his own literary history. If tradition "becomes an image of the heights by being driven down to the depths, or of the depths by being raised to the heights," can't this also be applied to Bloom's own dim view of the future prospects of our tradition to suggest that this is a means of defending the tradition, just as the valorization of anxiety is a means of defending against anxiety? And, in this context, if tradition is nonreferential, what does this suggest except that the "true" relation between defense, desire, and fact cannot be determined where discussions of tradition (or imagination or God) are involved?—that tradition cannot be demythologized finally and decisively any more than it could be mythologized beyond the capacities of revisionists like Bloom to demythologize it. What this means, of course, is that mythologizers and demythologizers alike are firmly within each other's traditions, really the same postcanonical tradition.

Bloom is not quite ready to assume such a position, at least not explicitly, and as he so often does, he uses the notion of psychic defense as his own defense against such a self-deconstruction. The salient fact about repression for Freud is that it never really works; it always readmits in intensified form what it seeks to repress. Now, in relation to tradition, he notes precisely that paradox we noted in Bloom's tropology in our earlier discussion of death and psychic defense (Chapter 1). In the case of tradition, low becomes high, high becomes low, and the daemonic, which Eliot and others consider tradition to defend against, is revealed at tradition's heart. Can we doubt that the "daemonic" referred to here is associated with the fear of mortality and the crushing sense of being isolated in our own doomed individuality that results?

How is it that tradition comes to be identified with death except through not being a sign? Like Imagination, like God, tradition marks the limit of a conceivable tropology—the point at which rhetorical substitution grinds to a halt and gnosticizing interpretation—systematic, internal, timeless—dies. Bloom remarks, as we have already noted: "When you declare a contemporary work a permanent, classic achievement, you make it suffer an astonishing, apparent, immediate loss of meaning" (KC, 100). We might gloss this remark by adding that it is true as long as we continue to regard meaning in the image of Bloom's apparently infinitely mobile identification of trope with psychic defense and fear of death. We might also take the apparent opacity or nonreferentiality of tradition from this perspective as evidence that it marks the point at which (as do imagination and God) a fundamentally ahistorical articulation of the workings of psychic defense and tropological substitution reenters history to encounter the mystery of its own very unsystematic manifestations among various people at various times.

We cling to God, Imagination, or Tradition not because they are inescapable but because we want to; they represent imperatives held in common that elude in the conventions of their own times—because we want them to—the reduction of knowledge to the fear of death. For Bloom then, it is history as a succession of opaque and monolithically authoritative terms subject to de-idealizing that offers his interpretation its dimension of freedom together with representing that death, that new deconstruction which it most fears.

Before we discuss any further Bloom's treatment of canon formation, it might be useful to clarify if possible the distinction between tradition and canon, terms that tend to overlap in use but which imply a distinction in theory. In the case of biblical canon formation, canon is the antithesis of tradition, which, fed by orality and the steady accumulation of apocrypha, had a dangerously destabilizing effect on nascent precanonical Christianity. The work of interpretation could not begin to construct a dogma distinct from Judaism because every such interpretation was potentially in direct competition with its original. In effect, the only way to add to the contemporary understanding of Jesus was to write a new life of Jesus.

The formation of the canon put a stop to this by fixing tradition in the Bible as the revealed form of the Christian religion. Subsequently, all new traditions are interpretive, stemming from the canon, rather than original. This absolute distinction between the canon and its interpretations is sustained by the Bible's sufficiency as the basis of a revealed religion. We can conclude from this not that there is no difference at all in our culture between text and interpretation but that, as Coleridge pointed out, because no secular work can fulfill this condition even for humanism, this distinction is in secular letters based on an ideologically loaded analogy of questionable validity.

As a result of this situation, secular writing, fictional and interpretive, is perpetually open-ended, its ends obscured, and tradition and canon are not clearly distinguishable, existing instead in an indistinct combination of identity and difference. Although Bloom does not distinguish very clearly between canon and tradition in the passages we have just discussed, what we know of the biblical canon suggests that they could just as easily be antithetical as coincident or, given the difference between sacred and secular, as easily neither as either. What we do know is that the biblical canon grows out of and is based on a tradition or genealogical handing down of sacred lore, against which it defends antithetically. After the formation of this canon, the tradition is interpretive, based on and gaining its coherence from a public, highly visible canon.

Part of our difficulty is alleviated if we remember that, although in a secular context we often speak as if books or even entire oeuvres are elements in a canon, the original biblical canon is a book, indeed defines "book" as we have come to idealize and understand it. In this sense, canon is the basis of the assumption of coherence and completeness that defines a book, authorizes the effort, and defines the immediate ends of interpretation. Critical works also constitute themselves in the image of this canonicity; they traverse the field of available texts or quotations within a text in order to constitute a canon of which the quotation/commentary combination is the revealed form.

Yet the fact remains that when we say that a work is canonical, we generally mean that it is one of the line of "great" works by "great" authors constituting the historical self-image of the tradition of literary humanism. In this light, tradition is a kind of self-image and canon the collection of texts sustaining and objectifying it. Since the eighteenth century, this tradition has periodically been constituted and reconstituted in canonical book form through anthologization. In modern anthologies, like the Norton or the Oxford, the addition of notes, glosses, and introductions presents the tradition in its "revealed" form with beginning, middle, and "end," toward which it all tends. Of course, such anthological canons are always open-ended, falling considerably short of the present in their comprehension, and they are thus perpetually subject to replacement—a rethinking of the "end" of the tradition, which may also require a rethinking of older, more established parts of the canon, such as the elevation of Donne at the expense of Milton. The secular tradition is a phenomenon of this open-endedness.

In *Agon,* Bloom assigns a threefold origin to the procedure of canon formation in the West: (1) in "the Jewish tradition of forming Scripture, with its Christian misprision and subsequent refinements"—the most important; (2) in "the Alexandrian Hellenistic tradition of literary scholarship . . . the most instrumental for us, since it inaugurated the canonization of what we would now call secular texts"; and (3) in "the Greek poets themselves, at least from Hesiod on," who "invented poetic self-canonization, or self-election." All poets who seek any permanence for their work, Bloom goes on to say, have, from Hesiod to the present, built "the canonical ambition, process, and agon" directly into their texts (*A,* 284).

There is something misleading in Bloom's characterization here of the Christian scriptural tradition as a misprision of the Jewish tradition. For one thing, the conclusion to the New Testament is so much more clearly and explicitly concerned with closure than that of the Old Testament that it seems probable that at least a prima facie case could be made (indeed has been made using different vocabularies) for the position that the New Testament is genuinely transumptive in relation to the Old. Conceivably, we might even yield to Bloom his point that figura and the notion of fulfillment are inadequate to overcome the strength of the Old Testament and still conclude that, from Bloom's own "poetic" point of view, the true authority of the New Testament lies elsewhere—in the success with which it has succeeded in imposing itself not only on our reading of Christian works but, throughout the Christian West, on our rediscovery and subsequent use of the Jewish scriptural tradition, of the Alexandrian tradition of secular canonization, and of the poetic tradition of self-election.

This brings us in turn to the recognition that if the Christian tradition of scriptural canon formation is a misprision, it has imposed misprision (that is, its own distinctive formulation of the problematic of interpretation) on our entire Anglo-American tradition, including Bloom's own contribution, which has misprision at its heart. Looking back from our present position, this Christian misprision is enormously more influential as a tradition than any other, a more shaping influence on the people and the works that brought us to our present point. To suggest that there is any way in which we can now retrospectively restore some kind of balance between origins is to ignore the fact that those alternative origins still exist largely within the limitations imposed by the Christian canonical/interpretive tradition. It is the continued effectiveness and authority of this tradition, even in secular letters, that stands between Bloom and the translation of his heterodoxies into a new, pragmatic gnosis.

Continuing his discussion of canon formation, Bloom presents what he calls "a highly compressed account of a theory of canonization" (A, 285), which makes clear his desire to see canon formation primarily as a function of poetic self-election—a necessary step if the question of canonicity is to be made fully available to Bloom's Oedipalizing mode of analysis. A canonical text is, he argues, one that has engendered strong misreadings over several generations. By "strong misreading," Bloom here means "strong troping"— one available only to the "agonistic striver in the reader, not to the reductionist who inhabits always the same reader" (*A,* 285–86). Thus, Bloom agrees with Longinus and Shelley that such poetry exists "in order to compel the reader to abandon easier literary pleasures for more difficult satisfactions" (*A,* 286).

Bloom's formulation differs from the conventional view that a canonical work is one that continues to be read *and* interpreted only in that it makes explicit, indeed reifies, the notion of difficulty already residing in our understanding of interpretation. We must wonder if this emphasis on the necessity to strive against difficulty does not suggest that poetry must become increasingly difficult in order to satisfy Bloom's "agonistic striver," in which case the goal of poetry is the steady reduction of its audience to a few "Gnostic" initiates. The alternative is to say that the agonistic striver brings to the text the difficulties and pleasures he seeks, in which case canonization is only by convention attributable to the text at all; primarily, canonization is an expression of the will-to-power and an interpretive self-image.

In connection with this second possibility, it should be pointed out, first, that Bloom still purports to make statements about how poems work and to attribute powers to them capable of overcoming all efforts at successful transumptive misprision and, second, that historically, Bloom's agonistic strivers have persistently tried to attribute both the difficulty and the pleasure to the text, at least in substantial measure. The convergence of Bloom's account of canonization with more conventional (and one is tempted to say, equally futile) accounts of poetic value indicates that the difficulty may well be with Bloom's emphasis on agon, struggle, difficulty. Elevating it as he does, Bloom seems dangerously close to idealizing what was originally for him *the* instrument of de-idealization. It could be argued that art is most mimetic when it is difficult, that agon is the imitation of reality and not the revealed form of poetry.

In any case, Bloom's notion of strong troping leads him to "a true law of canonization": "In a strong reader's struggle to master a poet's trope, strong poetry will impose itself, because that imposition, that usurpation of mental space, is the proof of trope, the testing of power by power" (*A,* 286). For the last three hundred years or so, he maintains, the nature of that strong troping has been transumptive and, by way of illustration, he elaborates his earlier accounts of Miltonic transumption, which

> crowds the imagination by joining Milton to an ancient and complete truth, and by making every poet's figuration that comes between the proper truth and Milton's text into a trope of belated error, however beautiful or valuable. By joining himself to an ever early candor, Milton thus assured not only his own place in the canon, but taught his poetic successors how to make themselves canonical by way of their transumptive imagery. This remains the canonical use of strong poetry: it goes on electing its successors, and these Scenes of Instruction become identical with the continuity of poetic tradition.
>
> (*A,* 286)

Bloom seems very close here to saying that Milton discovered poetic originality as we have come to understand it, or, perhaps more precisely, he forged the poetic instrument capable of achieving such originality. From him, his successors learned the paradoxical task, the self-defeating task, of trying to be original like Milton. This leads us to the rather ghoulish conclusion that the continuity of the modern tradition lies in the continuous failure of its poets—a conclusion already demonstrated in Bloom's brilliant reading of Browning's "Childe Roland to the Dark Tower Came" in *A Map of Misreading* (106–22).

His reflections on Milton lead Bloom into a brief historical review, stressing a shift in poetry toward Wordsworthian inwardness from the emphasis, dominant from Homer to Pope, on "the characters and actions of men and women clearly distinct from the poet who observed them" (A, 287). Bloom sees this new inwardness as "a necessity, perhaps a blight, of the broad movement that we see now to be called Romanticism or Modernism, since increasingly the latter would appear to have been only an extension of the former" (A, 287).

All of this paves the way for Bloom's ingenious answer to the questions facing any student of post-Miltonic literature, and especially one who adheres to an entropic literary history: why the destructive obsession with originality from the eighteenth century on? and why do post-Miltonic poets consent to invent and play with their predecessors this game they cannot win? Bloom argues:

> The traditional use of poetry in the Western world has been instruction through delight, where teaching has meant the common truths or common deceptions of a societal tradition, and where esthetic pleasure has meant a fulfillment of expectations founded upon past joys of the same design. But an individual psyche has its own accidents, which it needs to call truths, and its own necessity for self-recognition, which requires the pleasures of originality, even if those pleasures depend upon a kind of lying-against-time, and against the achievements of the past.
>
> (A, 287)

Such a historical explanation implies an equally important statement of the end of poetry:

> The use of poetry, for the reader as for the poet, is at a profound level an instruction in defense. Poetry teaches a reader the necessity of interpretation, and interpretation is, to cite the other great philosopher of modern poetry, Nietzsche, the exercise of will-to-power over a text.
>
> (A, 288)

If the poetry of inwardness requires the satisfactions of originality and if poetry is useful as instruction in defense, it can be argued that the same could be said of life itself. Perhaps there is merely a difference of degree, just as the poet, in Bloom's view, resents more the necessity of death. Beyond this difference in degree, the primary difference between poetry and life is that poetic desire is desire for power over texts rather than over reality. Apart from a tradition, like that of biblical canonicity, which privileges texts as a focus for the problems and satisfactions of existence, such a pursuit seems absurd.

By now, the entire tendency of Bloom's account of canon formation is toward the notion that the purpose of poetry is self-defense, even at the cost of "lying-against-time, and against the achievements of the past." What is odd about Bloom's argument is that, by his own account, poetry is a failure as a defense of the self—the younger poet is ultimately defeated by the precursor as a condition of the internalization making poetic election possible. If we take the Bloom of *The Anxiety of Influence* at his word, the self's best defense is not to become involved with poetry at all, especially since in Bloom's poetic history it can make little difference whether, as readers, we take an idealizing or de-idealizing stance toward literature—after all, neither ultimately works as a defense against life or death. Our best defense is to forget poetry, recognizing that since its inward turn it has had little to tell us except of the self's vulnerability to disillusionment and death—a lesson we are all too able to glean from life for ourselves.

Part of the difficulty with Bloom's view of canon formation as a defense of an indefensible selfhood is that his call for interpretive/poetic power as a goal and standard, when combined with a hostility to institutional definition of the ends of interpretation, becomes still another version of the doomed pursuit for originality, helplessly perpetuating what it seeks to revise.

Despite these difficulties, Bloom's description of canon formation is a perfect match for his historical explanation and his conception of the ends of poetry—a circumstance suggesting that the true purpose of secular canon formation is to match texts and commentary so as to imply a certain history and a certain end for literature. Indeed, this is exactly how Bloom's own account of canonicity works. As the transumptive trope of a transumption that, since Milton, has been accessible imperfectly at best, Bloom's canonization is the sign of its own absence, a sign that we are alienated from a canonization that is also the fulfillment of a desire.

Another way to approach this is to recognize that Bloom defines tradition in terms of the figure of hyperbole, involving images of height and depth, while he defines canon in terms of transumption, involving images of earliness and lateness. They combine to form a kind of grid, in which tradition is an ongoing qualitative justification/interpretation of the canon, whereas the canon arranges texts in order of priority to objectify the tradition. At every point, they are mutually and perpetually self-revising, their mutual, never quite attainable goal the revealed form of letters, ultimately based on an incomplete analogy with the biblical canon.

The success with which Bloom's discussions of tradition and canon formation promote his particular account of history and the ends of poetry by creating the illusion of inevitability has much to do, I think, with his exclusion of the third great institution (along with canon and tradition) central to our experience of secular letters, the library. For Michel Foucault, the library has long since replaced the canon as the form of our relationship with language and literature.

In "Language to Infinity," Foucault offers a brief history of his own. "For a long time," he argues,

> from the advent of the Homeric Gods to the remoteness of the divine in the fragment of *Empedocles*—speaking so as not to die

had a meaning now alien to us. To speak of heroes or as a hero, to desire to construct something like a work, to speak so that others speak of it to infinity, to speak for "glory," was indeed to move toward or against this death maintained by language; to speak as a sacred warning of death, to threaten men with the end beyond any possible glory, was also to disarm death and promise immortality. In other words, every work was intended to be completed, to still itself in a silence where an infinite Word re-established its supremacy. Within a work, language protected itself against death through this invisible speech, this speech before and after any possible time from which it made itself into its self-enclosed reflection. The mirror to infinity, to which every language gives birth once it erects itself vertically against death, was not displayed without an evasion: the work placed the infinite outside of itself—a real majestic infinity in which it became a circular mirror, completed in a beautifully closed form.

(LI, 59–60)

For us, the closure announced in the completion of the biblical canon is the definitive instance of this closure, which makes the completed work a "circular" mirror of a genuine infinity/divinity. When each book is a canon in this way, the text becomes that formulation of life most effectively defended against death, and mastery of the canon becomes a kind of power over the conditions of existence—a power, as Bloom would say, of divination. However, Foucault then says:

It seems to me that a change was produced in the relationship of language to its indefinite repetition at the end of the eighteenth century—nearly coinciding with the moment in which works of language became what they are now for us, that is literature. This is the time (or very nearly so) when Hölderlin became aware, to the point of blindness, that he could only speak in the space marked by the disappearance of the gods and that language could only depend on its own power to keep death at a distance. Thus, an opening was traced on the horizon toward which our speech has ceaselessly advanced.

(LI, 59)

Another way to put this is to say that infinity is internalized to become an aspect of language and, through this internalization, of selfhood as well. I am, in a sense, here combining Bloom and Foucault in order to demonstrate how their histories converge on the problematic of the sublime. And since what Foucault and Bloom describe is what is more broadly and conventionally known as secularization, we could add that Foucault's infinity within discourse brings with it Bloom's death within poetry as two key aspects of that historical process. Foucault continues:

> The space of language today is not defined by Rhetoric, but by the library: by the ranging to infinity of fragmentary languages substituting for the double chain of Rhetoric the simple, continuous, and monstrous line of language left to its own devices, a language fated to be infinite because it can no longer support itself upon the speech of infinity. But within itself, it finds the possibility of its own division, of its repetition, the power to create a vertical system of mirrors, self-images, analogies. A language which repeats no other speech, no other Promise, but postpones death indefinitely by ceaselessly opening a space where it is always the analogue of itself.
>
> (LI, 67)

Inclusion in the library, unlike inclusion in the canon, implies no (or at least minimal) judgment, only an accumulation aimed less at coherence than at making everything available as a potential analogue, antecedent, or descendant of everything else. Movement through the library is a potentially endless series of displacements. The absence of any Word, any revealed form combining tradition and canon, of which all these discourses are a part makes the library the antithesis of the closed biblical canon. But if the library faces the interpreter with the threat of being overwhelmed by the infinity of our discourses, it is also the domain of an extraordinary freedom, challenging him to traverse its spaces to construct one or a hundred canons and traditions to support any history and whatever ends we require.

It is the library that represents to us our condition, and interpretation, tradition, and canonization are still our tools to organize, defend against, and exploit it as best we can. Canon, tradition, and book no longer converge as in the closed, complete Bible. First, the closure is opened again by the accumulated weight of its interpretive displacements, then canon and tradition escape the limits of the book and divide. Finally, the library arises as the institution which, for secular humanism, stands in sacred surety for the ultimate, unifying Word, which has been rejected but still, paradoxically, guarantees the ultimate unity and value of all that goes on inside the library.

Here Foucault underestimates the resilience of that archaic tradition. For the library is still taken as if it comprised a wholeness, a complete canon and tradition, existing despite our inability to take it in through our "normal" intellectual senses—normal interpretation, normal canonization, and so on—in short, it is sublime as canon and tradition are no longer sublime; its unity, however limited, guarantees our ability to overcome what most threatens the integrity of the selfhood on which everything depends for us. Of course this is an illusion, for, as Foucault points out, the potential infinity of discourses within the library permanently ruptures the closure of whatever inclusive Word might be imagined (LI, 66–67)—canons are now inherently and permanently unstable. Or, to put it another way, for Foucault as for Bloom, we can go through the motions of canonization, but in the library we cannot truly canonize.

But before passing on to consider the relationship between the library and the sublime, we should note Foucault's claim that language in the library "postpones death indefinitely by ceaselessly opening a space where it is always the analogue of itself." Foucault articulates clearly how a quasi-mystical opposition between writing and death derives, before Hölderlin, from the relationship between a closed form, book or canon, and the external infinity that makes it possible—a relationship lost when the gods are lost to secular language. Yet here he seems to insist that language still holds death at bay, if not through closure, then simply through not stopping. How can this be if the analogy between language and life has been lost? How can language postpone death? Here Foucault seems in danger of idealizing his deidealizing instrument as much as Bloom idealizes struggle. Bloom, unlike Foucault, insists that once poetry is internalized and submitted to the conditions of selfhood (Foucault's internalization of the infinite in language), then death becomes internal to poetry, and the illusion that language can defend against death, however heroically maintained, is just that, an illusion.

Against the canon and the coherent, revealed history ultimately based on the closed unity of the Book, Foucault poses the multitextuality of the library and the history-as-mere-temporal-extensiveness it represents—"and," "and," and "and," and so on, ad infinitum, without subordination or hierarchy of any but the most arbitrary kind, if that. This puts us in the domain of what Neil Hertz identifies as an instance of Kant's mathematical sublime (NBLS, 62). Hertz's contemporary example of this version of sublimity is drawn from an omnibus review, "Recent Studies in the Nineteenth Century," by Thomas McFarland, in which McFarland pauses on the threshold of his task to complain that secondary discussion is accumulating at such a rate that not only does it seem impossible for anyone to master more than a small part of it; it seems to call into question the purpose of culture itself: "Just as the enormous increase in human population threatens all the values of individuality so carefully inculcated by centuries of humanistic refinement, so too does the flood of publication threaten the very knowledge that publication purports to serve" (quoted in NBLS, 63).[8] Clearly this is the lament of one who stands in the doorway of Foucault's library.

Kant's mathematical sublime involves a sense of cognitive exhaustion, brought on "by the fear of losing count or of being reduced to nothing but counting . . . with no hope of bringing a long series or a vast scattering under some sort of conceptual unity." This moment of blockage or cognitive exhaustion is "followed by a compensatory positive movement, the mind's exultation in its own rational faculties, in the ability to think a totality that cannot be taken in through the senses" (NBLS, 62). Perhaps another way to put this is to say that the mind confronting the potentially overwhelming number and diversity of impressions feels that it should be overcome and then realizes that it isn't—that such a standard of limitation is somehow irrelevant to its activities.

Certainly something like this happens in the case of McFarland. He does not go on to declare the exercise meaningless, nor, as Hertz points out (NBLS, 64), does he make any effort to clear the field of what is inessential; he simply proceeds to write his very competent review. This may be, Hertz suggests, because having expressed his anxiety, McFarland has done as much as he can in writing; or it may be because he has reached the point at which he glimpses "another sort of incommensurability," expressed in another passage cited by Hertz: here McFarland speculates that with the proliferation of secondary comment, the Emersonian ideal of the scholar as "man thinking" gives way to "man reading," an imbalance posing a profound threat to "the integration of awareness" as the aim of culture (NBLS, 65). After all we have said about secularization, internalization, and defense of the essential self, it is easy enough to see here

8. Internal citations refer to the page(s) in Hertz's essay where McFarland is quoted and discussed. For McFarland's original review, see *Studies in English Literature* 16(1976), 693ff.

in McFarland's concern with an ever-receding integration of awareness that another version of this fiction is at stake.

At this point, Hertz turns aside to seek clarification in a review of prominent theories of the sublime and in scholarly accounts of them, notably those of S. H. Monk and Thomas Weiskel. First, he establishes the similarity between the notion of difficulty, rooted in biblical interpretation and prevalent in eighteenth-century theories of the sublime, and the more modern phenomenon of blockage (NBLS, 66–71). Then, following Weiskel's argument, he notes how Kant finds in the fact that, despite the imagination's failure, a unity can nonetheless be thought evidence that "the agent of this thinking, the reason, must be the guarantor of man's 'supersensible destiny' " (NBLS, 73). Kant's terms are confusing to us because they are used in very nearly the opposite of the way in which the Romantics have taught us to use them. Nevertheless, the "reason" guaranteeing our supersensible destiny, which performs the leap over the numbers and diversity that threaten to overwhelm the senses and normal cognition, seems another instance of that *ineffable,* essential self. I stress "ineffable" because this essential self can only, as here, be negatively defined in terms of what it is not. If it resides anywhere, it is in that space leaped over between the collapse of the functions of imagination and the restoration of confidence accompanying the recognition that reason is *already* doing its work. Similarly, whatever enables McFarland to recover himself resides in the space leaped over between his recognition of blockage and his resumption of his reviewer's task.

This analysis leads Hertz to conclude that the notion of difficulty in the face of indefinite and disarrayed sequence is, in the sublime, transformed into an absolute blockage as the result of a *wish* to confirm "the unitary status of the self" through a "passage to the limit" that risks and evades "utter self-loss" (NBLS, 76). More specifically, in McFarland's case and in that of the scholar in general, the wish is for a "one-to-one confrontation," in which "numerical excess can be converted into that superogatory identification with the blocking agent that is the guarantor of the self's own integrity as an agent" (NBLS, 76). In effect, Hertz seems to suggest that there is a need both to exaggerate excess and disorder and to identify with it in order to achieve a negative definition sufficient to specify that integrated, essential self in whose name we then may act.

In an odd sort of way, it might even be thought that this movement of the sublime contrives to create an infinity, a supersensibility, which will bestow on the self through identification and internalization an integrity, in much the same way Foucault claims that an external infinity bestows on the written work the possibility of closure and its own integrity.

This impression is confirmed by the next step in Hertz's argument. Returning to the subject of McFarland's review, Hertz continues:

> What is generated is a rhetoric of interior totalization, the plea for "integration of awareness" and its embodiment in the figure of "man thinking." But at this point a further difficulty arises: for the scholar to contemplate the Emersonian description of "man thinking" is to be quite literally cast in the role of "man reading"; or, more accurately, to discern that one's thinking and one's reading are, in the best of scholarly times (and when would that have been? before what Fall?), hard to disentangle.
>
> (NBLS, 78)

It is at the point of this rather Coleridgean recognition that Hertz quotes McFarland quoting Schopenhauer:

> "The constant influx of other people's ideas . . . must certainly stop and stifle their own, and indeed, in the long run paralyze the power of thought. . . . Therefore incessant reading and study positively ruin the mind. . . . Reading no longer anticipates thinking, but entirely takes its place."
>
> (NBLS, 65)

If, Hertz asks, there is already too much secondary comment, why does McFarland quote Schopenhauer saying what he has just said; why not simply quote Schopenhauer and leave it at that? Clearly, it is the relationship between the same words or ideas in Schopenhauer's text and in his own that is important to McFarland here.

According to Hertz, Schopenhauer's words are necessary because "the self cannot simply think but must read the confirmation of its own integrity, which is only legible in a specular structure, a structure in which the self can perform that 'superogatory identification with the blocking agent' " (NBLS, 78). Thus, the enclosed, discrete, integrated self requires this external complement to itself in the way that Foucault's text requires for its closure and integrity an external, real infinity. That this confirmation must be read also tends to confirm the continued operation within the secular tradition of the privileged ontological status of the text and of reading based on analogies with the Bible.

If my comparison of Foucault and Hertz is valid, we should expect to find behind Schopenhauer's status as specular confirmation of the self's unity some kind of equivalent to Foucault's external infinity. This is indeed the case, for McFarland follows up his initial lament over the threatening proliferation of secondary comment with these remarks:

> What then will be the eventual disposition and use of most of these secondary studies? The answer seems clear: in due course their contents will be programmed into a computer, and, as time passes, will more and more be remembered by the computer and forgotten by men. And in a still further length of time, it will be possible not only to reproduce instantaneously any aspect of previous secondary work, but actually to produce new work simply by instructing the computer to make the necessary recombinations. The wheel will then have come full circle: computers will be writing for computers, and the test of meaningful publication will be to think and write in a way a computer could not.
>
> (quoted in NBLS, 64–65)

In other words, human thinking and writing, the foundations of the integrated self, are moving into a complementary relationship to the infinite accumulating, ordering capacity of the computer—our secular equivalent of that external, divine infinity. For Hertz, the computer is

> the machine inside the ghost of Schopenhauer, the system of energies that links "thinking" to "reading" to "remembering" to "citing" to "writing." It serves here as a figure for what makes scholars run, when that process is felt to be most threatening to the integrity of individual awareness, a threat from which even "the strongest are not free."
>
> (NBLS, 78)

This "system of energies," represented in its threatening aspect by the infinite repetitiveness of the computer, is in its institutional and benign aspect the library, in which the ordering work of scholarship, of reading in all its aspects, is set off against mere accumulation. We noted before the existence of a kind of implicit and necessary faith in the ultimate unity of the library in the Word—this unity corresponds at once to the unity of the self and to its essential ineffability. The whole process of writing, reading, interpreting literally humanizes that unity, ensures that the total form is a human form. In this context, what the computer represents as the antithesis of these recognizably human reading functions is the possibility that this ultimate and unified form is not human, not textual at all, which would in turn imply that that ineffable, essential self is not humane at all. From the point of view of the scholarly humanist, if the integrated human self is not the nearest analogue of that implicit totalizing force, if the text is not the true mediating form of this relationship, then the assumption shared by Christian and secular humanist alike that the text is the external, visible representation of the divinity in man is false, and humanism, literary and otherwise, has little or no explanatory value in defining what is essential in man, if indeed there is an essence and not simply a reducible series of biochemical functions.

In order to fully understand where we now stand, it is necessary to return to Foucault's conclusion in "Language to Infinity":

> Libraries are the enchanted domain of two major difficulties. They have been resolved, we know, by mathematicians and tyrants (but perhaps not altogether). There is a dilemma: either all these books are already contained within the Word and they must be burned, or they are contradictory and, again, they must be burned. Rhetoric is a means of momentarily postponing the burning of libraries (but it holds out this promise for the near future, that is, for the end of time). And thus the paradox: if we make a book that tells of all the others, would it or would it not be a book itself? Must it tell its own story as if it were a book among others? And if it does not tell its story, what could it possibly be since its objective was to be a book? Why should it omit its own story, since it is required to speak of every book? Literature begins when this paradox is substituted for the dilemma; when the book is no longer the space where speech adopts a form (forms of style, forms of rhetoric, forms of language), but the site where books are all recaptured and consumed: a site that is nowhere since it gathers all the books of the past in this impossible "volume" whose murmuring will be shelved among so many others—after all the others, before all the others.
>
> (LI, 67)

Canon, as we have described it, escapes both the dilemma of secular writing before and the paradox of secular writing after the eighteenth century. Clearly, for Foucault, the library is essentially what becomes of the biblical canon without closure and without the external authority of a divine infinity. As the biblical canon at once makes the Book possible and is internal to it, so the infinitely multiplied discourse of the library makes possible the perpetual open-endedness of the modern book and is internal to it as well.

As Foucault suggests, with the disappearance of that external infinity and of effective closure, the looked-for end of time, the closure of salvation history, also disappears; or rather, as our discussion of the sublime seems to suggest, it is internalized. But deprived of its analogues either in the book or in external divinity, what form can this hoped-for end take that is not immediately open to discredit and disillusionment? The most likely candidate is the ineffability at the center of the experience of the sublime. After all, if the ineffable can be said to have any positive characteristics at all, it is that of escaping determination. Indeed, we are tempted to speculate that the purpose of the sublime is to make credible the existence of such an ineffable but essential self, which is the form in which the wished-for end of time is internalized. It is also obvious that this strategy involves a radical, negative reduction in the presence of what is considered essential to being—a reduction that creates a permanent source of anxiety. Let us now turn to a closer, more historical examination of how this situation comes about and of the precise nature of the relationship between the canon and the sublime.

CANON AND THE SUBLIME

With the dramatic erosion of the Christian/humanist synthesis toward the end of the seventeenth century, the secular canon throws off its secondary role and vernacular literature takes for itself much of the cultural authority previously exercised by the Bible and the classics. This is especially true of England, where a highly developed appreciation for an impressive vernacular tradition is already a part of the national identity.

In this process, the distinction between the sacred and secular canons is clarified. Whereas the former protects and continues to protect the integrity and distinctiveness of God, the latter protects the conviction of an essential self—the foundation of a secular humanist ethic. The new ideological importance of such a selfhood opens up cultural and social institutions to the vicissitudes of the psyche, creating the need for a new, expanded psychology and decreeing a strong bias toward psychological or at least perceptional explanation. All of this finds literary expression in a near obsession with the psychology of genius and with the rhetoric of greatness, both important aspects of the vogue of the sublime.

From this perspective, the sublime represents the replacement in a new post-Christian secularism of divinity with the conviction of an absolute, inviolable self. The importance of the sublime, as we will see, also indicates a shift in authority away from the canon to this self. The great works of the secular canon stand as confirming monuments to the powers and achievements of a human essence that remains ineffable because it is yet to be realized at some future time toward which society progresses. Thus, the canon is not lionized in the service of contemporary literary achievement (or even literary achievement in the foreseeable future); it serves an idealized self, the perfected form of desire, to which no contemporary work can hope to do justice. Correspondingly, greatness or genius ceases to be an attribute of historical role or social function and becomes a defining characteristic of our "true" self.

This situation is the subject of Walter Jackson Bate's highly influential *The Burden of the Past and the English Poet,* a book that we will examine closely both for the historical perspective it affords and for the particular clarity with which it reflects the confusions and contradictions we have inherited from eighteenth-century and Romantic versions of literary humanism.

Bate poses the problem of the burden of the past in terms of the simple question, "What is there left to do?" He notes especially the deepening awareness of the past that begins with the preservation and dissemination of the classics in the Renaissance and, he implies, culminates in the eighteenth century as the past comes to exist as a densely compact, edited, highlighted, "eternal present" (*BPEP,* 4). According to Bate, this development poses the primary challenge to writers from the time of Dryden to the present—a challenge to which it is all too tempting to respond with a thorough-going pessimism about the artistic possibilities remaining. This pessimism, he suggests, frequently finds expression in modern criticism and literature in the notion of a second fall, attributed to all sorts of things but basically designed to express a sense that the historical and social context and hence the possibilities of art have been fundamentally altered for the worse (*BPEP,* 6–7).

This initial formulation alone raises several interesting questions. First, there is the odd fact of Bate's own dependence on the rhetoric of greatness sustaining the ideal of what he calls "magnanimous humanism" (*BPEP,* 7) in a book concerned with the problematic nature and effects of such a rhetoric. This alone should tip us off that something unusual is going on. After all, what are we to make of an unself-conscious book about the burden of self-consciousness?

Second, although the point is a perfectly obvious one, Bate ignores the fact that his own "magnanimous human-ism" is a part of that movement which by the eighteenth century brings about the intensified sense of the past result-ing in the "eternal present." In this sense, Bate's book might more frankly have been called "The Burden of Humanism" (insofar as humanism is identified with the notion that past greatness exalts the present instead of crushing it). Clearly, "the eternal present" has sinister implications that have to do, I think, with a threat to history as a means of ordering and giving an account of human experience. To put it another way, time is no longer used up in the living, and the past refuses to pass away; instead, it accumulates, and imaginative boundaries become necessary to protect the freedom of the present and the possibility of the future.

Third, it is not difficult to see in the notion of the second fall precisely such a defensive boundary since it puts much of what has gone before and which has now accumulated in another, not immediately relevant, category. Bate's use of the term *modern* is no less an instance of such a boundary. For him, it does not refer to the present or the roughly contemporary, nor even to the twentieth century; it refers to that period in which the burden of the past is a problem, a period separated off at least in degree from all previous history. Though Bate and the humanist in general pay a high price for it, the notion of the burden of the past and of a threat to literature itself allows him to reestablish the authority of history and the identity of literature in the face of the leveling challenge posed by Foucault's library.

But if, as the whole question of the past's refusal to be used up would suggest, there is a fundamental tension between history and humanism, between the rhetoric of temporal event and that of greatness or transcendent value, then why the costly attempt to save history? Why the dependence on an oxymoron like "eternal present"?

Humanism scans the past in order to distill a rhetoric of values and a canon to sustain it. Humanism is a demand made upon history that threatens constantly to put a greater burden on history than it can bear. Yet humanism needs history as the field of its reference, the space out of which it arises and into which it seeks to reenter. In this sense, history is humanism's defense against itself—against the idealizing, abstracting tendencies that threaten to separate a sense of value from the quiddity of life or sense of reality—and humanism names a relationship in which history and desire continually wound each other as they defend against each other. The closest and best analogue is the role of history in the prophetic books of the Old Testament. There, history is the common ground on which God chooses to intervene or refrain and man chooses to obey or disobey, the realm in which God and man constantly wound each other and by means of which each defends against the other. The burden of the past then can also be seen not as a particular stage in the history of humanism but as a true and permanently relevant representation of the relationship in humanism between history and the rhetoric of value or desire: antithetical and inseparable.

Bate quotes T. S. Eliot's famous remark: "Not only every great poet, but every genuine, though lesser poet, fulfills once for all some possibility of language, and so leaves one possibility less for his successors" (*BPEP*, 4). The circularity of this remark is staggering (clearly any poet who doesn't discourage others from writing is not only not great, he is not even genuine), and it aptly illustrates how the rhetoric of greatness quickly creates problems for anyone who commits himself to it. Indeed, if we take Eliot at his word, we are surely forced to conclude at some point that the great, genuine poet is the one who is smart enough to despair in the face of the past, not write poetry at all, and turn to some more "modern" endeavor.

It is also possible to conclude simply that Eliot's argument is not true. Repetition plays an enormous role in literature, and certain kinds of writing—westerns, mysteries, romances—retain their appeal to writers and readers through a seemingly endless number of repetitions. "But," the traditional humanist will quickly answer, "those writings not only are not great, they are not even genuine literature." And if we ask, "Why not?" what can he do but reply, "Because they do not burden subsequent writers and strangle their creativity," *or* drop the rhetoric of greatness in favor of some other standard for distinguishing books in terms of value—a standard likely to be more flexible and more historically specific. Bate, of course, disagrees with Eliot's im-

plicit pessimism, yet his commitment to the ideal of greatness issues in a rhetoric that sustains Eliotic pessimism rather
than any hopeful alternative.

Bate then goes on to pick up and extend his earlier observation that the advance of humane knowledge that presents
the artist with such a burden is if not simply and straightforwardly the source of "opportunity for us, as critics and historians" (*BPEP*, 4), then at least less anxiety-producing for
us than for them. Bate's distinction between critical/histori-
cal expository writing and literature proper is based on his
observation that in the case of the former:

> The discovery of even a handful of new facts, the correction of
> some others, or even the mere ability to rearrange details or
> arguments with some ingenuity for debate or supplement, will
> permit the writing, again and again, of a new work. In short,
> the "literature of knowledge" with its expository discussion is,
> even at its best, "provisional" and can always be superseded.
> (*BPEP*, 8)

But does this describe the works of exposition that we are
moved to read again and again, that are most important and
widely admired? In precisely what sense is Pater's *Renaissance*
or even Auerbach's *Mimesis* "superseded"? And, once again,
isn't Bate forgetting just how much of fiction and poetry is
given over to referring to, troping upon, or even outright
imitation of previous works? Once again, this distinction
between criticism and literature seems less something observed in historical practice than something determined in
Bate's own brand of humanizing. As this remark suggests,
there is obviously a relationship between the devaluing of
criticism and Bate's monumentalizing rhetoric of literary
appreciation:

> The *Iliad* or *King Lear* will not be dislodged with the same ease
> or excuse. They are, as de Quincey said, "finished and unaltera-
> ble"—like every other work of art, however minor. To feel

constraints in competition with even the greatest scholars and
critics of the last fifty years is not, in other words, the same
thing as to be in competition with Michelangelo, Shakespeare,
Rembrandt, Bach, Beethoven, Dickens or Mann and with the
finalities that the works of such men represent.

(*BPEP*, 8)

Certainly in comparison with this Mount Rushmore in
prose criticism and history writing seem ephemeral, yet
when we consider with what gusto writers have plundered
each other's work and related endlessly among themselves,
the monumental analogy lurking in Bate's rhetoric seems
highly tendentious. Indeed, if we take the position that exposition is primarily concerned, or at least deeply concerned,
with ideas or knowledge, we might even argue that the
writer in prose who must generate a new idea—an idea,
which, once generated, need never be generated again and
which, if simply repeated, could be branded, horror of hor-
rors, a plagiarism—is in an even more straitened position
than the writer of fiction.

Now we are approaching a perspective on the burden of
the past from which it appears to express and to cloak the
critical thinker's anxiety about the limited field of possible
abstraction and, therefore, a sense of the diminishing value
of commentary. It may be that the more that is written, the
less there is left to write; it is certainly the case that the more
is written about a limited corpus, the less it seems necessary
to add. Can it be that great literature and a self-wounded
"ephemeral" criticism are not separate entities but a single
narcissistic self, an anxious humanism contemplating its own
ideal self with an almost lyric intensity?

Naturally enough, much of Bate's discussion is devoted
to a variety of possible explanations for the sense of decline
haunting poetry from Dryden on. He begins by rejecting the
notion that Neoclassicism is somehow to blame, arguing
rather that English authors seize upon Neoclassicism because

it provides them with a defense against a sense of the burden of the past that is already present: "It gave the English poet a chance to be different from his immediate predecessors while at the same time it offered a counter-ideal that was impressively, almost monolithically, systematized" (*BPEP*, 17–18). Later, Bate concludes: "The point is that, where there was inhibition or retrenchment in the arts, the theoretical premises, however strict, were not the cause, though they could be overwhelmingly persuasive if one was prepared to accept them; and that, when inhibition and retrenchment occurred, there were other, more directly personal reasons" (*BPEP*, 32).

First, I think that it is worth our while to note that although Bate denies Neoclassical ideas—indeed, ideas in general—a strictly causal status, he nonetheless presents them as the only definitions of that otherwise undefined psychological state that he presents as the real cause of the poets' malaise.

Unfortunately, having embraced Neoclassicism as a means of defining as yet unexplored artistic possibilities keyed to notions of decorum, elegance, etc., and as a highly rationalized defense against the greatness of the native tradition, poets soon discovered in their classical models qualities of generic scope and originality that brought to the fore once again the achievements of Shakespeare, Spenser, and Milton and raised anew the question, "Why not in our time?"

Still seeking an explanation, Bate launches into a survey of contemporary speculations on why the eighteenth century was producing no poets of comparable stature. The writings of the time seem especially to emphasize a painful contrast between art and continuing progress in other areas—in all other aspects of intellectual achievement and the increasing perfection of society in general. As William Collins notes in his poem on Sir Thomas Hanmer's edition of Shakespeare, it was beginning to seem as if poetry alone was the exception to the pattern of progress everywhere discernible in society (*BPEP,* 45).

In response to such perceptions, a number of theorists developed variations of the idea that poetry is a primitive contraction, perhaps a synecdoche of the entire field of modern intellectual activity. As society is advanced, this portmanteau is slowly unpacked, and the synecdoche is progressively literalized until the field of intellectual activity is completely articulated into its component disciplines, and poetry becomes a kind of archaic curiosity. In its linguistic aspect, this idea takes the form of a belief that primitive language suffered from a paucity of denotative terms, and, therefore, things frequently had to be referred to by means of metaphorical extensions of existing terms. As man progressed, these metaphors were replaced by names and forms of writing, like poetry, based on metaphor moved increasingly to the periphery of intellectual activity (*BPEP,* 50–52).

Bate also presents a number of views from the time and later that range themselves against this prevalent view, but, nonetheless, he concludes (despite the cogency of these arguments) that it is still impossible not to feel that something really has hampered the poet. He begins by citing Schiller's argument in "On Naive and Sentimental Poetry" that the present suffers in relation to the past only because it is selectively judged in terms of those standards in which the past excelled. If those aspects of present poetry that are most finely realized were held up as models of what art *can* be, then ancient works would similarly suffer accordingly (*BPEP,* 71).

Then Bate expands this argument with reference to Arthur Koestler's observation that all such inflated estimations of the past in relation to the present have to do with valuing the context rather than the intrinsic value of the work, offering the fascinating example of the art forgeries perpetrated by Lothar Malskat, which were praised by experts for displaying all those virtues so impossible to achieve in our own time (*BPEP*, 72–73). Yet the point is not nearly so decisive as it may seem. The experts were led astray by their appreciation of intrinsic merits; their mistake was simply in connecting these merits with a particular time. Perhaps we might say that they took too literally a rationale guiding their experience of art that was ultimately only incomplete or figurative.

More interesting, however, is the question of whether Malskat's works, having been recognized as possessing all the intrinsic qualities of old masters, are to be treated as masterpieces. The answer is clearly no because a great work of art is not so by virtue of intrinsic qualities but by virtue of being monumentalized. This brings us to David Hume's *Rise and Progress of the Arts and Sciences,* which Bate seems to endorse as the eighteenth century's most clear-sighted and intelligent analysis of its own situation. Central to Hume's argument is the observation that, contrary to what we might expect, the amount of genius displayed by people varies dramatically from generation to generation. He goes on from there to describe how productive emulation is crushed by a preceding generation when its greatness is such that individuals either abandon poetry or turn aside into the decadent pursuit of novelty for its own sake. As true greatness is achieved in area after area, the range of possibly great endeavor shrinks and the manifestations of genius become increasingly rare, though not impossible (*BPEP*, 80–82).

The centrality of genius for Hume, as well as the eighteenth century's near obsession with the psychology of genius, is clarified by the example of Malskat's brilliant forgeries. Just as greatness in art is not intrinsic but an act of monumentalization performed on a work or artist, genius is not, as Hume implies, an intrinsic attribute of individuals and their works; it is an act performed upon them, and the problem with a psychology of genius is that genius is not a psychological entity at all—it is as interpretive and ideological as canonization.

Bate is willing to endorse, within limits, Hume's argument because he argues the inevitable decline of the arts not on the basis of some deterministic view of the zeitgeist but on an account of human psychology in its perversity. Where Bate sees himself most profoundly in agreement with Hume is in holding psychological inhibition responsible for the failure of eighteenth-century poetry in the face of past achievement (*BPEP*, 82). If we have to see this idealizing of the past at the expense of the present as a part of the "incorrigible nature" of man, our inner darkness, we can only think back to Bate's insistence on the shared uniqueness of that time and our own and wonder how it is that human nature became more incorrigible in the eighteenth century, decreased in incorrigibility for the Romantics, and blossomed into incorrigibility again for us. Why should human nature be any different; why should we suddenly become modern?

The reason that Bate cannot give clearer definition to this psychological condition is that it is exhaustively defined in the theories of decline, which he rejects as deterministic. In truth, these determinisms and Bate's psychological inhibitions are mirror images of each other, distorted just enough in the passage from one rhetorical order to another to disguise the fact that Bate's explanation of the causes of the eighteenth century's sense of decline is essentially deterministic, even though it ostensibly rejects the rhetoric of determinism as antihumanistic.

But what brings Bate to this impasse? What else could he have done? Simply, he could have chosen the most liberating interpretive path, as he would have the poets do with poetry; he might have considered the possibility that something was gained in this stance of minority, that it purchased poets a new kind of power over their predecessors or at least compensated them for their own loss of power. But this is precisely the line that Bate cannot follow because it is inconceivable in the context of his essentially Longinian humanism that a poet should avoid greatness, evade canonization, and pursue a poetic purpose outside the bounds of literature as Bate perceives it. My point here is not so much that this speculation is necessarily true, only that Bate is unable even to consider this possibility.

When Bate goes on to admonish us for avoiding the knowledge that we, with our sense of diminished possibility, are self-wounded, we must ask why Bate's act as a critic/historian, in placing this issue at the center of his own work and, as it turns out, at the center of his field, is any less obsessed with and implicated in the burden of the past than the acts of the poets he admonishes. Finally, we must also wonder if the inadequacy of Bate's subsequent explanation of why the Romantics recovered from the poetic lethargy of the eighteenth century is not due to the fact that Bate himself is still thoroughly enmeshed in the problematic of pastness, which he has defined—a problematic indistinguishable from the ideal of greatness.

Bate begins the final stage of his argument by reiterating his conviction that the essential problem remains the artist's relationship with his own art—a matter of disordered psychology or creative will, rather than historical, social, economic, or intellectual determinants (*BPEP*, 95). Yet if the problem of the tradition's crushing greatness is largely self-created, we must still wonder what created the will that created the problem. To put it another way, how is it that the creative will was re-created in so many eighteenth-century poets in precisely this negative, self-effacing form?

It is also here that Bate outlines for us the factors in the Romantics' dramatic recovery from the creative paralysis of the late eighteenth century. These factors include a turning outward to nature, which involves a broadening and deepening of that concept to include a new concern with the inner life of the individual and with the whole process by which the personal dawns into the general. Also included as contributing factors are the development of a variety of new subject matters and a renewed concern with the concrete and the particular (*BPEP*, 116–18).

I hesitate to expand on this brief summary because Bate himself more or less dismisses these as symptoms or effects rather than causes when he says that all this still does not explain the Romantic rebirth. What is missing, he continues, is the real essential element, that "boldness of spirit that seizes upon opportunities and creates new ones" (*BPEP*, 127). So, inaccessible to historical, intellectual, or even psychological explanation is an ineffable something—a nothing—that brings about the recovery of the creative will. Nor, Bate tells us, is this "nothing" explainable as an irrational, arbitrary convergence of circumstance, nor even as an accident of genius.

Like an instance of grace visited on the will from some still more subliminal force within, this "nothing," known only by its result, intervenes. And now we find ourselves recognizing some of the elements of the sublime as Weiskel describes it in *The Romantic Sublime*. We cannot but wonder if we are not now confronting some sort of interpretive, humanistic sublime, the ideological heart of Bate's Longinian humanism. Can it be that greatness and this "nothing" within, this significant absence, are correlatives in an attempt to construct a rhetoric of divinity in a secular age, a negative theology? It is certainly the case that the more we read of Bate, the clearer it is that his entire history of the burden of the past stands in representation, negatively of course, for the power of this invisible self.

If all this is so, what we are now confronting is the intensely problematic nature of humanism's favorite self-image and instrument of historical analysis, secularization.

The burden of the past emerges from this point of view as the permanent disability of the secular present in relation to the divine past. Bate's modernism then names a permanent distinction in history between the present and past. The phenomenon that Bate chronicles would simply not have been possible if humanism had actually succeeded in replacing the rhetoric of divinity with a secular, rational rhetoric. But divinity continues to reside, untransformed, potent because unacknowledged, at the heart of secular humanism.

The discontinuity at the historical level between a secular, burdened modernity and a divine past finds its corollary in the discontinuity characteristic of Bate's argument and of humanist discourse in general, between the continuity of rational explanation (in this case, the accessible factors of the Romantic "recovery") and the rhetoric confirming and authorizing the values of the whole secular/rational edifice.

Beyond this analysis there is also the point that Bate argues for the impermanence of the Romantic recovery. Indeed, he argues that the very success of the Romantics closed off still more poetic possibilities and thus intensified the burden of the past. It certainly begins to seem that in explaining how it is that our contemporary situation is so much like that of the eighteenth century, Bate is adopting literally the logic of explanation that he ostensibly rejects earlier. No matter what weight we choose to place on this point, we must still wonder if a sustained literary recovery is even conceivable for Bate. Would not a reading of literary history that found there a sustained level of creative energy and continuously healthy literary commonwealth undercut the whole phenomenology of heights and depths upon which the rhetoric of greatness that sustains Bate's values depends?

This contradiction can be more clearly understood if we examine more closely Bate's sense of the nature of the Romantic achievement, which corresponds largely to the widely held institutional/humanistic understanding of the

Romantic enterprise currently under attack by revisionist critics. The fundamental goal of Romantic poetry, Bate argues, is the renewed perception of "the unity of being," which involves a protest on behalf of organic nature (*BPEP*, 125). Organicism is ideologically important because in insisting on the unity of the organism in time and space, it argues the comprehensibility of the world; it is, of course, imagination that allows us to comprehend the myriad aspects of nature as a unity. The function of this relationship between unity of being and organicism is exactly like that in the Christian tradition between monotheism and the continuity of history. Unfortunately, the ideal of "unity of being" is hopelessly at odds with the antinomian nature of humanism's secular, rational, postdivine self-image. What emerges again and again in Bate's argument is the irresolvable conflict between the ideal unity (the immortal free masonry, perpetually benevolent) and historical antinomianism (the divine or religious past versus the secular present).

In this context, the first sentence in Bate's penultimate paragraph—"the essence of neurosis is conflict" (*BPEP*, 133)—seems particularly ironic since, in Freud's view, the conflicts that create the possibility of neurosis are largely inherent in our culture. Freud's psychoanalysis tries and fails to purge the residues of divine mystery from secular culture. Indeed, the gradual reconstitution of the language of divinity within psychoanalysis may be seen as a precondition of its broad acceptance. Bate's infinitely more naive humanism most wants to deny the fundamental reality of conflict between individual and collective modes of existence, yet in order to posit a unity beyond conflict, he must have recourse to a mystery that only intensifies the conflict endemic to secular humanism; he must literally have recourse to that about which humanism cannot speak, even in the form of psychoanalysis—to that which is below the threshold or, more accurately, beyond the pale. This is the primal nothing at the heart of humanism and upon which Nietzsche built his negative theology that finally unites us in this negative relation to articulate being.

In *Criticism in the Wilderness,* Hartman pithily remarks: "The specter of a discontinuity between labor and grace, artistic genius and religious truth, threatens the Christian-humanist synthesis and forces the poetic genius back on its own" (*CW*, 94). The poet then has the choice between becoming humanism's victim by renouncing his poetic ambitions or its Satan by asserting them.

Thomas Weiskel's *The Romantic Sublime,* like Bloom's *Anxiety of Influence,* is at once immensely more sophisticated theoretically than *The Burden of the Past and the English Poet* and quite dependent on Bate's literary history. Certainly one of the most instructive things about Bate's book is the way in which it marks the intersection of the anxieties of an idealizing criticism with the founding myth of contemporary critical revisionism—an intersection suggesting that despite radical differences in method and perspective, both critical modes remain firmly embedded in a single, highly ambivalent critical tradition, originating in the problematic humanism first formulated in the eighteenth century. Similarly, one of the most interesting things about Weiskel's book is its account of how this same ambivalence is carried over into and is given its definitive form in Romantic poetry, most especially that of Wordsworth. In Weiskel's account, Wordsworth's dual formulation of the sublime into its egotistical and liminal aspects is at once a complex defense against the threat posed by the eighteenth-century sublime to the distinct poetic ego or identity and its creative possibilities—an antisublime—and the means of putting the problematic of the sublime firmly at the center of literary humanism—an arch-sublime.

Weiskel begins by noting that the sublime "claims that man can in feeling and in speech transcend the human, though what lies beyond is uncertain," goes on to say that an interest in the sublime arises as God withdraws from direct participation in the experience of men, and concludes his introduction by remarking that the need for a sublime is related to the unease of minds involuntarily secularized—a remark we might gloss by adding that the heyday of the sublime seems to be associated with a sense that the secularization of society proceeds more rapidly than the changes it brings about can be assimilated.

Our discussion of Bate has prepared us to question or adjust this account on a number of grounds. First, when Weiskel says that "without some notion of the beyond, some credible discourse of the superhuman, the sublime founders or becomes a 'problem' " (*RS,* 3), perhaps it is necessary to add that the sublime is always problematic because it seeks from the beginning to make of itself the discourse of the superhuman upon which its authority is to be based. Second, if a humanistic sublime is an oxymoron, as Weiskel suggests, it is for reasons already discussed *the* humanistic oxymoron (*RS,* 3). Third, we should note the connection between the "uncertainty" or nothing that lies beyond and the equally ineffable quality to which Bate attributes the Romantic recovery. As Weiskel goes on to point out, the discourse of the sublime is the discourse of significant absence, and we might further speculate that what is absent is the divine, irrational mystery that secular, rational humanism consigns to a superstitious, divinity-laden past. In this context, it should be clear that, in the eighteenth century at least, the sublime is equally the servant of those who find themselves involuntarily secularized and of those who find themselves involuntarily daemonized.

Weiskel offers a summary introduction to his treatment of the sublime:

> The Romantic sublime was an attempt to revise the meaning of transcendence precisely when the traditional apparatus of subli-

mation—spiritual, ontological, and (one gathers) psychological and even perceptional—was failing to be exercised or understood. It was the most spectacular response of the literary mind to the dualisms that cut across post-Renaissance thinking and made so much authoritative doctrine suddenly in need of interpretation. It was not least a hermeneutic, a remarkably successful way to read, offering formulas which preserved the authority of the past within the ramified structures of dualism. It provided a language for urgent and apparently novel experiences of anxiety and excitement which were in need of legitimation. In largest perspective, it was a major analogy, a massive transposition of transcendence into a naturalistic key; in short, a stunning metaphor.

(RS, 4)

Given what we have already seen, this last sentence should tip us off that in the sublime we are confronting the primary ideological vehicle of secularization in the eighteenth and early nineteenth centuries, in effect, an effort to substitute transcendence for divinity and ultimately to remove the analogical need for the divine by making transcendence a metaphor for itself. Metaphor, Weiskel tells us (RS, 4), is a compromise between old and new, allowing us to grasp experience in terms sanctioned by the past, so the sublime offers itself not only as a metaphorical representation of transcendence; it operates as a metaphor for the relationship of present to past: the metaphorical transcendence of divinity by the metaphor of transcendence.

There are, in the Romantics especially, powerful alternatives to the sublime, two of which Weiskel notes in particular. First, there is the aesthetic of beauty, which horizontalizes the vertical bias of the sublime in an attempt to achieve a sense of value without recourse to eye/object, spirit/sense dualisms. Second, there is the literalism of the visionary tradition best represented by Blake's insistence that the transcendental nothingness or void is predicated on the defeat of the imagination since, by linking the immeasurability of space to our supersensible faculty, it transforms imagination into a metaphor for its own emptiness. Blake preferred to reject entirely the sight/insight dichotomy and to understand imagination quite literally as a seeing. In this way, he avoids making imagination into a metaphor for itself, as the sublime transcendence is a metaphor for itself (*RS*, 6–7).

Milton is particularly important for the eighteenth century, Weiskel argues, because he marks the last time that traditional theological terms were freely available to express and encompass the guilt of modernism. Thus, he marks the great divide between a divine past and a secular present, in which guilt remains but no clear locus of authority can guarantee either correction or disaster (*RS*, 10).

For Weiskel, Wordsworth is the key figure in the sublime after Milton, and he begins his long, final chapter by suggesting that Wordsworth's distinctive poetic discovery is

> a mode of conversation, now most easily recognized outside of poetry in the domains of the authentic psychoanalyst and a certain kind of expert teacher too tentative to know or say for sure what he "really" thinks. This conversation is not a "communication" (the cant word of our social world); its aim is not the transmission of knowledge or a message but the springing loose of an efficacious spirit which haunts the passages of self-knowledge, however shallow or deep.
>
> (*RS*, 167)

This efficacious spirit is linked to Wordsworth's real interlocutor in *The Prelude*—not Coleridge but himself, "a part of himself, archaic or prospective but in any case alienated from his present, who beckons to him across a 'vacancy' " (*RS*, 170).

> That "other Being" is in part a remembered state of mind, a previous consciousness, and in part the preferred protagonist of visible scenes of whom he is now conscious for the first time.

For the first time because that other Being did not exist in the past, though he now exists there; he is a creation of the present.
(*RS*, 170)

If the "other Being" is, at least in part, a creation of a present busily engaged in revising, even creating, the past in its own image, this goes far to explain why this other Wordsworth remains inaccessible except through the highly mediated languages of memory and desire—after all, the other exists only in this present conversational discourse.

Even where scenes that are unquestionably a part of Wordsworth's literal experience are discussed (the Simplon Pass episode, for instance), there are misconstructions, distortions pointing not to faulty remembering but to evasions designed both to preserve the mysterious power of this "other Being" and to prevent it from taking over his own present speech, or from forcing him into a stance of alienation.

In all of this, nature hovers in the background as the guarantor of the dialogue—the principle that redeems its discontinuities and the screen against which the multiplicity of its representations is projected. Whenever the "forms" of literal nature begin to become "characters" or symbols of something beyond themselves, nature as nature has already disappeared, for behind every symbol is an absence, the death of the thing whose place it takes. Thus, speech itself is founded on the withdrawal of the primordial object (*RS*, 172).

It is in this liminal passage from forms to characters, from image to symbol, that the efficacious spirit, this "other Being," lurks:

> *The Prelude* as a whole is an attempt to negotiate the strait leading from remembered images, and from the power of mind to which these images continue to testify, to capable speech. "I have seen such things—I see them still (memory)—and see moreover deeper into them, as if anew (imagination)—I therefore was and am a favored being (identity)—and I can speak (be a poet)."

This argument, here abstractly reduced and overemphasized, presides over each rememoration in the poem, as if this poem were in fact a prelude, achieving its unforeseen finalities only under a propaedeutic pretense. In a way the argument serves as "profoundest knowledge" to orient and occasion the "efficacious spirit" which is the poem itself.

(*RS*, 172)

Paradoxically, even though this passage from image to symbol is blocked or occluded in Wordsworth, this moment is, nonetheless, that of his essential poetic greatness—the sole province of his "visionary power." His landscapes hover on the edge of symbolic revelation, and the hovering becomes a replacement for the missing revelatory climax. Central to Wordsworth's poetry is the image threatening to become symbolic, a transparent signifier, but which never does so. If such images were to lose their opacity and the invisible world stand fully and symbolically revealed, there would be nothing left to pursue (and, one might add, no further occasion for such poetry). Thus, Weiskel concludes, Wordsworth's gestures toward interrogating such images about their meaning are merely the feints of a "mind learning how knowledge is opposed to efficacious power" (*RS*, 175). The passage from image to symbol involves a confrontation with the power of symbolicity itself, and the imagination may be identified with the resistance to symbolicity that keeps the poet's quest and his poem from grinding to a halt.

The threshold between image and symbol in which Wordsworth is poised at the moments of his greatest poetic power is the domain of the liminal sublime. Essentially, the liminal sublime is a compromise formation, both an extension and the antithesis of the eighteenth-century or negative sublime and of what Keats termed Wordsworth's "egotistical sublime." On the one hand, it extends the distinct identity, bound to the order of the image, as far as possible in the direction of the absolute power of the symbolic to transform and negate the natural world. But the movement toward the symbolic must be occluded in order to prevent the symbolic transformation and consequent negation of the poet's individuality. On the other hand, the ineffability that can find only negative representation in the eighteenth-century sublime achieves embodiment in the powers of the individual poetic personality. This movement too must be occluded at the threshold, lest the transformative, divinatory poetic power be reduced to something merely psychological. Such a stance, deeply divided within itself, is inevitably marked by ambivalence and the consequent anxiety.

On the basis of this analysis, Weiskel examines the famous Spots of Time passage (*Prelude* XII, lines 198ff.) in terms of the line of association linking them to death. In Weiskel's readings, it is easy enough to see that writing does, in some sense, equal death or, to put it another way, that the recognition of a signifier equals the intimation of death. But we must ask why "it is against the fact that things may come to signify" that Wordsworth must "force his way" (*RS*, 180). To a degree, we have already answered the question by noting that if forms or substances are to take on whatever superadded power symbolization has to bestow, they must die out of the imaginary or perceptional order and into the symbolic order of verse. As Weiskel observes: "For the speaker or poet this passage appears to involve the intimation of sacrifice and the assumption of guilt" (*RS*, 181).

It may be, as Weiskel suggests, that in the second of the famous Spots of Time episodes what is repressed is a presentiment of, perhaps even wish for, the father's death that links visionary power with guilt, but why this should necessarily be so remains unclear. Weiskel begins his answer to this question by remarking in a discussion of Book V that Wordsworth's solicitude for the vulnerability of poetry, especially in its ability to exhilarate and soothe, seems rather to mask a fear of poetry based on its alliance with apocalyptic destruction: "Poetry is not threatened *by* Apocalypse: poetry threatens Apocalypse, at least insofar as it is prophetic poetry" (*RS,* 187). We can go beyond the Freudian assumption about such expressions of solicitude to the biblical prophecies themselves in order to confirm this. Surely prophecy would not have been necessary or even possible in its familiar form if the relationship between society, God, and nature had not been in disarray; it bespeaks an alienation from the perceptional order of the image in the name of a transcendent, symbolic reality.

Weiskel then goes on in Bloomian fashion to argue that since the poetry referred to in the opening of Book V is the poetry of Wordsworth's great precursors, it is his fear that this achievement will annihilate him that is being screened by his solicitude. As for these poets, Weiskel writes:

> The mystery embodied in their words is still a literal one; their archaic power comes from the fact their prophecy points to a literal fulfillment. . . . Their word is, or is in touch with, the Word. More than the enlightened conditions of belief, more than the general and gregarious advance of intellect makes this impossible for Wordsworth. It is a question, not of scepticism, which can be (as in Keats) generous and liberal, but of fear. As the first great humanizer of the mystery, Wordsworth has priority, but his very priority exposes him to the terror and literalness of the archaic sublime.
>
> (*RS,* 188)

Weiskel adds:

> Wordsworth's fear is specifically, though not exclusively, a fear of the Word. The epiphany of the signifier intimates death (the apocalyptic destruction of nature and of natural man) because that showing forth is charged with the only creative power that is absolute—the power to create literally and the power of the literal. For what, displacements aside, is the manner of the

Word? *God said, Let there be light; and there was light:* the most
remembered of Longinus' examples, marked for its simplicity
by Boileau. In a change of mood, from subjunctive to indica-
tive, reality is born. That is the "Omnific Word," identified by
Milton and tradition with the Son, the filial Godhead.

(*RS,* 189)

In Keats's "The Fall of Hyperion," the fallen Saturn is
pathetic not only because he has lost his power but because
he continues to envision a future in terms of such power,
not realizing that it is superannuated, replaced by the new
"subjunctive" regime of an Apollonian poetry that creates
in the mind and in the mind alone (*RS,* 189). Such reflec-
tive poetry is always subjunctive, and "no doubt," Weiskel
remarks, "even Wordsworth was content with second place
to Godhead, if not to Milton" (*RS,* 189). But—and here
Weiskel differs from both Bloom and Hartman—the terror
inhabiting Wordsworth's perception of past poetry is not
the result of an obsession with priority, nor of the necessary secondariness of the earthly or humanizing mind.
After all, Wordsworth's ambition is quite consciously identified with sublimation or the displacement of the traditional high argument into the human mind and heart. What
threatens is the fact that "the mystery still lays claim to
him; it is still in the mist that he finds the power, and the
power is still, as it was for Collins, 'dark power' " (*RS,*
189–90). He continues:

> Knowledge and power are opposed in Wordsworth in a way
> that to Keats will seem itself archaic and rugged, superstitiously
> egotistical. Not only is knowledge purchased by loss of power,
> but power is purchased by terror, and terror assaults the possi-
> bility of perception or insight. Here in ampler lineaments is the
> very structure of the negative sublime, which exists in Keats
> only as affectation or a stage of the mind to be recapitulated in
> wonder.

(*RS,* 190)

The power is dark because it requires the assumption of archaic guilt, which, Weiskel argues, Wordsworth identifies with the earliest convergence of symbolicity and power in acts of (human) sacrifice—at once the origin of culture and of symbolicity. In Book XIII of *The Prelude* (lines 312ff.), Weiskel points to the well-known passage in which Wordsworth imagines himself a participant in a druidical sacrifice and sees, as Weiskel puts it, "the power alienated in time"— an alienation cured only by the sacrifice uniting living and dead (*RS*, 191–92).

In this characteristic Wordsworthian movement into "terror, followed by a saving sharpness of sight (prototype of imagination's silence)," we are told that "Wordsworth seems to recapitulate and perform the Enlightenment all on [his] own" (*RS*, 194). Weiskel goes into greater detail, arguing that in *The Prelude*'s quest for the efficacious spirit, there are two stages or movements:

> First, there is a movement *toward* power, from image to symbol, from ordinary seeing, through self-consciousness (ambition), to the locus or spot of power, manifested in a symbol of sacrifice or guilt. Second, there is a movement, the Imagination's proper movement, *away* from power, from symbol back to image: this is the humanizing direction Wordsworth consciously celebrates in his claim that the Imagination is redemptive.
>
> (*RS*, 194)

Wordsworth wants to believe that the second movement is the genuine one for the mind, allowing it to feed on power without being annihilated by it. In contrast with this project of exaltation is that, associated with the older, prophetic poets, of finding (or assuming) the voice absolutely strong of godhead, which continues to haunt Wordsworth's humanizing enterprise (*RS*, 194). Weiskel concludes:

> The paradox thus roughly thrust into view is that Wordsworth's search for efficacious power was opposed to the humanizing

originality which was his historical opportunity and necessity. . . . We read poetry both for the exaltation of wisdom and
for the renovation of power, and I, for one, would not know
how to choose between the two.

(*RS*, 195)

Weiskel ends his discussion of Wordsworth and his book
with a detailed treatment of the famous Simplon Pass episode in Book VI of *The Prelude* as the instance par excellence
of a passage in which the movement of image to symbol is
not successfully occluded and Wordsworth's humanizing
stance is placed in real jeopardy. As Weiskel observes:

The aspect of eternity checks and supersedes the evidence of
things seen, so that the image of process, change, or motion
evokes and indeed signifies its supratemporal contrary. The
woods themselves are decaying, but decay itself is eternal: in the
aspect of Eternity there is no future tense. Water itself falls, but
falling itself is "stationary." The elements come and go, passing
through the *order* of nature which, abstracted, is Eternity.

(*RS*, 197)

The Wordsworthian "I," which usually makes the progress
of the verse the dramatic progress of a consciousness, has
disappeared (*RS*, 199).

It is precisely this annihilation of the "I" that explains
why, in Weiskel's account, Wordsworth should provide his
regret at the premature crossing of the Alps as a screen for
his wish to be already across the Alps, that is, already past
the Gondo Gorge, scene of this traumatic annihilation of
poetic self-consciousness (*RS*, 200). The assumption upon
which all this rests is that the greatest threat to Wordsworth
would be the experience that denies him the possibility of
self-consciousness.

In order to explain how this failure to block the passage to
symbol paradoxically confirms Wordsworth's sense of himself, it is necessary to begin with the recognition that the

screen memory is in fact a failure and that when memory fails in the service of imagination, then imagination must work against it "with such intensity as to occlude sight" (*RS,* 202). Imagination rises in flight from the Word and may be structurally defined as a power of resistance to the Word, in which sense it coincides with the necessity of originality. Experientially, imagination is the extreme consciousness of self that "mounts in recoil from the annihilation of self which imminent identification with the symbolic order enjoins" (*RS,* 202-3)—a rejection, rather than evasion, of the Oedipus complex, which is at the center of symbolicity for Weiskel.

Weiskel is quick to add that such a rejection is, from the point of view of literary history, a fiction that founds the self and ensures that originality is possible. Weiskel comes to rest then with the necessity of fiction as defense: "In life, it is our defenses that enable us to exist and therefore to create; so in poetry, the fiction of originality founds the poet" (*RS,* 208). Thus, the imagination rises to occlude the memory of the gorge, securing both self-recognition and self-vindication as a usurpation, which remains in a domain properly human, of the power that lurks beyond the threshold of the supersensible (*RS,* 204). In the Simplon Pass episode, imagination evades or leaps over the mediating signs at the threshold— from sight to the invisible without passing through the domain of types and symbols, of the Word—and thereby achieves an exaltation, which is to say a transcendence without an anxiety of originality (*RS,* 204).

But Weiskel adds one last turn to his argument as he concludes. Imagination is successful enough in answering the terror of the gorge so that the experience can reappear in Wordsworth's poem without destroying it. But, in a way, the experience will not be denied, returning to answer the claims of imagination as it has itself been answered by imagination. There is no uniting the two kinds of greatness that these imply, "the positive and negative poles of the Romantic sublime" (*RS,* 204).

Weiskel's argument in the final chapter of *The Romantic Sublime* is guided by his sense of Wordsworth as the great humanizer of previous transcendent mysteries, as the cutting edge of poetic humanism (humanistic literature, as opposed to humanism merely using literature). This sense of Wordsworth's historical mission is closely related to his sense, detailed by Weiskel, that knowledge is somehow opposed to efficacious power. This conflict between the claims of knowledge and of power is, I think, the distinctive anxiety haunting the humanist imagination.

For traditional Christianity, clinging to the notion of God's absolute goodness, the existence of evil was the anomaly that haunted the Christian mind with the specter of God's guilt. Thus, the theodicy becomes the imaginative form underlying all Christian literature. Similarly for humanism, moving beyond the divine mystery, with its model of absolute power and authority, toward the assertion of the primacy of knowledge over belief, of a reflective/investigative over a hieratic stance, the central anxiety was that this knowledge was being purchased by the loss of that primal power and that the exaltation of wisdom is vastly inferior to the power of the creating Word.

So in the poetry of Wordsworth, most spectacularly in *The Prelude,* the imaginative form of literary humanism becomes a reflection on poetic origins, which is further developed into a self-consciousness enforcing the assumption that these origins are in and of the self. But as we will see, not only does self-consciousness become the primary vehicle for literary humanism; it also becomes humanism's defense against itself.

According to Weiskel, Wordsworth sees in prophetic poetry—that is, in the archaizing, God-enamored poetry of his great precursors, striving to get in touch with the creating Word or to achieve a literal vision—an intimation of death. More generally, this is the death of nature and natural man as their substance is transformed into the transparent signs of a transcendent reality. More personally, it represents the fall into a mode of discourse already occupied and, in any case, perhaps not suited to his time and place—in short, it represents the loss of the fiction of originality.

Wordsworth's problem arises because that archaic power, despite the threat it poses to his humanizing project and the sense of originality it supports, still attracts. This power is seen as fundamentally dark because it involves elements of guilt and sacrifice. What Weiskel does not sufficiently emphasize is that Wordsworth seeks out this darkness *in order* to be surprised by it. The archaic guilt and sacrifice are the founding events of Wordsworth's poetic selfhood—the dark pleasures and hence the ghosts of the humanizing mind that rejects them and yet has already succumbed to them as the price of its being. Even, perhaps especially, in the poetry of this most humanizing of poets, there lurks a vestige of the archaic, the darkly perverse, in that the founding fiction of originality always requires the sacrifice of the past and the assumption of guilt; whereas the Christian fiction of the single sufficient sacrifice, the Word in which Wordsworth fears his precursors and which is embodied in Christ, holds out the promise of a new origin without guilt. Ranged against this archaic mystery, humanism paradoxically needs sacrifice, and that humanizing poetry is doomed to self-contradiction is the implicit message of Wordsworth's poetry as Weiskel understands it. Thus, the apparent opposition between efficacious power and humanistic knowledge screens the origins of humanism in what it rejects.

Humanism itself is the problem, for without the unifying fiction of the creating Word, uniting literal and creative and making all future sacrifices in order to achieve such a union unnecessary, in terms of what discourse can knowledge and power be brought together? It is precisely the symbol as locus of this union that Wordsworth elides in his imaginative passage through (actually, a leaping over or going around) the threshold. The Simplon Pass episode is an excellent example of this, an example that proves the elision to be necessary because the darkness cannot finally be kept out. And the internalization of self-consciousness that is so important in the humanistic poetic actually exacerbates the problem as psychologizing reveals itself at bottom to be a form of archaizing—as the Freudian notion of the unconscious so richly confirms.

Imagination, however, is posited as the means by which both power and knowledge are possible. It is known by its effects, never clearly distinguishable from a desired ideal. Therefore, it authorizes knowledge without itself becoming the object of knowledge—in effect, a God term. Weiskel defines Wordsworthian imagination as a power of resistance to the dark allure of the Word, a resistance to primal guilt and the need to propitiate the dead. In this sense, it coincides with the poetic need for originality, the founding gesture of the poetic self. An imminent identification with the symbolic order enjoins the annihilation of this original self-hood—a threat of annihilation countered by the extreme self-consciousness embodied in the double structure of the liminal sublime. This ultimate rejection of the symbolic, which is also a rejection of any identification with a father or precursor, is for this reason also a rejection of the Oedipal conflict as a representation of the fundamental structure of the self. This rejection is a necessary fiction of the poetic self and also of the humanist, postreligious worldview. Freud's continuing relevance for literary humanism has much to do with the unconscious's role, speaking through the Oedipus complex, of the archaizing voice within.

Bate's Longinian humanism, enjoining us to believe in the redemptive power of the tradition, seems to exhort us to accept a fiction similar to that of Christ's sufficient sacrifice—a lie against a primal knowledge of conflict. Indeed, Bate implicitly defines humanism as a lie against primal knowledge or the experience of natural man. Wordsworth's poetic humanism embraces such primal knowledge in order to evade it. He attempts to deny the authority of the past by evasion, yet he accepts the necessity of overcoming, if only by evasion, the authority of the fathers in order to gain it for himself, thereby reopening himself to their influence. In short, Wordsworth presents us with humanism as an archaic struggle to evade archaism. Unlike Bate's Longinism, Wordsworth's internalized humanism requires that the symbolic domain of the ancestors be elided. This is the difference between Bate's critical humanism and Wordsworth's poetic humanism—Wordsworth is trying to envision humanism as something more than the defeat of poetry—a hopelessly archaic, burdened discourse. The contrast suggests that the criticism/poetry split, like the knowledge/power split, is built into the ideological structure of humanism. The implicit burden of Weiskel's account of Wordsworth is that poetry is archaic and that this archaism infects literary humanism as a whole. We can go even farther to argue that literature is both central to and contradicts the pretensions of all humanizing projects. On the other hand, this subversive archaism also keeps humanism's abstracting, idealizing tendencies under control, just as it counters the progress of the devouring "I" that threatens in the egotistical sublime to devour so much that it becomes invisible itself.

The triumph of the secular canon in the eighteenth century, as the vernacular tradition, especially in England, decisively establishes its unquestionable authority, is a precondition both for Bate's burden and for the negative sublime. Perhaps for the first time, the canon of secular humanism has the authority to assert its value independent of reference to traditional, biblical notions of transcendent value. Yet the denial of the transcendent mystery (like Bate's denial that the canon is exclusive and belittling) must itself serve as the content of that new transcendence (which Weiskel calls the exaltation of wisdom). Hence its existence is merely the negation of the perceptional, which becomes, as in every transcendence, a metaphor for the status quo. Such a negative transcendence invites most particularly in poetry a flooding back in of the archaic. And the role of poetry becomes to segregate that archaism so that the progress of rational humanism can continue in other areas. The negative sublime then, with its attendant psychologizations, is both the primary ideological vehicle of humanism and its primary defense against itself.

Wordsworth's great humanizing project was the discovery of self-consciousness as the vehicle of a humanizing verse and also as a defense against it. The egotistical sublime discovers reflexive self-consciousness as a way of avoiding the flight into the vacuum of negative transcendence. As such it represents a reformulation of the ideology of humanism. Because of its own self-negating tendencies, it becomes necessary, in effect, to become self-conscious about self-consciousness. This prevents self-consciousness from intensifying to the point where it becomes symbolic, no longer an attribute of a distinct human self. Furthermore, this helps to explain the peculiar role of self-consciousness as an apparent threat to literature in its potential to deprive it of the ability to be about anything but itself and also as literature's primary defense against this fate.

The liminal sublime then is the form of a distinctive Romantic articulation of a literary humanism, giving it real depth by transforming the ideology into a problematic, which we have received as a part of our own humanism and which helps to protect it from ideological deconstruction of all but the most determined kind.

3

ROMANTIC LOSSES

If literature, as it has traditionally been regarded, really is dying (Little Nell-like, has been dying for the last two hundred years), it would be reasonable either to abandon it entirely as an activity central to culture or to revise fundamentally our notions of its nature and purpose. Yet Romanticism represents virtually the only vigorous and apparently successful post-Enlightenment attempt at such a redefinition. And even the Romantics, as I will argue, ultimately fall well short of the reconstitution of literature on any grounds radically different from those of the eighteenth century against which they rebelled. The continued coexistence in the new age of secular letters of traditional conceptions of literature with the conviction that such a literature is no longer possible suggests some disturbing parallels with melancholia as Freud describes it in his 1917 essay, "Mourning and Melancholia."

Mourning is the familiar process by which the affections are painfully withdrawn from their lost object and redirected elsewhere. In melancholia, however, the mourning process does not end since the affections refuse to redirect themselves. Melancholia is further distinguished by the fact that the melancholiac may be unaware of the precise nature of his loss or even that a loss has occurred. Freud concludes: "This would suggest that melancholia is in some way related to an object-loss which is withdrawn from consciousness, in contradistinction to mourning, in which there is nothing about the loss which is unconscious" (MM, 245). In the context then of our discussion of the burden of the past, the poet's insistence on clinging to an object—poetry—which he believes is in decline and, for all intents and purposes, lost for modern society suggests that behind the anticipated end of literature, there lurks a different and even more deeply feared loss.

Although the mental state of the melancholiac resembles that of the mourner—for example, a lack of interest in the outside world and a turning inward—it is perhaps most clearly distinguished by a marked lack of self-esteem, suggesting that "in mourning it is the world which has become poor and empty; in melancholia it is the ego itself" (MM, 246). This too finds a parallel in the late eighteenth-century poet's self-denigrating attitude. Freud cannily hastens to add that it is fruitless to contradict such self-denigrations because a person in this condition really *is* unpleasant and ineffectual. Similarly, we would be hard-pressed to contradict Gray or Collins when they scourge themselves insistently with unfavorable comparisons to Milton or to the tradition combining Shakespeare, Spenser, and Milton. Still, for the poet as for the melancholiac, there is something odd in pursuing an activity in which he is doomed to inferiority from the start and in insisting on a particular conception of greatness that can only deepen that inferiority. But, Freud goes on to say, the accuracy of such self-denigration "is secondary; it is the effect of the internal work which is consuming his ego— work which is unknown to us but which is comparable to the work of mourning" (MM, 246).

We might expect that someone afflicted with such a sense of inferiority would take pains to hide it. Surprisingly: "One might emphasize the presence in him of an almost opposite trait of insistent communicativeness which finds satisfaction in self-exposure" (MM, 247). This too seems applicable to the work of the Sensibility Poets. The inappropriate violence of the melancholiac's self-reproaches leads Freud to "the key to the clinical picture," which is that "the self-reproaches are reproaches against a loved object which have been shifted away from it on to the patient's own ego" (MM, 248). This brings us back to our earlier conjecture that behind the apparent anxiety over the end of literature there lurks the fear of a different, greater loss, to which we can now add the tentative conclusion that the self-accusations of the poet are actually aimed elsewhere, perhaps at the loved object, literature itself.

Having established the presence of "a mental constellation of revolt" underlying the melancholiac's surface contrition, Freud argues:

> There is no difficulty in reconstructing this process. An object-choice, an attachment of the libido to a particular person, had at one time existed; then, owing to a real slight or disappointment coming from this loved person, the object-relationship was shattered. The result was not the normal one of withdrawal of the libido from this object and a displacement of it to a new one, but something different, for whose coming about various conditions seem necessary. The object-cathexis proved to have little power of resistance and was brought to an end. But the free libido was not displaced onto another object; it was withdrawn into the ego. There, however, it was not employed in any unspecified way, but served to establish an *identification* of the ego with the abandoned object. Thus the shadow of the object fell upon the ego, and the latter could henceforth be judged by a special agency, as though it were an object, the forsaken object. In this way an object-loss was transformed into an ego-loss and the conflict between the ego and the loved person into a cleavage between the critical activity of the ego and the ego as altered by identification.
>
> (MM, 248–49)

This account presents us with something of a contradiction since "on the one hand, a strong fixation to the love-object must have been present; on the other hand, in contradistinction to this, this object-cathexis must have had little power of resistance." Freud solves the problem by noting, after Rank, that "this contradiction seems to imply that the object-choice has been effected on a narcissistic basis, so that the object-cathexis, when obstacles come in its way, can regress to narcissism" (MM, 249).

Freud's conclusion that the disposition to melancholia originates in a narcissistic object-choice seems to suggest, at least in terms of our present comparison, that literature is being accused for the loss of the poet's narcissistic ego-ideal—a dream of greatness, of more-than-human creative achievement. A sad solicitude for the fate of poetry, like the poet's self-denigrations, masks a hostility toward literature for its "failure" to sustain the possibility of this ideal.

Not surprisingly, things are somewhat more complicated than this because, in arguing that their burdened situation is the result of the impersonal historical process of social progress, eighteenth-century thinkers erect a profoundly ambivalent defense: they are able to rail endlessly against literature even as they are able to defend it against their accusations by taking the (exaggerated) responsibility on themselves—a roundabout self-aggrandizement. This is very like the strategy that Bloom attibutes to the Kabbalah—a similarity suggesting that this may be a stance common to all revisionisms, Bloom's own included.

It is important to realize that like the narcissistic wound that always occurs too early to be avoided, the discrediting of the narcissistic poetic self-image has always already occurred. In other words, one does not become a poet and fail; this failure is the beginning of poetic identity—a conclusion, contrary to the pretensions of *The Prelude*, which lurks just beneath the surface of Wordsworth's "Intimations" ode and which that great poem strives, contra Gray, to hold at bay.

Ironically, it is Wordsworth, striving to refute Gray's melancholy view of poetic possibility, who actually completes the terms of our analogy between melancholia and the post-Enlightenment poet's relationship with literature and the tradition. Freud notes that the melancholiac does not realize that a change has taken place; he revises his past to show that he has always been inferior or unworthy. This is clearly at odds with the treatment of literary history elevating the past as a means of making it serve to represent the ego-ideal. But the revisionary design of *The Prelude,* appropriating Wordsworth's past identities to the present idealized identity of poet, in effect internalizes the ambivalence of the Sensibility Poets, rendering invisible and unconscious a formerly visible and, if not entirely conscious, at least more accessible relationship. Thus, the possibility of mourning and redirection is blocked and the sense of loss internalized as in melancholia—a process graphically acted out at the end of Shelley's "Alastor," when that poem confesses its failure to escape the determining influence of Wordsworth.

In Gray's "Elegy," the origin of poetic identity in a failure that has already occurred is represented initially by the accident of birth that so limits the possibilities of achievement for the rustic. By the end of the poem, this theme has managed to appropriate to itself the "greater" theme of the universality of death, the fatal limitation or narcissistic wound that is with the greatest of us from birth. For Gray, the inevitability of death extends to poetry, which is moving inexorably throughout the poem toward its ultimate reduction to epitaph. This poetic death refers us to the fatal compromising of the ineffable, essential, idealized self—its failure to externalize itself adequately. Such a failure or narcissistic wound has always already occurred because this self is founded on ineffability, and, hence, its externalization as such is impossible.

This ineffability is nonetheless necessary to defend an extreme self-idealization, which is projected onto the tradition of the great precursors both as a self-reproach and as a revenge, since it allows them to suffer the same "death" when poetry as a contemporary activity comes to an end and the pretensions of poetic greatness are destroyed by their final elevation out of this world. Furthermore, the ineffable, essential self is at a permanent disadvantage in the face of the tangibility of the precursors' texts or even of its own—a recognition reflected in the revisionist's view of interpretation as a defense, comprehending both reading and writing, of the self, rather than of creed, country, or social interest.

Before the Sensibility Poets, death frequently appears as the measure of what we most fear to lose; it is the great antagonist trying to frighten us into self-betrayal. For Homer's Sarpedon and Glaukos as for Richardson's Clarissa Harlowe, honor and the integrity of social role are more important than life itself. But, with the later eighteenth century, the situation is complicated: death comes to be measured against death and becomes a synecdoche of itself, just as the self becomes a synecdoche of itself, in which the essential, idealized, and ineffable self is measured against the mundane, externalizable self. Consequently, the end of poetry portends the ultimate failure of this idealized self, even as the death of each poet becomes an increasingly ominous portent of the coming end of poetry.

THOMAS GRAY

Completed in 1750 when Gray was thirty-four, "Elegy Written in a Country Churchyard" became one of the best-known poems of the later eighteenth century and, as such, made Gray an influence to be reckoned with for the first-generation Romantics. As we will see, this is especially true for Wordsworth, who singles Gray out for criticism in his famous preface to the *Lyrical Ballads* and whose "Intimations" ode is perhaps most profitably seen as a revisionary response to the "Elegy."

Gray's poem begins in that imaginative space ably defined by Geoffrey Hartman in his essay "Evening Star and Evening Land"—the liminal state, separating the full light of day from the coming darkness, so admirably suited to convey the sense of diminished poetic possibility appropriate to the final stages of a declining poetic tradition:[1]

> The Curfew tolls the knell of parting day,
> The lowing herd wind slowly o'er the lea,
> The plowman homeward plods his weary way,
> And leaves the world to darkness and to me.
>
> (lines 1–4)

Here, the twilight state, as it is epitomized by William Collins's "Ode to Evening" (1747), is even further condensed as Gray crowds right up against the moment when darkness finally blots out sense—"Now fades the glimmering landscape on the sight" (line 5)—and does entirely without the Hesperidean promise of the Collins poem.

Throughout the "Elegy," Gray displays an intense formal self-consciousness, manifested in a remorseless process of reduction. An entire tradition of temporal poetry, dealing with the cycle of the seasons and the times of day, shrinks into the form of the evening poem, which is itself further reduced to this moment on the edge of darkness. Similarly, the shaded and secluded bower, privileged for poetry since the beginnings of pastoral, is first transformed into the churchyard and then further reduced to the grassy grave plots with their epitaphs: "Where heaves the turf in many a mould'ring heap, / Each in his narrow cell for ever laid, / The rude Forefathers of the hamlet sleep" (lines 14–16). Finally, all poetry written in the twilight of the tradition is necessarily elegiac—the form appropriate to the penultimate or evening stage of poetic progress, just as the epitaph with

1. Geoffrey Hartman, *The Fate of Reading* (Chicago: University of Chicago Press, 1975), pp. 147–78.

which the poem ends is appropriate to its ultimate, purely nostalgic night.

As the locus peculiar to poetry in his own age, Gray presents the churchyard as a place in which the poet confronts the future he shares with all men and becomes a part of the tradition, himself a "Forefather" to someone. Death is especially privileged in this vision as the intersection of the poet's personal fate and the fate of poetry in the imminent future. The result is a kind of compensation granted to the later poets as the proximity of encompassing death eases the burden of past greatness and the giants of the tradition are similarly chastened by their new vulnerability as the "rude Forefathers" of the poetic hamlet. For this reason, the tone of the poem is more melancholy than sad, which is to say that there is a pleasurable element of new freedom mixed into the sadness—the freedom accompanying a defeat for which one cannot be blamed and against which no amount of genius can prevail.

On a somewhat more superficial level, the poem proceeds with the poet appealing to his audience to appreciate the humble virtues of these good rural farmers and laborers and not to diminish them by inappropriate comparisons with the greatness associated with opportunities they never had. The increasing eloquence and urgency of the poet's appeal reveals an identification beyond mere sympathy, which is, of course, based on his own wish to be judged in terms of the diminished poetic possibilities available to him. His too are the virtues of the good workman, making the most of his limited station:

> Oft did the harvest to their sickle yield,
> Their furrow oft the stubborn glebe has broke;
> How jocund did they drive their team afield!
> How bow'd the woods beneath their sturdy stroke!
>
> Let not ambition mock their useful toil,
> Their homely joys, and destiny obscure;

Nor grandeur hear with a disdainful smile,
The short and simple annals of the poor.
The boast of heraldry, the pomp of pow'r,
And all that beauty, all that wealth e'er gave,
Awaits alike th' inevitable hour.
The paths of glory lead but to the grave.

Nor you, ye Proud, impute to These the fault,
If Mem'ry o'er their Tomb no Trophies raise,
Where thro' the long-drawn isle and fretted vault
The pealing anthem swells the note of praise.

Can storied urn or animated bust
Back to its mansion call the fleeting breath?
Can Honour's voice provoke the silent dust?
Or Flatt'ry sooth the dull cold ear of Death?
(lines 25–44)

Since all, including the greatest, are ultimately reduced to dust, death becomes the poet's most effective defense, however pyrrhic, against the crushing greatness of the tradition. But the poetic *tu quoque* defends the modern poet by reviving in lines 41–44 the very dangerous question also addressed by Milton in "Lycidas": what good is poetry in the face of death? In that poem, Milton grants poetry's detractors their most damaging premise, characterizing it, in essence, as a dallying with "false surmise." In a brilliant reversal, he goes on to argue that it is the very artificiality, the unreality of poetry that makes it the language of faith, which is, after all, "the substance of things hoped for, the evidence of things not seen" (Hebrews 11:1).

What is so pyrrhic in Gray's way of stating the problem is that in attacking the pretensions of greatness in the face of death, he calls into question poetry's most fundamental compensatory myth. In effect, Gray is challenging the notion prevalent since Homer and (probably) before of the value of poetic fame—that poetic greatness somehow provides an immortality in the minds of men that trancends the limits of mortal existence. Gray, despite his later insistence on the saving value of commemoration, raises the possibility that poetry itself and hence poetic fame are also mortal.

Clearly, Gray's is the fear that there will be no one to perform for him and the others of his generation the acts of commemoration that he performs for those before. He is struggling to preserve a faith in posterity sufficient to ensure that even if he can no longer have the fame of a Milton, he can at least anticipate some modest existence in the poetic memory after death.

Yet this desire to believe in a poetic posterity is belied by the use of death as a leveling defense against the accusation represented by past greatness. If "the paths of glory lead but to the grave," then the very notion of fame is undercut, and the pretensions of any poetic fame whatever could scarcely be more absurd.

As a defense, the universality of death is a dangerous failure, calling into question the myth of fame on which all poets depend in order to express the desire that makes them poets; it is also a failure necessary to the freedom peculiar to the poet late in the tradition. In order to understand this, we must look a bit more closely at the nature of defense. Repression, for example, is not known in and of itself but through the consequences of its failure—a failure that suddenly transforms the literality of behavior into something interpretable. Indeed, it is precisely the failure of defense that makes possible the interpretive activity of psychoanalysis. To put it another way, the existence of such an interpretation requires both that there be something like defenses and that they fail. From the point of view of literary criticism, whether carried out implicitly by poets or explicitly by critics, what this suggests is that there is a paradoxical interpretive relationship between failure and the will to power.

The damage done to the myth of fame by the power Gray grants to death opens up a new area of poetic endeavor: to

make up for the loss of faith in fame by redefining poetry in
order to give it different goals and to identify it with new
bases of value and authority. In this sense, the stance of
lateness or minority is clearly a way of making space, although we have yet to determine if the cost is not too high.
From this point, Gray speculates:

> Perhaps in this neglected spot is laid
> Some heart once pregnant with celestial fire;
> Hands, that the rod of empire might have sway'd,
> Or wak'd to extasy the living lyre.
>
> But knowledge to their eyes her ample page
> Rich with the spoils of time did ne'r unroll;
> Chill Penury repress'd their noble rage,
> And froze the genial current of the soul.
>
> Full many a gem of purest ray serene,
> The dark unfathom'd cares of ocean bear:
> Full many a flower is born to blush unseen,
> And waste its sweetness on the desert air.
>
> Some village-Hampden, that with dauntless breast
> The little Tyrant of his fields withstood;
> Some mute inglorious Milton here may rest,
> Some Cromwell guiltless of his country's blood.
>
> (lines 45–60)

We are tempted to respond immediately that a "mute inglorious Milton" is not a Milton at all, yet here Gray prepares
the way for the Wordsworth of the Preface in arguing that
one is not a poet by virtue of actually having written poetry
but by virtue of an essential disposition of the self. Such a
view is an important compensatory complement of a fundamentally impersonal and deterministic view of history. In
the lines above, Gray emphasizes that impersonal circumstances of birth, time, and place are sufficient to overpower
even genius. Clearly, it would be intolerable if the individual
were held responsible for the limits imposed by history. On
the other hand, to remove the identity of the poet from its

objective manifestation in having written is also to move away from a visible canon as the shape and source of literary authority toward an altogether vaguer, internal standard.

However, the poem continues: if circumstance kept these villagers from recognizing their own potential greatness, it also prevented them from indulging in the excesses of greatness (lines 61–76). Recognizing the essential violence of greatness, Gray goes on to suggest a connection between that excess and a revolt against death:

> Yet ev'n, these bones from insult to protect
> Some frail memorial still erected nigh,
> With uncouth rhimes and shapeless sculpture deck'd,
> Implores the passing tribute of a sigh.
>
> Their name, their years, spelt by th' unletter'd muse,
> The place of fame and elegy supply:
> And many a text around she strews
> That teach the rustic moralist to die.
>
> (lines 77–84)

The alternative recommended by Gray is a poetry of acceptance, a poetry freed by its final defeat at the hands of death and history. But this reduction of poetry to elegy deprives poetry of its due seasons—gone are the stages of growth (pastoral, georgic, epic) with their unique concerns corresponding to the times of life. In the twilight of the tradition, all poetry is aimed at being reconciled to its fate:

> For who to dumb Forgetfulness a prey,
> This pleasing anxious being e'er resigned,
> Left to the warm precincts of the chearful day,
> Nor cast one longing ling'ring look behind?
>
> On some fond breast the parting soul relies,
> Some pious drops the closing eye requires;
> Ev'n, from the tomb the voice of Nature cries,
> Ev'n in our Ashes live their wonted Fires.
>
> (lines 85–92)

Here Gray returns to a much muted version of the myth of fame, in which poetry is no longer seen as striving against mortality but as easing our acceptance of death by assuring that someone cares. Poetry becomes the privileged language of this anxiety/caring because it too is in decline toward death.

Begun the year after the publication of "Elegy" and completed in 1754, Gray's long Pindaric ode "The Progress of Poesy" makes explicit the idea of poetic history underlying the melancholy of the earlier poem. It traces the westward progress of the focus of poetic greatness from Greece, to Rome, to England and, after extolling the virtues of Shakespeare, Milton, and Dryden, concludes:

> Oh! lyre divine, what daring Spirit
> Wakes thee now? Tho' he inherit
> Nor the pride, nor ample pinion,
> That the Theban Eagle bear.
> Sailing with supreme dominion
> Thro' the azure deep of air:
> Yet oft before his infant eye would run
> Such forms, as glitter in the Muse's ray
> With orient hues, unborrow'd of the Sun:
> Yet shall he mount, and keep his distant way
> Beyond the limits of the vulgar fate,
> Beneath the Good how far—but far above the Great.
> (lines 112–23)

The convoluted syntax of that last line very nearly succeeds in obscuring Gray's conviction that the progress of poesy represents for moderns a permanent decline in greatness. This new Pindar anticipated by Gray, though soaring far above the merely good, is nevertheless doomed to remain far below the truly great. Indeed, although he does not slight Shakespeare and Milton by saying so, Gray manages to suggest that the power and spontaneity of the Greeks was never recaptured in later poetry, for all its virtues.

Before launching into his account of the actual progress, Gray devotes his first sixty-five lines to rehearsing the original, undiminished powers of poetry, including the power to alleviate care, control passion and distract from violence, and give voice to love and desire. Once, he even suggests, poetry was a sufficient answer to death itself:

> Man's feeble race what Ills await,
> Labour, and Penury, the racks of Pain,
> Disease, and Sorrow's weeping train,
> And Death, sad refuge from the storms of Fate!
> The fond complaint, my Song, disprove,
> And justify the laws of Jove.
> Say, has he giv'n in vain the heav'nly Muse?
> Night, and all her sickly dews,
> Her spectres wan, and birds of boding cry,
> He gives to range the dreary sky:
> Till down the eastern cliffs afar
> Hyperion's march they spy, and glitt'ring shafts of war.
>
> (lines 42–53)

The translation of Milton's intention, expressed in the famous invocation of *Paradise Lost,* to "justify the ways of God to Man" into the gratuitous and sadly self-conscious classicism of "And justify the laws of Jove" suggests not only the poetic weakness of Gray's classicism but also the pedantic rather than imaginative foundations of much of his verse.

The decision to add in the 1768 edition notes to "The Progress" and its companion ode, "The Bard," serves only to emphasize the way in which the poems are, in a sense, already footnoted, if not partially reduced to footnotes themselves, by the many echoes of previous poems, unrelated in meaning to their immediate context, which they contain—echoes clearly designed to be recognized as evidence of an erudition shared by reader and poet as the basis of their relationship.

Not only does this indicate the need for new poetic myths to give imaginative life to Gray's subject matter; it also suggests that a poem, whatever its ostensible subject, will inevitably become a poem about its own status as poetry. And what are we to make of the "Advertisement," also added in 1768?

> When the author first published this and the following Ode, he was advised, even by his Friends, to subjoin some few explanatory Notes; but had too much respect for the understanding of his Readers to take that liberty.

We can only assume that between 1757 and 1768 Gray was persuaded that his faith was misplaced and the distance between himself and his audience somewhat greater than he had imagined. We do know that his nonoccasional poetry after 1754 is dominated by a search for extracanonical and nonclassical sources in various northern traditions. The first and most important of these efforts, "The Bard," was completed in 1757 and published along with "The Progress of Poesy." "The Bard" was followed in 1761 by "The Fatal Sisters," "The Descent of Odin," and "The Welsh Odes."

"The Bard" is particularly interesting for our purposes because it promises to redefine the tradition outside the deterministic history and overburdened self-consciousness of "The Progress," but it ultimately fails to seize the opportunity and ends up reinforcing and extending the pessimism implicit in the earlier poems.

In his "Advertisement" Gray tells us:

> The Following Ode is founded on a Tradition current in Wales, that Edward the First, when he compleated the conquest of that country, ordered all the Bards, that fell into his hands, to be put to death.

As the poem begins, the last of the Welsh bards curses the king with a prophetic vision of the disasters to befall his line before it dies out to be replaced by the new promise of the Tudors. The contrast between Edward and Elizabeth is a contrast between poetry at odds and allied with temporal power and the forces of history. But it is difficult to know what conclusions we are to draw. On the one hand, the story seems to suggest a compensatory principle at work in history, with present memories to be replaced by future glories; on the other hand, since Gray's "history" stops with Shakespeare, "The Bard" is a kind of complement to rather than replacement for the view expressed in "The Progress of Poesy," especially since it makes the canonical Shakespeare the fulfillment of the bard's hopes.

There also seem to be certain parallels between Gray's vision and that of Collins at the end of "Ode to Evening" and in "The Manners" (1746). In the final lines of the former poem, Collins associates the new, muted poetic of evening with the social virtues of "Fancy, Friendship, Science, smiling Peace" (line 50). In "The Manners," he begins by bidding farewell to the self-involvement of larger intellectual and imaginative ambitions and turns outward to cultivate a harmony, antithetical to the aggressivity of greatness, of the natural and social worlds:

> Youth of the quick uncheated sight,
> Thy Walks, Observance, more invite!
> O Thou, who lov'st that ampler Range,
> Where Life's wide Prospects round thee change,
> And with her mingling Sons ally'd,
> Throws't the prattling page aside:
> To me in Converse sweet impart,
> To read in Man the native Heart,
> To learn, where Science sure is found,
> From nature as she lives around:
> And gazing oft her Mirror true,
> By turns each shifting Image view!
> Till meddling Art's officious Lore,
> Reverse the Lessons taught before,

208 · Literary Revisionism

Alluring from a safer Rule,
To dream in her enchanted School:
Tho' Heav'n, whate'r of Great we boast,
Has blest this social Science most.

(lines 19–36)

Gray draws a distinction between the old bards' powers
and those of Spenser, Shakespeare, Milton, and those who
follow them. Before the massacre of the old bards, there was
"Cadwallo's tongue, / That hush'd the stormy main" (lines
29–30) and "Modred, whose magic song / Made huge Plin-
limmon bow his cloud-top'd head" (lines 33–34). The great
revival of poetry ushered in by Elizabeth promises:

The verse adorn again
Fierce War, and faithful Love,
And Truth severe, by fairy Fiction drest.
In buskin'd measures move
Pale Grief, and pleasing Pain,
With Horrour, Tyrant of the throbbing Breast.
A Voice, as of the Cherub-Choir,
Gales from blooming Eden bear;
And distant warblings lessen on my ear,
That lost in long futurity expire.

(lines 125–34)

In light of "The Progress of Poesy," this last line may
seem a trifle ominous since the five hundred years between
the thirteenth and eighteenth centuries seem sufficient to
qualify as a "long futurity." But the bard's song, his prophetic curse, is itself the best example of the gap separating
the earlier greatness from the later. If those who could actually bend nature to their wills by song are gone, the lone
survivor can speak a prophecy of five hundred years' duration and bring disaster down on his enemy's line. It is this
sense of poetry as power that is missing from Gray's account
of the more modern greats.

The difference seems to suggest that poetic power of the

prophetic kind is intimately linked with disaster. A prophecy like this requires an occasion, and it is difficult to imagine a suitable occasion that could be anticipated with any pleasure. Thus, the conditions of poetic power seem completely at odds with the natural and social harmony envisaged in "The Manners."

Much in this poem hinges on the necessity of the bard's suicide:

> Enough for me: With joy I see
> The different doom our Fates assign.
> Be thine despair, and scept'red Care,
> To triumph and to die, are mine.
> He spoke, and headlong from the mountain's height
> Deep in the roaring tide he plung'd to endless night.
>
> (lines 139–44)

The truth of the prophecy and efficacy of the curse, the sheer poetic power, is not enough to give the bard any vision of his own future or even to allow him to contemplate his own survival. He knows that his poetic identity, his fellowship with the poets of power, binds him to the past by excluding him from a future in which he can have no part except by becoming another kind of poet entirely. And, finally, it is not the evident truth of the prophecy or power of its utterance that validates it, but the death of the poet—the ultimate evidence of sincerity.

Defeated by history, yet seeking a literal validation of poetic power outside poetry itself, the bard can prove this power only by his willingness to die—a gesture that mortgages the poetic future by committing it in advance to eulogize him, even as Gray is now doing. There is no sublimation of death here, no metaphorical drive to be elsewhere, and hence nothing to compete with the reality of death. "The Bard" rejoins the vision of "Elegy Written in a Country Churchyard" in conceiving poetry as the means by which, like Huck and Tom, we contrive to be spectators at our own funerals. This helps to explain our peculiar position in this poem as those who bear witness and, in doing so, recognize that we are the living fulfillment of the bard's prophecy. In this view, history is prophecy fulfilled, beyond revision or, to put it another way, history is death.

All of this, especially the sense of history as death, encourages us to see in "The Bard" a dark allegory of originality as disaster. Indeed, the bard's originality is inseparable from the disaster that befalls his tradition and leaves him trapped in a past whose obsolescence he is even now declaring but without which his prophetic vision could not be. Tied to that origin defining his originality, he is powerless to join the future he envisions. The bard's is the trap of all prophecy: realized, it ceases to be prophetic and becomes history, and, hence, the original poet is a Moses who cannot enter his promised land.

Thus, the link between the ideal of originality and the ineffability of the ideal self becomes apparent. The heroism of the defeated bard is internalized, and this internalized heroism, founded in a despair of the present, is originality, which eternally finds its ultimate triumph somewhere just beyond its reach and so seeks to postpone indefinitely its final defeat. Such an internalization, stripping heroism of its external supports, its points of reference in a living community, cuts off the avenues of externalization, the opportunities for the adequate gesture, and leaves the hero of origins alone with death, at once the end of ambivalence and the threshold of a desired future. Here, in germinal form, we have the origin of Wordsworth's effort to redeem originality by sublimation—an evasion implicitly confirming the connection of originality with death—and of Shelley's attempt to overcome Gray and Wordsworth both by severing this connection.

From the point of view of the Romantics who follow, Gray represents an exhausted orthodoxy. He makes no attempt to subvert the reality of death by rendering it a figure of itself, nor does he strive to keep alive in any vital form the poetic ambition to surpass death, either by sublimating it (in order to forestall disappointment) or by rejecting sublimation altogether (in order to seek an alternative reality). Nevertheless, as Bate points out, Gray's poetic is very much a part of the secular revisionism of the eighteenth century, which the Romantics both extend and define themselves against.

Wordsworth's conservative revisionism is based on sublimation just as Shelley's radicalism is based on the rejection of sublimation. As we have already seen, Bloom's rejection of sublimation as the doctrine of the second chance marks his as an extreme Gnostic revisionism and seems to set him apart from the tradition of sublimation dominating literary humanism after Wordsworth. For all of this, Shelley through Wordsworth and Bloom through Shelley remain powerfully bound to Gray's reformulation for secular poetry of the revisionist problematic of gain-through-loss.

WILLIAM WORDSWORTH

In my book on Coleridge, *Vision and Revision*,[2] I stressed Wordsworth's failure to sustain a stance sublimating poetic desire in order to highlight by contrast Coleridge's adherence to the ideal of immanence. Coleridge self-consciously regarded his project in terms of this theological conception of the nature of God's being in the world. Yet the complexities resulting from the fact that because of the limits of individual identity, man's mode of being could at best approximate this ideal, suggest that for Coleridgean man, immanence is finally a kind of sublimation, though it remains to be seen whether immanence has more to suggest about sublimation or vice versa.

2. *Vision and Revision: Coleridge's Art of Immanence* (Berkeley: University of California Press, 1982).

In Wordsworth's case, the sublimation of imagination into nature is necessary in order to prevent the apocalypse, which unrestrained imaginative desire would surely bring on—a catastrophic revelation of imagination's ultimate helplessness in the face of the material world and death. The moment in which imagination stands revealed and triumphant—as in the Simplon Pass or on Mount Snowdon—is also the moment in which it is exposed to the most devastating contradiction, the universal "so what?"

Wordsworth's situation is further complicated by his conception of the nature of the poetic, which brings us to his preface to *Lyrical Ballads* as a response to Gray. In our discussion of "Elegy Written in a Country Churchyard," we noted that his emphasis on greatness, poetic or otherwise, as a function of an inner disposition rather than of actual performance has profound implications for poetry and poets. In the preface of 1800, Wordsworth typically takes what was, for Gray, a defensive stance and goes on the offensive by insisting that a poet

> is a man speaking to men: a man, it is true, endowed with more lively sensibility, more enthusiasm and tenderness, who has a greater knowledge of human nature, and a more comprehensive soul, than are supposed to be common among mankind; a man pleased with his own passions and volitions, and who rejoices more than other men at the life that is in him; delighting to contemplate similar volitions and passions as manifested in the goings-on of the Universe, and habitually impelled to create them where he does not find them. To these qualities he has added a disposition to be affected more than other men by absent things as if they were present; an ability of conjuring up in himself passions, which are indeed far from being the same as those produced by real events, yet (especially in those parts of the general sympathy which are pleasing and delightful) do more nearly resemble the passions produced by real events, than anything which, from the motions of their own minds, other men are accustomed to feel in themselves:—whence, and from

practice, he has acquired a greater readiness and power in expressing what he thinks and feels.

(737)

There is a tremendous tension here between likeness and difference; the poet is like other men except that he is their superior in virtually every humane quality—his is a sublimated transcendence of mere humanity. On the one hand, the desire for greatness and to realize the distinctiveness of his special poetic identity drives Wordsworth away from the rest of humanity; on the other hand, the efficacy of poetry and the eventual recognition of poetic greatness depends on being like others. This highlights another danger inherent in Wordsworth's greatest moments of imaginative power—the danger that his superiority will overpower the similarity. If we follow Bloom in arguing that the poet wishes at least to transcend death figuratively by claiming that he has achieved a kind of compensation, the poet's success in this would also mark the moment in which he ceases to be a poet. Thus, even as he presents each poem to the public as sufficient (that is, a representation and explanation of common experiences good enough for *readers*), in his own mind he sees it as a failure—the necessary prelude to writing again. In his sense, every poem is, for the Wordsworthian poet, necessarily a "Prelude," haunted by the lingering specter of the inauthentic or the insincere.

In *The Prelude,* if the Snowdon episode represents the triumph of difference, of what Keats was to call the "egotistical sublime" (recognizing that, for Wordsworth, it was more important finally to possess poetry as an attribute of his particular selfhood than of people in general) over sameness, the conflict of the two in its most desperate and evasive intensity is typified by episodes of apparent but false identification. One such episode, commencing at line 370 of Book IV,

involves an old soldier whom the young Wordsworth meets
on the road:

> . . . an uncouth shape,
> Shown by a sudden turning of the road,
> So near that, slipping back into the shade
> Of a thick hawthorne, I could mark him well,
> Myself unseen. . . .
>
> (lines 387–91)

The initial impulse to prolong the advantage of seeing without being seen sets the tone for the whole encounter. After
hearing of the soldier's trials and observing the contrast between his obvious suffering and calm demeanor, Wordsworth secures shelter for him in a nearby house—one of
those highly ambiguous acts of kindness composed partly of
sympathy and partly of a desire to avoid identifying too
closely with any victim of the very real risk of failure attend-
ing our existence. The rather priggish way in which the
youngster "entreats" the veteran—"that henceforth / He
would not linger in the public ways, / But ask for timely
furtherance and help / Such as his state required" (lines 454–
57)—reflects in its condescension the desire to differentiate
himself not just from the individual but from the vulnerability of the human condition, which is a threat to his budding
sense of his own unique powers. Ironically, the soldier's
response—"My trust is in the God of Heaven, / And in the
eye of him who passes me!" (lines 459–60)—can, under the
circumstances, only emphasize the vulnerability from which
Wordsworth hastens to disassociate himself.

A similar episode, following soon after, early in Book V,
seems to emphasize the complementary danger of identifying too closely with imagination and its idealizing power in
a material world. This episode involves the famous Arab
dream, in which Wordsworth falls asleep while reading *Don
Quixote* and dreams of an encounter on a vast desert with a

bedouin, who carries a stone, representing "Euclid's Elements" (line 88), and a shell, representing poetry. Holding the shell to his ear, Wordsworth hears:

> A loud prophetic blast of harmony;
> An Ode, in passion uttered, which foretold
> Destruction of the children of the earth
> By deluge, now at hand. . . .
>
> (lines 95–98)

A poetic imagination alienated from existence as it is here cannot prophecy anything except destruction since its own purity requires the negation of the world, and the refusal of the world to go away threatens perpetually to destroy the purity of the imaginative vision. Caught in this destructive relationship, the Arab is hastening to bury the stone and shell in order to preserve them from the apocalypse, which they themselves require.

The dream itself is a means for Wordsworth to place himself at a distance from this dangerous tendency of poetic desire—a defense against identification that finds expression in the poem when Wordsworth, who has been "with" the Arab throughout, is suddenly a spectator, looking on as he flees, "hurrying o'er the illimitable waste, / With the fleet waters of a drowning world / In chase of him" (lines 136–38). This new distance is confirmed as Wordsworth immediately awakens. From this safe vantage point, he is able to assert a carefully hypothetical identity between himself and the Arab:

> . . . in the blind and awful lair
> Of such a madness, reason did lie couched.
> Enow there are on earth to take in charge
> Their wives, their children, and their virgin loves,
> Or whatsoever else the heart holds dear;
> Enow to stir for these; yea, will I say,
> Contemplating in soberness the approach
> Of an event so dire, by signs in earth

Or heaven made manifest, that I could share
That maniac's fond anxiety, and go
Upon like errand. Often times at least
Me hath such strong entrancement overcome,
When I have held a volume in my hand,
Poor earthly casket of immortal verse,
Shakespeare, or Milton, labourers divine!

(lines 151–65)

We should also note how, in emphasizing the importance of those in whom poetry finds a home and a defense against the fragility of books themselves, Wordsworth manages to return us to the notion that poetry exists essentially by virtue of the inner qualities of the poet and continues to reside there in its purest form.

The difficulties created, or emphasized at least, by Wordsworth's insistence that the poetic finds its source not in other poetry but in the nature of the poet naturally raise the question of why he felt that such a redefinition was needed and direct our attention once again to the 1800 preface, so much of which is devoted to the nature of poetry and of poetic diction.

If Wordsworth's emphasis on the feelings of the poet tends to pull poetry back into the self, his notion of poetic language represents a counterforce that tends to tie poetry to nature and humanity by insisting on the commonality of language. As every student knows, Wordsworth begins by characterizing the language of *Lyrical Ballads* as "a selection of the real language of men in a state of vivid sensation," fitted to a metrical arrangement (734). From there, he goes on to blast the "gaudiness and inane phraseology of many modern writers . . . who think that they are conferring honour upon themselves and their art, in proportion as they separate themselves from the sympathies of men and indulge in arbitrary and capricious habits of expression, in order to furnish food for fickle tastes, and fickle appetites of their own creation" (734, 735).

Although superficially this would seem to apply only to those addicted to innovation for its own sake, Wordsworth sees a fundamental connection between pointless innovation and the burdened poetic self-consciousness of the late eighteenth century, so heavily dependent on what he characterizes as "a family language which writers in metre seem to lay claim to by prescription . . . phrases and figures of speech which from father to son have long been regarded as the common inheritance of Poets" (736). As we noted in our discussion of Gray, this situation leads poets to be "poetic" by echoing previous poems even where sense is not enhanced and there is no necessity to do so. Paradoxically, this dependence on the poetic qualities of an inherited diction also leads to a facile but basically inane capacity for innovation, as the later poet varies existing formulas in order to make them "new" (though still recognizable as echoes—for example, Gray's "Jove" for "God" in "The Progress of Poesy"). By this intermediate step, the very straitening conservatism of late eighteenth-century poetic diction can be seen as a contributing factor in creating a taste for innovation for its own sake that leads to the complementary fashion of "frantic novels, sickly and stupid German tragedies, and deluges of idle and extravagant stories in verse" (735).

Gray is especially singled out by Wordsworth as one who has helped drive poetry back in upon itself by emphasizing the distinction between an exalted poetic language and a prose mired in the mundane. As a result, poems can only be about other poems and reflect the preconditions of being poetic rather than any deeper truth of our existence (736). When he came to write an appendix to the preface, on poetic diction, for the 1802 edition of *Lyrical Ballads*, Wordsworth recast his indictment as a capsule "history" of poetic language:

The earliest poets of all nations generally wrote from passion excited by real events; they wrote naturally, and as men: feeling powerfully as they did, their language was daring, and figurative. In succeeding times, Poets, and men ambitious of the fame of Poets, perceiving the influence of such language, and desirous of producing the same effect without being animated by the same passion, set themselves to a mechanical adoption of these figures of speech, and made use of them, sometimes with propriety, but much more frequently applied them to feelings and thoughts with which they had no natural connection whatsoever. A language was thus insensibly produced, differing materially from the real language of men in *any situation*.

(741)

By contrast, Wordsworth seeks to base the language of *Lyrical Ballads* on the language of real men, modified by the imagination and by the demands of propriety. This "reality" is specifically the reality of country life:

Humble and rustic life was generally chosen, because, in that condition, the essential passions of the heart find a better soil in which they can attain their maturity, are less under restraint, and speak a plainer and more emphatic language; because in that condition of life our elementary feelings coexist in a state of greater simplicity, and, consequently, may be more accurately contemplated, and more forcibly communicated; because the manners of rural life germinate from those elementary feelings, and from the necessary character of rural occupations, are more easily comprehended and more durable; and, lastly, because in that condition the passions of men are incorporated with the beautiful and permanent forms of nature.

(735)

If the artificial poetic diction of Gray represents a self-enclosed poetry, cut off from the world around, then a poetic language springing from the greatest possible proximity to the "beautiful and permanent forms of nature" promises not only to open poetry up to the world but also to put it in touch with the self-renewing diversity of nature. And, in light of the internalization of the poetic, which is another prominent feature of the preface, it also promises to complement and counterbalance the dangerous solipsism and tendency to push beyond nature toward apocalypse of unbridled imaginative desire. Yet from the point of view of that imaginative desire, the same language that saves it from itself must also appear perpetually as the demiurgic force that traps and restrains the imagination in this material world. Such is the ambivalence of Wordsworth's stance that language is at once the means by which a poet is a poet at all, and the demiurge preventing the attainment of the desire that drives the poet to poetry to begin with.

This ambivalence is perhaps clearest in the famous poem "The Solitary Reaper," published in 1807. At the heart of the poem is the connection between the poet's ignorance of the song's meaning ("Will no one tell me what she sings?"[line 17]) and his sense that it could go on forever ("Whate'r the theme, the Maiden sang / As if her song could have no ending" [lines 25–26]), which implies a corresponding relationship between poems' dependence on words and the fact that they must end. From here, it is only a small step to the recognition that the inevitable ending of poetic song is a kind of falling back of the pure, untrammeled imagination into the natural world ruled by its principle of closure, death. But the "pure" poem is incomprehensible and hence, by definition, not a poem at all.

For the Wordsworth of "The Solitary Reaper," vision, fantasies of fulfillment, or belief in transcendence, religious or otherwise, become poetry only when desire is thwarted and surrendered to language and comprehensibility. Furthermore, language is most demiurgic in tying the imagination, through the demands of comprehensibility, to closure and, ultimately, to death.

Despite the importance of this ambivalence for Wordsworth's poetic practice in *The Prelude* and elsewhere, it is confronted only indirectly in "The Solitary Reaper"—much less directly than by John Keats in his 1819 poem "Ode to a Nightingale," which echoes "The Solitary Reaper" in some of its most crucial lines:

> The voice I hear this passing night was heard
> In ancient days by emperor and clown:
> Perhaps the self-same song that found a path
> Through the sad heart of Ruth, when, sick for home,
> She stood in tears among the alien corn;
> The same that oft-times hath
> Charmed magic casements, opening on the foam
> Of perilous seas in fairy lands forlorn.
>
> (lines 63–70)

The corresponding lines from the Wordsworth poem are:

> No Nightingale did ever chaunt
> More welcome notes to weary bands
> Of travellers in some shady haunt,
> Among Arabian sands:
> A voice so thrilling n'er was heard
> In spring-time from the Cuckoo-bird,
> Breaking the silence of the seas
> Among the farthest Hebrides.
>
> (lines 9–16)

Desiring to be one with the pure, incorporeal song of the invisible nightingale, Keats comes to realize that to do so would be to lose precisely that which, however burdened, allows him to hear, to feel, and to savor the nightingale's song. At this point, he is vouchsafed a kind of imaginative vision of the timelessness of the song, which shades off into a kind of fantasy vision of "fairy lands forlorn" and out of which he is inevitably called back to his "sole self." Keats's acceptance of his natural self and of the fleeting nature of imaginative vision is leading him toward the greatest of Romantic sublimation poems, "To Autumn." In "The Solitary Reaper," Wordsworth is clearly suggesting that poetry *is* sublimation, the sublimation of imaginative desire into the forms of the universe of death. Unlike Keats, however, Wordsworth tends to displace his confrontations with death, with imagination, and with the necessity of sublimation into memory or dream, or onto Lucy, or the Boy of Winander, or the Arab, because he must delay as long as possible the revelation that it is poetry as a personal attribute of William Wordsworth that is most valuable to him—a revelation ruinous to the sublimation of poetry into the general run of humanity upon which Wordsworth's account of its redemptive powers is based. This result is most apparent at the end of *The Prelude,* in which Wordsworth, the "Prophet of Nature" to the antlike masses below, resembles nothing so much as a Moses who cannot bring himself to carry the tables down from the mountain, lest he lose his special closeness to God.

In this context, we can see that when the quality of being poetic is shifted inward, away from the objective, unitary identity imposed by the standard of poetic diction, the poetic becomes as problematic and multiform as inwardness itself, re-creating in the humanist tradition the same insatiable need to interpret, to get the "real word," that was created in the religious tradition by the complex immanence—at once everywhere present, absent, and invisible—of God.

Most of all, Keats seems to be willing to face, as Wordsworth is not, that a poetic of sublimation is finally a poetic of acceptance and, most especially, of the acceptance of death. At best, it implies that given the same external conditions, one can still respond to them internally either for the better or for worse. In order to become a prophet and to satisfy the demands of his poetic selfhood, Wordsworth must step outside the mode of sublimation and destroy the delicate balance of imagination and nature upon which his poetry rests. He must contradict himself and therefore fail by his own definition in revealing for all to see the irreconcilable conflict at the heart of his poetic practice. For all these reasons, as we shall see, Shelley rejects the sublimating mode of Wordsworth and Keats.

It also remains to be pointed out that sublimation demands repression—the repression of the fear that the best that our inner resources can do with the conditions of existence is simply not enough. Wordsworth must maintain the sublimating mode of the bulk of his verse, despite the protests of a poetic ego always trying to capture the poetic as an aspect of its own distinct identity, because sublimation postpones the confrontation with the fact that no change in the internal quality of experience truly compensates us for the fact of death and that to accept the external status quo is ultimately to accede to one's own death.

In order to avoid this confrontation, it is necessary for sublimation to incorporate into itself as much as possible, thus limiting the number of vantage points from which idealization is confronted by the absolute nature of death. One unintended (at least for the Romantics) consequence of this tendency is to limit or even eliminate the external vantage points from which effective critiques of society can be carried out.

Wordsworth's great poem of sublimation and, along with "To Autumn," perhaps the greatest such poem in the post-Enlightenment tradition is, of course, "Ode: Intimations of Immortality from Recollections of Childhood." The large Pindaric in English (especially if we place "Lycidas" more in the tradition of the Italian canzone), the "Intimations" ode achieves the stature for that form in English that Gray had sought in "The Progress of Poesy" and "The Bard." The poem's composition was divided, with stanzas 1 to 4 dating from 1802 or 1803, before the completion of The Prelude and the composition of "The Solitary Reaper," and the remaining seven stanzas from 1806. Those initial, early stanzas read as follows:

1

There was a time when meadow, grove, and stream,
The earth, and every common sight,
To me did seem
Apparelled in celestial light,
The glory and the freshness of a dream.
It is not now as it hath been of yore;—
Turn whereso'er I may,
By night or day,
The things which I have seen I now can see no more.

2

The Rainbow comes and goes,
And lovely is the Rose,
The Moon doth with delight
Look round her when the heavens are bare,
Waters on a starry night
Are beautiful and fair;
The sunshine is a glorious birth;
But yet I know, where'er I go,
That there hath past away a glory from the earth.

3

Now, while the birds thus sing a joyous song,
And while the young lambs bound
As to the tabor's sound,
To me alone there came a thought of grief:
A timely utterance gave that thought relief,
And I again am strong:
The cataracts blow their trumpets from the steep;
No more shall grief of mine the season wrong;
I hear the Echoes through the mountains throng,
The Winds come to me from the fields of sleep,
And all the earth is gay;
Land and sea
Give themselves up to jollity,
And with the heart of May
Doth every beast keep holiday;—
Thou Child of Joy,
Shout round me, let me hear thy shouts, thou happy
  Shepherd-boy!

4

Ye blessed Creatures, I have heard the call
Ye to each other make; I see
The heavens laugh with you in your jubilee;
My heart is at your festival,
My head hath its coronal,
The fulness of your blisss, I feel—I feel it all.
Oh evil day! if I were sullen
While earth herself is adorning,
This sweet May-morning,
And the children are culling
On every side,
In a thousand valleys far and wide,
Fresh flowers; while the sun shines warm,
And the Babe leaps up on his Mother's arm;—
I hear, I hear, with joy I hear!
—But there's a Tree, of many, one,
A single Field which I have looked upon,
Both of them speak of something that is gone:
The pansy at my feet
Doth the same tale repeat:
Whither is fled the visionary gleam?
Where is it now, the glory and the dream?

(lines 1–57)

The first stanza confesses to an unexpected sense of loss, and it is important to note that, unlike the conventional elegy, it refers to nothing in the situation that implies a preceding narrative or history to account for this sense of loss—it simply is. Beginning with loss as something always mysteriously already there, Wordsworth moves away from traditional ways of accounting for such feelings.

In the Christian tradition, for example, the notion of original sin names the mysterious reverberation of the Fall down through history by which we feel guilt and responsibility—a sense of loss—and are tempted to despair even in advance of personal sin. Wordsworth's reordering contrives to suggest that we do not feel this obscure loss because there was a Fall but that we have a myth of the Fall in order to account for the feelings of loss. Nor is it from the anticipation of the catastrophe of death that this melancholy springs, as in Gray's rather more stoic and literal account; rather, it is from some as yet unrealized (or uncreated) catastrophe in the past that we must trace our emergence—a catastrophe corresponding to the loss of the narcissistic ego-ideal that is the origin of poetic identity. For Gray, that loss is a literal event reconfirmed in the reality of death. For Wordsworth, it is a myth, a creation of desire to account for its own emptiness.

In any case, what has been lost, Wordsworth tells us, is not anything specific but a way of perceiving that apparels in "celestial light" and lends "The glory and the freshness of a dream." But Wordsworth hastens to prove by the richly appreciative descriptions of the next two stanzas that this is not the situation of Coleridge in "Dejection: An Ode" (1802), who sees but cannot feel the beauty around. Wordsworth is careful to let us know "My heart is at your festival, / My head hath its coronal, / The fulness of your bliss, I feel—I feel it all." Neither sin, nor death, nor alienation from nature can account for his sense of loss.

In the third stanza, Wordsworth returns to the pastoral mode and explores its value as a means of coping with his melancholy. Is this, he seems to ask, the familiar pastoral situation? If I give my dark thoughts "timely utterance," will I be able to return to the natural joy all around? The answer is only a qualified yes, and the melancholy is momentarily lifted only to reassert itself in the midst of joy in the fourth stanza. Because the pastoral provides only temporary relief, it must endlessly recapture the same ground as the gap between the burdened adulthood of the poet and the "happy Shepherd-boy" narrows, widens, and narrows again. As Wordsworth presents it, loss is not finally a function of our relationship with history or God or nature; it seems to refer, if anything, to our very constitution, as if loss was not only prior to our experience of everything external but always already there in consciousness itself.

Wordsworth concludes the first movement of his poem by reasserting his sense of loss: "Whither is fled the visionary gleam? / Where is it now, the glory and the dream?" Words like "visionary," "glory," and "dream" tend to identify what is lost with transcendence or with the dream of a transcendent fulfillment of desire and point us in the direction of a new myth in which life itself is seen as a sublimation of such aspiration, burdened by its insistent struggle to become literal "once again." In other words, life is not the anticipation of a final apocalypse, personal or collective, but the aftermath of an apocalypse or what Bloom calls "catastrophe creation."

The implications of the problematic of loss as it is understood by the end of stanza 4 are rather substantial. Clearly, there is the danger that such a sense of loss, as in Bloom, will be transformed into a permanent sense of belatedness and a powerful, perhaps overpowering, retrospective bent, seriously crippling any sense of futurity. It remains to be seen whether such a defense against the future catastrophe of death is not finally too expensive, or if Wordsworth can generate a myth capable of restoring the middle ground, absent in Gray, between the lost pastoral of youth and the elegiac poetry of old age.

To this end, in the next four stanzas, Wordsworth goes all the way back to Plato's *Phaedro,* which he begins by echoing ("Our birth is but a sleep and a forgetting"), in order to generate the mythical heart of his poem:

5

Our birth is but a sleep and a forgetting:
The soul that rises with us, our life's Star,
Hath had elsewhere its setting,
And cometh from afar:
Not in entire forgetfullness,

And not in utter nakedness,
But trailing clouds of glory do we come
From God, who is our home:
Heaven lies about us in our infancy!
Shades of the prison-house begin to close
Upon the growing Boy
But He beholds the light, and whence it flows,
He sees it in his joy;
The Youth, who daily farther from the east
Must travel, still is Nature's Priest,
And by the vision splendid
Is on his way attended;
At length the Man perceives it die away,
And fade into the light of common day.

6

Earth fills her lap with pleasures of her own;
Yearnings she hath in her own natural kind,
And, even with something of a Mother's mind,
And no unworthy aim,
The homely nurse doth all she can
To make her Foster-child, her Inmate Man,
Forget the glories he hath known,
And that imperial palace whence he came.

7

Behold the Child among his new-born blisses,
A six years' Darling of a pigmy size!
See, where 'mid work of his own hand he lies,
Fretted by sallies of his mother's kisses,
With light upon him from his father's eyes!
See, at his feet, some little plan or chart,
Some fragment from his dream of human life,
Shaped by himself with newly-learned art;
A wedding or a festival,
A mourning or a funeral;
And this hath now his heart,
And unto this he frames his song:
Then will he fit his tongue
To dialogues of business, love, or strife;
But it will not be long

Ere this be thrown aside,
And with new joy and pride
The little Actor cons another part;
Filling from time to time his "humorous stage"
With all the Persons, down to palsied Age,
That Life brings with her in her equipage;
As if his whole vocation
Were endless imitation.

8

Thou, whose exterior semblance doth belie
Thy Soul's immensity;
Thou best Philosopher, who yet dost keep
Thy heritage, thou Eye among the blind
That, deaf and silent, read'st the eternal deep,
Haunted forever by the eternal mind,—
Mighty Prophet! Seer blest!
On whom those truths do rest,
Which we are toiling all our lives to find,
In darkness lost, the darkness of the grave;
Thou, over whom thy Immortality
Broods like the Day, a Master o'er a Slave,
A presence which is not to be put by;
To whom the grave
Is but a lonely bed without the sense or sight
Of day or the warm light,
A place of thought where we in waiting lie;
Thou little Child, yet glorious in the might
Of heaven-born freedom on thy being's height,
Why with such earnest pains dost thou provoke
The years to bring the inevitable yoke,
Thus blindly with thy blessedness at strife?
Full soon thy Soul shall have her earthly freight,
And custom lie upon thee with a weight,
Heavy as frost, and deep almost as life!

(lines 58–132)

The effectiveness of Wordsworth's myth resides less in
the fact that it clearly refutes Gray's pessimism or resolves
the questions of the ode's earlier stanzas than in rendering
the relationship among death, anxiety, melancholy, desire,

and poetry once again problematical enough to sustain a body of verse—a new poetic.

For instance, the new importance, very un-Platonic, granted to childhood might be seen as another eighteenth-century-style privileging of earliness over lateness. But the focus on the child's lack of awareness concerning his own condition shifts the focus of greatness to the adult, whose burdened but more comprehensive perception allows him to perceive it for what it is. Also, since the myth presents itself rather self-consciously as something derived to meet the need defined in the first four stanzas, it tends to dramatize Wordsworth's point that "greatness" or "prophecy" is something attributed out of need rather than "residing in"— a myth of compensation in which even the ability to regret what has been lost springs from the humanizing effects of loss.

Stanza 6 refines Wordsworth's earlier comments on the role of nature in a way that suggests at once a Gnostic conviction that the earth is not our proper home and a very un-Gnostic determination to hold to sublimation by refusing to accuse the created world, which does the best it can for us. But the poem itself must represent the (at least) partial failure of sublimation, of the complacent, accepting interpretation of life, which is necessary for adult consciousness to be born. This failure is already built in as the loss that gives the lie to all settled arrangements with life. Since the acceptance of this world turns back from the apocalyptic alternative, there remains only to reinterpret and then interpret again or, from the writer's view, write and write again.

Stanza 7 then takes up a theme central to English literature, at least from Shakespeare, the theme of inauthenticity. In Shakespeare, the emphasis tends to fall on the sense of inauthenticity caused by the gap between public roles and private feelings. In Wordsworth's poem, this gap and the

230 · Literary Revisionism

sense of inauthenticity associated with it preexists any specific social arrangement and is internal to life itself. If this is so, it implies rather forcefully that we attribute greatness in such extravagant measure, wounding ourselves in the process, as an expression of a sense of inauthenticity that is a function not of historical inferiority but inner constitution. We erect the greats of the past as images of an integrated authenticity that we desire but cannot have. There is nothing, Wordsworth implies, to prevent any of us from serving the future in precisely this way, despite our misgivings and sense of inadequacy.

But Wordsworth's myth is only static enough to gain the upper hand on a disadvantageous literary history; where something is to be gained, it is historical in assuming both change and growth. It is only by becoming adult and questioning his sense of loss that the child finally knows himself. The unself-conscious, daemonic child gives way to the humane adult and the poetry of spontaneous power to a poetry of gain-through-loss. It is difficult to avoid concluding from all this that, from Wordsworth's point of view, old poetry—unconverted, uninterpreted—would not be poetry at all in the humane adulthood of the tradition.

The pitfalls of such a view should be obvious. Clearly, Wordsworth's myth can be seen as only a delaying action since the movement from childhood to adulthood implies an eventual dotage and death. On the other hand, by internalizing the life of poetry into the pattern of the individual life rather than of social development, Wordsworth does imply an alternative model of poetry as the endless repetition of that pattern for every poet. The two alternatives are of enormous importance: the first suggests that poetry is a direct reflection of the nature and state of society; the second implies that poetry only indirectly reflects society through its more primary function as an expression of the realities of individual experience and, frequently, of the conflicts arising from the distance between the quality of that experience and the pretensions of society. Wordsworth's own ambivalence over whether poetry reflects or corrects reality is everywhere echoed in our post-Romantic understanding. Although it is important to add that a progressive view of society, with everything that implies about the increasingly peripheral status of poetry, almost decreed that the alienated, critical view would seem increasingly sufficient in and of itself.

Except for implying in his own success the capacity of poetry to renew itself in unexpected ways, Wordsworth's sense of the futurity of poetry, while having the advantage of being more vague than Gray's, is nevertheless just that—vague; it reconstitutes a present for poetry without guaranteeing its future.

And this brings us to the subject of death, rather conspicuous in its relative absence from Wordsworth's poem given its omnipresence in Gray's. I have already alluded to the close connection in Wordsworth between the necessary sublimation of visionary or imaginative desire and the sublimation of death. Clearly, by making life a gradual discovery of the vision always there, he also makes of birth a kind of death and converts death from an abrupt end of life to a process indistinguishable from life itself, almost as if only the whole of life was sufficient to render death figurative.

The Gray/Wordsworth relationship signals an important shift in the nature of death as a poetic theme. In Milton, death is treated at once as a challenge to faith and to the value of poetry. The very uselessness of poetry becomes a means of saving faith as it becomes first a metaphor for the apparent futility of life in the face of death and then a means of replying to that futility. But in Gray and Wordsworth, the themes of death and the fate of poetry are inextricably linked. The virtual disappearance of death from the picture in the "Intimations" ode suggests that once a sufficiently rich poetic present has been created, the death of poetry and the death of the poet alike recede into the distance. However, it is also apparent that a sense of futurity is also sacrificed in order to keep the end that lurks there at bay.

In this connection, it is interesting to note the controversy over lines 121–24 in stanza 8, the only lines in the poem implying that Wordsworth's is actually a reincarnative myth. According to most accounts, these lines, included in the editions of 1807 and 1815, were left out in 1820 because of Coleridge's complaints about their heretical nature (*Biographia* XXII). But I find it hard to believe that Wordsworth would have done so unless he had in the meantime recognized some sense in which they were at odds with his larger purpose in the poem. In fact, the removal of the lines is in keeping with the poem's attempt to reconceive "immortality" retrospectively, rather than in anticipation, as a means of delaying indefinitely the imagination's confrontation with its future end.

The whole project of indefinitely delaying the imagination's confrontation with the fact of death (by sublimating it into life as a series of lesser losses) is threatened by the desire for immortality, for an absolute that must shatter sublimation. Thus it is only by renouncing or at least sublimating this desire that we can be any of the things we celebrate in our own humanity. The traditional poetic version of the wish to be immortal is the myth of fame, which the poet and poetry must outgrow in order to come into their maturity. Fame is a fiction of youth, the opiate of the young, and the true challenge, Wordsworth seems to be saying, is to reconceive poetry apart from the desire for and the traditional assurances of fame, in terms of an entirely new compensatory myth.

The eighth stanza concludes by recognizing that the burdens of adult existence are "almost" as deep as life itself. Out of this narrow difference, marked by that sense of loss without occasion, our redeeming and humane maturity arises:

9

O joy! that in our embers
Is something that doth live,
That nature yet remembers
What was so fugitive!
The thought of our past years in me doth breed
Perpetual benediction: not indeed
For that which is most worthy to be blest;
Delight and liberty, the simple creed
Of Childhood, whether busy or at rest,
With new-fledged hope still fluttering in his breast:—
Not for these I raise
The song of thanks and praise;
But for those obstinate questionings
Of sense and outward things,
Fallings from us, vanishings;
Blank misgivings of a Creature
Moving about in worlds not realised,
High instinct before which our mortal Nature
Did tremble like a guilty Thing surprised:
But for those first affections,
Those shadowy recollections,
Which, be they what they may,
Are yet the fountain-light of all our day,
Are yet a master-light of all our seeing;
Uphold us, cherish, and have power to make
Our noisy years seem moments in the being
Of the eternal Silence: truths that wake,
To perish never:
Which neither listlessness, nor mad endeavour,
Nor Man nor Boy,
Nor all that is at enmity with joy,
Can utterly abolish or destroy!
Hence in a season of calm weather
Though inland far we be,
Our souls have sight of that immortal sea
Which brought us hither,
Can in a moment travel thither,
And see the Children sport upon the shore,
And hear the mighty waters rolling evermore.

(lines 133–71)

In light of the implications of his poetic myth, stanza 9, the poem's central affirmation, is something of a retrenchment; it could well be the credo of literary humanism as it is understood by M. H. Abrams or W. J. Bate, a doctrine of the saving remnant, viewing poems as fragments of something not of this time and place, all but gone. The stanza makes clear, I think, the potential connection between the myth of secularization and a nostalgic view of art as the revival of the lost essence, reluctant to anticipate what time might bring in exchange for what has been lost.

Yet the stanza is not a complete retrenchment; it does free a poetic present lost in Gray, and, insofar as it maintains a certain ambiguity over whether we are talking about an actual remnant to be saved or only about the absences leading us to imagine their source, it sustains the idea of a new adult poetry, grounded in gain-through-loss. What is gained is first and foremost a richer experience of self, based on a privileged relationship between that past, which, by definition, cannot survive in the present except indirectly, and an essential, better, deeper self. This relationship is sustained by reinforcing rather than breaking down differences between past and present, self and other; it creates an extraordinary number of imperatives necessary to its survival.

The tenth stanza returns us, presumably as proof of the efficacy of the preceding affirmation, to the pastoral mode of stanzas 3 and 4 and to the appreciation of the natural world:

10

> Then sing, ye Birds, sing, sing a joyous song!
> And let the young Lambs bound
> As to the tabor's sound!
> We in thought will join your throng,
> Ye that pipe and ye that play,
> Ye that through your hearts today
> Feel the gladness of the May!
> What though the radiance which was once so bright

Be now forever taken from my sight,
Though nothing can bring back the hour
Of splendour in the grass, of glory in the flower;
We will grieve not, rather find
Strength in what remains behind;
In the primal sympathy
Which having been must ever be;
In the soothing thoughts that spring
Out of human suffering;
In the faith that looks through death,
In years that bring the philosophic mind.

II

And O, ye Fountains, Meadows, Hills, and Groves,
Forebode not any severing of our loves!
Yet in my heart of hearts I feel your might;
I only have relinquished one delight
To live beneath your more habitual sway.
I love the Brooks which down their channels fret,
Even more than when I tripped lightly as they;
The innocent brightness of a new-born Day
Is lovely yet;
The Clouds that gather round the setting sun
Do take a sober colouring from an eye
That hath kept watch o'er man's mortality;
Another race hath been, and other palms are won.
Thanks to the human heart by which we live,
Thanks to its tenderness, its joys, and fears,
To me the meanest flower that blows can give
Thoughts that do often lie too deep for tears.

(lines 172–207)

This return to the pastoral mood should come as no surprise since the most the poem of sublimation can insist on is
that we now experience the same world differently. In this
case, we experience this traditional poetic mode in terms of a
new inwardness. Nor, we are assured, has Wordsworth's
attachment to nature been diminished. Indeed, it has been
enriched so that "To me the meanest flower that blows can
give / Thoughts that do often lie too deep for tears."

This bit of hyperbole is perhaps as expressive of the problematical nature of Wordsworth's stance as any two lines in the poem. Far from turning on the enhancement of nature, as it seeks to imply, it turns on the dramatic reduction of nature, revealing that the self is at the heart of all that we most admire out there. Wordsworth's ultimate affirmation hinges on the absolute distinction between the external reduced to mere occasion ("the meanest flower that blows") and the limitless grandeur of the inviolate self ("thoughts that do often lie too deep for tears"), which is absolutely necessary to maintain the fiction of an essential self in a secular context.

At the risk of heresy, we must ask if, taken literally, there is not something rather absurd in so lionizing the capacity to exceed extravagantly the actual occasion. To value this capacity more highly than seeing clearly, estimating fairly, or any other social virtue is to ensure the tangentiality of poetry as the price of its sanctity. Surely the interpretive complement of such a poetic would hinge on the disparity between the most reductive view of the literality of poetic language or the adequacy of unaided understanding and an exaggerated view of interpretation's role in making literary experience possible. Again, as in Wordsworth's poem, the function is to preserve the gap between literary and other activities and the fiction of essentiality it sustains.

As I have tried to suggest, one of the most important features of the "Intimations" ode is its apparent recognition that much of the pessimism felt by Gray and his contemporaries was the result of an unfortunate combination of a continuing dependence on the notion of poetic fame with the absence of any faith in the survival of the necessary preconditions, especially in the continuity of the tradition. "Intimations" aims at redefining the immortality that poetry offers away from the highly social notion of fame toward the ultimately rather solipsistic notion of intensified perception in the present. Among the distinctions between these two views is, to my mind, the highly significant one between a view requiring a carefully cultivated investment in the future and its continuity with past and present and one that may positively require a corresponding discontinuity as evidence of its power.

Interestingly, Wordsworth's real retrenchment comes seven years later, with the 1814 publication of *The Excursion*. "Essay on Epitaphs," a lengthy note attached to Book VI, "The Churchyard Among the Mountains," invites comparison with Gray's "Elegy" and, through this common referend, with "Intimations."

The desire to live in the memory of one's fellows signified by the epitaph, Wordsworth begins, could not exist "without the consciousness of a principle of immortality in the human soul" (728). If we look back to childhood, he goes on, we can see that there is a sense of the self's immortality from the very beginning, which cannot be dismissed merely as the result of the child's ignorance of death (729). Our ability to love, to live in a community, in short, all of what we consider the human virtues, depend upon a faith in immortality that counterbalances the impression of death. All commemoration gives voice to this faith and could not exist without it (729).

So powerful is the bond between these contraries that one passes "insensibly" into the other:

> As, in sailing upon the orb of this planet, a voyage towards the regions where the sun sets, conducts gradually to the quarter where we have been accustomed to behold it come forth at rising; and, in like manner, a voyage towards the east, the birthplace in our imagination of the morning, leads finally to the quarter where the sun is last seen when departing from our eyes; so the contemplative Soul, travelling in the direction of mortality, advances to the country of ever lasting life; and, in like manner, may she continue to explore those cheerful tracts, till

she is brought back, for her advantage and benefit, to the land of
transitory things—of sorrow and of tears.

(729-30)

As a description of the dynamics of the "contemplative
Soul," this describes a kind of enclosed, steady-state system in which too extreme a movement in one direction or
the other automatically triggers a saving reaction. Wordsworth remains intentionally vague about whether this reincarnative scheme merely describes the dynamics of our
thinking on mortality or applies literally to the fate of the
soul. What is clear is that in either case to privilege the
conviction of immortality as a human trait, perhaps *the*
human trait, is also to magnify the terror of death. And it
should be pointed out that nowhere does Wordsworth allow himself to consider the distinction between a desire to
believe in immortality and an actual conviction of its existence. In fact, Wordsworth's emphasis on the near-univer-
sality of commemoration among those peoples with writing seems almost to strive to establish that the soul is
immortal by consensus.

If it does not necessarily attest to a belief in immortality,
the epitaph does at least assume a continuity of sorts. Attest-
ing to the human virtues of the deceased and placed in close
proximity to the physical remains, it establishes the connection between body and soul, dead and living, past and present. In order to achieve this, it is also necessary that the
epitaph have the further virtue of seeking a congruence between the individual being praised and the universal feelings
and concerns of people (731).

Wordsworth warns against any attempt to weigh virtues
and vices as alien to the spirit of reconciliation proper to the
epitaph's occasion (731-32), nor is it necessary, in the case of
famous men, to elaborate achievements that live in public
memory and are perpetuated in their works (733). Here he

tips his hand by quoting Milton ("On Shakespeare") on Shake-speare's proper monument:

> What needs my Shakespeare for his honoured bones
> The labor of an age in piled stones,
> Or that his hallowed relics should be hid
> Under a star-ypointing pyramid?
> Dear Son of Memory, great Heir of Fame,
> What need'st thou such weak witness of thy name?
> Thou in our wonder and astonishment
> Hast built thyself a livelong monument,
> And so sepulchred, in such pomp dost lie,
> That kings for such a tomb would wish to die.
>
> (733)

As the alert reader will have suspected for some time, the "Essay on Epitaphs," with its warnings against overpraise and its urgings to appeal to the experience of all people in all times as much as possible, is a kind of primer on how to praise for the ages, which begins from the recognition that fame has appeal only to those who can maintain some faith in a form of immortality. In turn, this means that to lose this faith is to find mockery in one's own fame. That such a loss of faith is a real possibility and that the test of belief in the real value of fame must be postponed as long as possible are reflected in the way that Wordsworth tropes on Gray's rather more literal humility in order to treat the common epitaph as a sublimated rhetoric of fame.

This allows Wordsworth, especially toward his essay's conclusion, to carry on with himself a disguised debate over exactly what he wants or should want from posterity. The center of this debate is a comparison between the two most common kinds of epitaph: the one in which the deceased is portrayed speaking directly from the grave and the one in which the survivors speak of the deceased. The first, to which poets seem particularly prone, creates the fiction of a continu-ing presence, of an immortality of voice, and hence insists on a literality in its survival. But this is an all-too-fragile fiction, and so Wordsworth recommends the second mode, in which the desire for immortality is sublimated into the memory of those who survive—life becomes a kind of commemoration, and an obligation to remember is imposed.

To this point, except for an implicit recognition that in a time of diminished faith in immortality the rhetoric of greatness must also be diminished to be credible, Wordsworth's position is not markedly different from that of his precursors. But in quoting Milton's lines on Shakespeare, Wordsworth displays his customary inability to be satisfied with sublimation. To begin with, it is ironic, indeed, that he should wonder what use Shakespeare would have for a pyramid when, in the preface to *The Excursion,* he has just finished comparing the completed edifice of his works to a gothic cathedral (in which, presumably, he would lie in state). The "livelong monument" of which Wordsworth speaks is obviously not simply Shakespeare's reputation but the works themselves.

In a very real sense, Wordsworth has sacrificed the more limited survival of the voice-speaking-from-the-grave mode of epitaph in order to apply the conceit to the body of his work. So familiar is this notion to us now, that we scarcely bother to realize that Wordsworth is calling back all those books that he has sent out into the world and conceiving them all as ideal epitaphs; he wants to take it with him.

Refusing the comforts of conventional praise/commemoration, Wordsworth refuses to separate himself from his poetry, and the man remains to haunt his work, demanding that it serve as the vehicle for a personal and imperfectly sublimated immortality. If we wish to read, we must remember.

In our tradition, the Romantics are distinctive as poets whose poetry is (or is treated as) inextricable from personality. If the circumstances of the lives of the second-generation poets had much to do with this, it was still Wordsworth who taught those who followed to seek the man in the poetry so assiduously. And as critics we should not forget that biographism dominated the critical reading of poetry for one hundred years after the Romantics. Nor can we ignore the personal struggle for the "possession" of poems that even now dominates relations between authors and critics.

For Wordsworth, the epitaph is an important metaphor because it emphasizes the way in which poetry may be seen as the perpetuation of personality through apparent universalization; yet to view poetry in so reductive a way is to re-create it, rather simply, as the wanting of what we cannot have. In this context, Bloom is the greatest, truest of modern Romantics, seeing poetry in precisely this way and, for his part, cleaving to that poetic history that denies poetry the future he would wish for it.

PERCY BYSSHE SHELLEY

Wordsworth's poetic possessiveness makes for a deeply ambivalent relationship with the canon, which depends for its authority in our secular tradition on a depersonalizing of the poetic voice so that it may speak *sub specie aeternitatis*. The depersonalizing effect of canonization brings with it a kind of immortality, which, unfortunately, requires if not always the actual death of the poet then of the living, changing poetic identity.

It is over the willingness to die, out of life as well as out of poetry, that Shelley fights his battle against the poetic of sublimation. Shelley's concern with the willingness to test the reality of death as a barrier to consciousness is linked to his recognition that what the Wordsworthian poet of sublimation wants above all else is not to die. When all is said and done, Shelley feels, compared with reforming society or cleansing perception, this is not much of an ambition.

Shelley's is a poetic insistent on change, and he hurls himself against death as the limit that forces poetry into sublimation. In this, he rather accedes to Wordsworth's sense that poetry as we know it is sublimation; so often in Shelley, going beyond death necessarily corresponds to falling silent. There can be no report from the grave because poetry ceases to exist when sublimation is removed. Shelley also seems to recognize with Wordsworth that for poetry, death and futurity are all but indistinguishable. For Shelley, there is a direct relationship between poetry's willingness to harrow death and the possibility of envisioning a future.

Central to this vision is the characteristic Shelleyan gesture of giving up the defensive selfhood of the individual in order to risk, not death per se but nothingness, the permanent silencing of poetry and the poet. In "Alastor," the poet has followed his earthly quest as far as possible, to the ends of the earth, where he gives up his life as the only gesture remaining. In "Mont Blanc," when the imagination has been temporarily thwarted by the distance between the poet and the overpowering literality of the mountain, he gives the spirit up to the winds, and it is "Driven like a homeless cloud from steep to steep / That vanishes among the viewless gales!" (lines 58–59). By this means, he makes the leap to the universe of power and death at the mountain's top, which no man can literally see. In "Ode to the West Wind," he pleads to be taken up, to surrender the insistent striving of imaginative selfhood in order to test, in a kind of imaginative harrowing, whether it has the capacity for self-renewal: "Scatter, as from an unextinguishable hearth / Ashes and sparks, my words among mankind! / Be through my lips to unawakened earth / The trumpet of a prophecy" (lines 66–69). And in "Adonais," his great elegy for Keats, Shelley concludes with his other most common gesture of de-sublimation and casts himself adrift, surrendering himself to an unknown destination.

In each case, Shelley undoes poetic sublimation's implicit acceptance of the present in order to go in search of some otherness, a future that may satisfy imaginative need. Although too skeptical to claim knowledge of what cannot be known, he is clearly driven by a kind of faith that the degree of imaginative desire must signify some actual possibility of existence—there must be, either elsewhere in the present or in the future, something more. This is very different from Wordsworth's sublimation of desire in "Intimations." There, imaginative desire is seen as loss, as always defeated, and it only remains to reconcile it with life's limitations.

The Wordsworth of *The Prelude* is clearly a revisionary poet with regard to Milton and the epic and with regard to his own life. Poised on the edge of what he hopes will be the fullness of his poetic power, he goes back to subsume into the present all of his previous identities. The fiction at the heart of *The Prelude* is "I have always been a poet, even before I wrote—I have always been as I am now." In achieving this fiction, however, Wordsworth generalizes the history of his own existence such that past and present combine to thwart any vision of a fundamentally different future. I have said that Wordsworth is the progenitor of a properly humanist poetry, and this characteristic is not noticeably different from the way the generalizing bent of interpretation and history as we practice them tend to defeat faith in future difference by attributing a kind of sameness to all present and previous difference. This is the trap Shelley seeks to evade.

Shelley's earliest extensive critique of Wordsworth's poetic is offered in the 1815 (published in 1816) poem "Alastor; or The Spirit of Solitude." The youthful poet who is the "hero" of "Alastor" is presented as a kind of Romantic paragon, a cross between Wordsworth's Boy of Winander, the privileged child of nature, and Byron's Childe Harold, the quester graced with every virtue, who has apparently seen everything, done everything, and learned everything this world has to offer. In his preface, Shelley gives this account of the poem's action:

> The magnificence and beauty of the external world sinks profoundly into the frame of his conceptions, and affords to their modifications a variety not to be exhausted. So long as it is possible for his desires to point towards objects thus infinite and unmeasured, he is joyous, and tranquil, and self-possessed. But the period arrives when these objects cease to suffice. His mind is at length suddenly awakened and thirsts for intercourse with an intelligence similar to itself. He images to himself the Being whom he loves. Conversant with speculations of the sublimest and most perfect natures, the vision in which he embodies his own imaginations unites all of wonderful, or wise, or beautiful, which the poet, the philosopher, or the lover could depicture. The intellectual faculties, the imagination, the functions of sense, have their respective requisitions on the sympathy of corresponding powers in other human beings. The Poet is represented as uniting these requisitions, and attaching them to a single image. He seeks in vain for a prototype of his conception. Blasted by his disappointment, he descends to an untimely grave.
>
> (14–15)

Thomas Weiskel is surely right when he remarks that. "Alastor" "exhibits one of the clearest narcissistic careers in the Romantic canon" (*RS*, 144), but the coalescence of diverse external objects of desire into a single visionary object is more than a function of the poet's sudden recognition of "their irreducible otherness, their residual externality" (*RS*, 145); it is also the result of a realization that the "infinite and unmeasured" variety of natural objects does not imply the corresponding infinity of the consciousness that perceives them. The poet's sudden discovery is of the negation of self implicit in everything in a world ruled by death. In short, the formation of this narcissistic, idealized self-image coincides with the recognition that he must die, no matter how perfect he is. This is the revelation, as Shelley later puts it, of "that Power which strikes the luminaries of the world with sudden darkness and extinction" (15).

As long as "his desires point towards objects thus infinite and unmeasured," conception is renewed and transformed by the variety of the external world—desire is duped by a constant stream of false satisfactions. The poet's vision of a woman, not only a poet like himself but an idealized, perfected version of himself—"Her voice was like the voice of his own soul" (line 153)—ruins all this. Or, rather, the narcissistic overtones of this ideal suggest that the dream represents not so much a change in as a logical extension of what has always been a narcissistic relation to the world, in which what is always sought in diverse experience is an image enabling the self to experience itself more intensely. The idealized vision of the woman is that perfect image in which the self is perfectly present to itself.

We have already seen in our discussion of Wordsworth how the dream or vision can serve to isolate and distinguish threatening possibilities from the poet's "normal" self. The failure of the dream in "Alastor" to isolate the disastrous narcissism of the young poet ultimately reflects on Shelley's own poetic project, despite the defensive precaution of inserting between himself and the poet the device of a somewhat Wordsworthian narrator. Consider this description of the poem's hero, offered by its narrator:

> By solemn vision, and bright silver dream,
> His infancy was nurtured. Every sight
> And sound from the vast earth and ambient air,
> Sent to his heart its choicest impulses.
> The fountains of divine philosophy
> Fled not his thirsting lips, and all of great,
> Or good, or lovely, which the sacred past
> In truth or fable consecrates, he felt
> And knew . . .
>
> (lines 67–75)

. . . Nature's most secret steps
He like her shadow has pursued . . .
            (lines 81–82)

. . . And the green earth lost in his heart its claims
To love and wonder . . .
                                (lines 97–98)

    His wandering step
Obedient to high thoughts, has visited
The awful ruins of the days of old . . .
                        (lines 107–9)

He lingered, poring on memorials
Of the world's youth, through the long burning day
Gazed on those speechless shapes, nor, when the moon
Filled the mysterious halls with floating shades
Suspended he that task, but ever gazed
And gazed, till meaning on his vacant mind
Flashed like strong inspiration, and he saw
The thrilling secrets of the birth of time.
                                (lines 121–28)

Given the easily recognizable selections of achievements, virtues, and so on, culled from idealized poetic alteregos of Wordsworth, Coleridge, and Byron, this could easily be an instance of Shelleyan irony, a sly parody of his elders' excesses—but it's not. Shelley needs the pathos of this gap between the young man's virtues and his fate to make his own poem work; he too has much invested in what he seeks to deplore, and this fact is at the heart of this poem's importance and complexity.

This impression is more than borne out by the truly extraordinary second paragraph of Shelley's preface to "Alastor":

The picture is not barren of instruction to actual men. The Poet's self-centred seclusion was avenged by the furies of an irresistible passion pursuing him to speedy ruin. But that Power which strikes the luminaries of the world with sudden darkness and extinction, by awakening them to too exquisite a perception of its influences, dooms to a slow and poisonous decay those

meaner spirits that dare to abjure its domination. Their destiny
is more abject and inglorious as their delinquency is more con-
temptible and pernicious. They who, deluded by no generous
error, instigated by no sacred thirst of doubtful knowledge,
duped by no illustrious superstition, loving nothing on this
earth, and cherishing no hopes beyond, yet keep aloof from
sympathies with their kind, rejoicing neither in human joy nor
mourning with human grief; these, and such as they, have their
apportioned curse. They languish, because none feel with them
their common nature. They are morally dead. They are neither
friends, nor lovers, nor fathers, nor citizens of the world, nor
benefactors of their country. Among those who attempt to exist
without human sympathy, the pure and tender-hearted perish
through the intensity and passion of their search after its communities, when the vacancy of their spirit suddenly makes itself
felt. All else, selfish, blind, and torpid, are those unforeseeing
multitudes who constitute, together with their own, the lasting
misery and loneliness of the world. Those who love not their
fellow-beings live unfruitful lives, and prepare for their old age a
miserable grave.

(15)

And here is Thomas Weiskel's splendid comment:

This is astonishing, outrageous prose. I should be the last to
deny its rhetorical power or the force of its bitterness, but ethically it makes no sense and it shows a deeply fractured mind
defending itself. That "Power" intends death, either way. Yet
Shelley refuses to question, examine, or sublimate the "irresistible passion," though he insists that its objects are uniformly
treacherous. The split results in the oxymoronic phrases—"deluded by no generous error, instigated by no sacred thirst of
doubtful knowledge, duped by no illustrious superstition"—that
surely raise a question of bad faith. Attempting to exist without
human sympathy: this means trying to exist *given that* there is no
human sympathy, but it also suggests deceptively that the "pure
and tender-hearted" have made the attempt to accept this condition in good faith. The Poet makes no such attempt. Though it
leads to disaster, his desire remains generous, sacred, and illustrious. Shelley's equivocation—the Poet is "led / By love, or
dream, or god, or mightier Death" (ll. 427–28)—exhibits a narcissism compounded by denial. I need hardly add that the poem

was the beginning and not the end of Shelley's maturity and that its schizoid structure is sublimated into genuine irony in the later poems. Yet the fear of identity persists throughout the Shelleyan oeuvre, and undoubtedly is to be referred as much to his struggle with Wordsworth as to his own fascinating psychological constitution.

(*RS*, 148)

To Weiskel's remarks it is important to add that the passage just quoted from the preface, quoted as Weiskel quotes it, actually ends with these lines from Book I of *The Excursion:* "The good die first, / And those whose hearts are dry as summer dust, / Burn to the socket" (lines 500–502). It requires no great leap to see in this Shelley turning Wordsworth's own words against him, especially if we consider the short poems to Coleridge and Wordsworth, accusing them of selling out their poetic missions, that were published with "Alastor" in the 1816 volume. But the real irony here is that the accusation threatens to rebound on Shelley himself if he cannot succeed in distinguishing himself from Wordsworth, his most threatening precursor, as "Alastor" is intended to do.

In her note affixed to the 1839 edition, Mary Shelley says of her husband:

> In the Spring of 1815 an eminent physician pronounced that he was dying rapidly of a consumption; abscesses were formed on his lungs and he suffered acute spasms. Suddenly a complete change took place; and, though through life he was a martyr to pain and debility, every symptom of pulmonary disease vanished. His nerves, which nature had formed sensitive to an unexampled degree, were rendered still more susceptible by the state of his health.

(30)

After his close call, Shelley was surely thinking of the contrast between his own ill health at the threshold of his poetic maturity and Wordsworth's robust good health in his poetic apostasy. But he also realized, judging from what we will see of the poem, that if he failed to distinguish himself poetically, the pathos of his early death would alone be the final ground of his "superiority"; he would himself be another Wordsworthian paragon, like the Boy of Winander. Ultimately, Shelley's struggle with Wordsworth is over how poetry should be read and used by readers. Judging by the myth that Victorians and subsequent readers built around the early deaths of the second-generation Romantics, the greater purity and intensity of commitment to poetry attributed to them remains a sign that it is Wordsworth who emerges as the poet who most determines how poetry is to be read by serious readers. All of this helps to explain why the convergence of the Wordsworth/Coleridge ideal of poetic desire sublimated into nature with the Byron/Shelley reluctance to accept this world as a fit home for the imagination is such a potential threat to Shelley's poetic independence. Despite what might be considered Shelley's failure, "Alastor" remains one of the subtlest and most penetrating critiques of Wordsworth's poetic sublimation, aimed particularly at the "Intimations" ode.

The narrator opens the poem with a Wordsworthian testimony to his special relationship with nature and invokes her as his muse:

> Mother of this unfathomable world!
> Favour my solemn song, for I have loved
> Thee ever, and thee only; I have watched
> Thy shadow, and the darkness of thy steps,
> And my heart ever gazes on the depth
> Of thy deep mysteries. I have made my bed
> In charnels and on coffins, where black death
> Keeps record of the trophies won from thee,
> Hoping to still these obstinate questionings
> Of thee and thine, by forcing some lone ghost
> Thy messenger, to render up the tale
> Of what we are. In lone and silent hours,

When night makes a weird sound of its own stillness,
Like an inspired and desperate alchymist
Staking his very life on some dark hope,
Have I mixed awful talk and asking looks
With my most innocent love, until strange tears
Uniting with those breathless kisses, made
Such magic as compels the charmed night
To render up thy charge: . . . and, though ne'er yet
Thou hast unveiled thy inmost sanctuary,
Enough from incommunicable dream,
And twilight phantasms, and deep noon-day thought,
Has shone within me, that serenely now
And moveless, as a long-forgotten lyre
Suspended in the solitary dome
Of some mysterious and deserted fane,
I wait thy breath, Great Parent, that my strain
May modulate with murmurs of the air,
And motions of the forests and the sea,
And voice of living beings, and woven hymns
Of night and day, and the deep heart of man.

(lines 17–49)

For the Wordsworthian poet, or any poet committed to nature as sublimation, there is really only one mystery—the mystery of death—here intensified until the fascination with death becomes inseparable from the love of nature. From within nature, death necessarily undergoes mystification as the absolute limit of imagination, as that beyond which it cannot go. It is this combination of the fear of death with the imaginative desire to test and move beyond this limit, to sublimate and to transcend, that characterizes a Wordsworthian poetic in which imaginative desire is ultimately stronger than its ties to the natural and social worlds. Such an erotic melancholy marks a devotion not to nature for itself but as protective coloring for an imagination fully capable of destroying itself by its demands. Yet if this is true for Wordsworth, how much more true for the second generation, in which the rejection of Wordsworthian sublimation, especially by Shelley, leaves him so openly exposed to the excesses of the imagination.

At the end of his invocation, the narrator is isolated, rapt, waiting in the deserted dome, anticipating an inspiration, which, given the action of the poem, one cannot help but feel will never come because it is not so very different in what it desires from the vision of the young poet.

The story proper begins with a clear Wordsworthian echo:

> There was a Poet whose untimely tomb
> No human hands with pious reverence reared,
> But the charmed eddies of the autumnal winds
> Built o'er his mouldering bones a pyramid
> Of mouldering leaves in the waste wilderness
>   (lines 50–54)

Wordsworth's 1800 lyric "There Was a Boy" was expanded to become the well-known Boy of Winander passage of Book V of *The Prelude* (lines 364ff.). The boy is one of Wordsworth's paragons, representing a spontaneous and privileged relationship to nature much like the one he claims for his youthful self. But the boy's death at an early age raises the possibility, carefully hedged about and displaced by Wordsworth, that nature not only betrays the heart that loves her; she also kills it. You cannot be young enough, natural enough, virtuous enough, brilliant enough, or even poetic enough to be excused—being a paragon is of no value except as a part of a narcissistic desire to evade mortality through a self-enclosed perfection. We have already spoken of how such narcissistic self-idealizations, however parodistic they may seem, are for all poets, Shelley included, perilously close to real desire. The passage gives us a clue to Shelley's difficulty in distinguishing himself from Wordsworth: Wordsworth, for himself and those who follow, succeeds in redefining what the poet wants from poetry. With-

out a substantially different vision of poetic success, Shelley
is all too easily drawn back into the problematic of which
the other poet is the master. And the argument that Wordsworth is, by his own standards, finally a sellout is not an
effective defense against such imaginative hegemony.

The solitude of the death described here and the grave
tended only by nature herself are also strongly reminiscent
of Wordsworth's "Lucy" poems, especially of "She dwelt
among untrodden ways" and "Three years she grew," poems in which Wordsworth's own death anxiety and his re-
sentment of what he likes to think of as his natural, "mortal" part (as opposed to the "immortality" of creative
imagination) are displaced onto Lucy, for whose obscurity
and vulnerability he displays a concern in direct proportion
to his own anxiety ("Strange fits of passion have I known").
Here too Shelley faces an uphill struggle since his own efforts to displace his poetic fears onto Wordsworth are subject to deconstruction by the same critique.

The dangerous nature of poetic desire is reflected in the
song in the poet's dream:

> . . . A vision on his sleep
> There came, a dream of hopes that never yet
> Had flushed his cheek. He dreamed a veiled maid
> Sate near him, talking in low solemn tones.
> Her voice was like the voice of his own soul
> Heard in the calm of thought; its music long,
> Like woven sounds of streams and breezes, held
> His inmost sense suspended in its web
> Of many-coloured woof and shifting hues.
> Knowledge and truth and virtue were her theme,
> And lofty hopes of divine liberty,
> Thoughts the most dear to him, and poesy,
> Herself a poet. Soon the solemn mood
> Of her pure mind kindled through all her frame
> A permeating fire: wild numbers then
> She raised, with voice stifled in tremulous sobs
> Subdued by its own pathos: her fair hands

Were bare alone, sweeping from some strange harp
Strange symphony, and in their branching veins
The eloquent blood told an ineffable tale.
The beating of her heart was heard to fill
The pauses of her music, and her breath
Tumultuously accorded with those fits
Of intermitted song. Sudden she rose,
As if her heart impatiently endured
Its bursting burthen: at the sound he turned,
And saw by the warm light of their own life
Her glowing limbs beneath the sinuous veil
Of woven wind, her outspread arms now bare,
Her dark locks floating in the breath of night,
Her beamy bending eyes, her parted lips
Outstretched, and pale, and quivering eagerly.

(lines 149–80)

Of course, in the next moment, unable to restrain himself, the poet leaps to embrace her, whereupon she disappears and he faints. "Ineffable" and "strange," the song is like that of Wordsworth's solitary reaper, which is beyond language and meaning and, therefore, need never end. Initially at least, this dream too holds out the possibility of a poetry transcending language, purified of the mundane and escaping sublimation.

As the dream continues, however, the singer and the song become indistinguishable; she no longer has to sing, only be the poem. Subsuming the body, imagination can sublimate into itself to become song; it no longer need contaminate itself with the other in order to be poetry. But the drive toward imaginative fulfillment entirely on its own terms is inimical even to the residual otherness of the self. At one point, it seems almost as if the immense inner pressure of that desire might burst the heart, consuming the self that tries to contain it. Offering, impossibly, the sublimation of what cannot or will not endure sublimation, the dream presents poetry rather nakedly as wanting, no insisting on, what we cannot have.

On this score, Shelley himself is quite vulnerable. How-ever, the dream also aims itself rather specifically at the Wordsworthian insistence on internalizing poetry and at-tempting to subordinate it to personality—an effort, which, the dream suggests, will inevitably fail since imagination is more than an individual ego can contain. To attempt to do so is to create the possibility of an inner division of the sort everywhere apparent in *The Prelude*. This is why the theme of solitude is so important in "Alastor." It is the poet's means of defending his conviction of specialness from con-tradiction. But the distance it places between the poet and other people is a mere reflection of the distance between poetic desire and the inadequate self it inhabits.

Shelley's young poet has rejected the Wordsworthian sub-limation into nature, revolted ˙ by the omnipresent death lurking behind the intractable otherness of the world. Now he begins the process of realizing that his very self is intrac-tably other as well, burdened by its own natural existence. Here the movement beyond sublimation to self-sublimation threatens to fragment the self—the maid's "bursting heart" or the schizoid personality of which Weiskel speaks—or, whatever else it might be, the song ceases to be poetry. In this context, the faint is literally and significantly a fall out of poetry as it bursts the bounds of sublimation and then a fall back into poetry as the dream ends and poetic sublimation reasserts itself. As I have already suggested, Shelley rebels against the terms of sublimation, but he wounds himself in seeming ultimately to agree, against his will, that poetry, if not life itself, is sublimation. This is why Shelley at his most Gnostic is always testing the limits of poetry and of life as if, imperceptible from where we stand in a demiurgic creation, something else perhaps more amenable to the imagination, its true home, lies just beyond.

When the poet awakens, Shelley refers us to one of the best-known lines in the "Intimations" ode:

> . . . Whither have fled
> The hues of heaven that canopied his bower
> Of yesternight? The sounds that soothed his sleep,
> The mystery and the majesty of Earth,
> The joy, the exultation? His wan eyes
> Gaze on the empty scene as vacantly
> As ocean's moon looks on the moon in heaven.
>
> (lines 196–202)

The corresponding lines in Wordsworth's poem—"Whither is fled the visionary gleam? / Where is it now, the glory and the dream?"—refer us to Wordsworth's own complex poetic myth, a myth, Shelley seems to suggest, ultimately as dangerous as the young poet's dream, which would sacrifice life to death by sublimation as the price of preserving the myth of an essential poetic being.

It is one of the difficulties of this poem that the young poet, so Wordsworthian in his error, is so Shelleyan in his response. Wandering over the face of the earth seeking his ideal, visionary "love" and finding that everything now seems hopelessly alien to him, he decides to cast himself adrift "And meet lone Death on the drear ocean's waste; / For well he knew that mighty Shadow loves / The slimy caverns of the populous deep" (305–7).

After the poet casts himself adrift, Weiskel tells us, the action "falls into two phases, an upward, regressive journey to origins (ll. 222–468), and a downward course, following a river that is meant to image the progress of his life (ll. 492–671). In the middle is a suspended, womb-landscape of the most extreme regression. A rivulet leads us there, by narrowing banks 'whose yellow flowers / For ever gaze on their own drooping eyes, / Reflected in the crystal calm' (ll. 406–8), and toward one 'darkest glen' in which there is a deep, darkly gleaming well" (*RS*, 146):

> Hither the Poet came. His eyes beheld
> Their own wan light through the reflected lines

Of his thin hair, distinct in the dark depth
Of that still fountain; as the human heart,
Gazing in dreams over the gloomy grave,
Sees its own treacherous likeness there.
(lines 469–74)

The contrast between the flowers, perfectly reflected back at themselves, and the man, whose natural self so contradicts desire, could not be clearer. Furthermore, the lines seem to intimate the connection between desire and death in a secret conspiracy. Weiskel sees this as a moment of clarity and the poet's opportunity to escape his compulsion:

> Here, if anywhere, is a moment of recognition that intimates release from the Poet's erotic compulsion. But the moment doesn't deepen; the only identity the Poet can envision is a "treacherous likeness"—an evanescent imitation but also a frightening revelation of the heart's faithlessness. In the normative resolution one would renounce the unacceptable desire of the heart in favor of a new identification. And a new possibility does enter, as if to resolve the Poet's self-perception and rescue him:

A Spirit seemed
To stand beside him—clothed in no bright robes
Of shadowy silver or enshrining light,
Borrowed from aught the visible world affords
Of grace, or majesty, or mystery;—
But, undulating woods, and silent well,
And leaping rivulet, and evening gloom
Now deepening the dark shades, for speech assuming,
Held commune with him, as if he and it
Were all that was,—only . . . when his regard
Was raised by intense pensiveness, . . . two eyes,
Two starry eyes, hung in the gloom of thought,
And seemed with their serene and azure smiles
To beckon him.
(ll. 479–92)

But the poet is too far gone; the eyes (his own) return as the Other, and the erotic relation is reinstalled. For a moment he had teetered and almost moved into dialogue with that rather Wordsworthian Spirit—a nonerotic ideal, a kind of superego.

Instead, he succumbs again to "the light / That shone within his
soul" (ll. 492–93).

(RS, 146-47)

This is all very well, but Weiskel's advice is also a bit
Wordsworthian, missing the point about the treachery of
desire and ignoring the autoerotic nature of Wordsworth's
"nonerotic" idealism. True, the Shelleyan poet fails to establish a genuinely erotic relationship with the other, but the
solipsism into which he recedes is a distillation of the Wordsworthian stance.

In Chapter 1, I spoke of the disordering of desire, the
splitting of desire within itself. Here we confront that split
directly. What natural man, the ego, desires is to live, to
cling to this world as long as possible. What creative or
poetic desire wants is not to be imaginatively subject to
death and to the limitations of natural being. These two
desires can be profoundly at odds since it seems that creative
or poetic desire can decide that not the denial of death but its
embrace is a possible means of passing beyond the limitations of natural being.

The desire not to die, the love of this world, is a block to
every transcendence-based ethic or poetic, sacred or secular.
The belief in and pursuit of a better "elsewhere" as the
proper home of an essential self necessarily involves something very like a death wish—frequently, the end of poetry,
expressed not as a wish but as a fear. Part of Shelley's difficulty in distinguishing himself from Wordsworth has to do
with the interpenetration of these two desires, disordering
desire itself.

For Weiskel, the essential point

is that the Spirit implicates the Poet in a dialogue; the landscape
becomes "speech." The threshold the Poet fails to cross is the
threshold of discourse in which he could have been inscribed as
a speaking subject, as an "I." But that would have required

renouncing the beckoning smiles of desire. The Poet fears identity—fears being constituted in the continuity of discourse—
because he cannot bear its cost.

(*RS,* 147)

The dialogue the poet fears to enter into is poetry itself,
a sublimation that would compromise desire in its drive
beyond natural limitation. But behind this there is Shelley's
own difficulty with the "Wordsworthian Spirit," which
haunts poetry itself for Shelley. Ironically, this testament to
Wordsworth's poetic power also exposes the naïveté of his
own faith, expressed in the preface to *Lyrical Ballads,* that
poetry can address itself to the world, unhaunted by the
ghosts of dead poets. The temptation is then to return to a
dialogue with Wordsworth, to return to poetry as established; instead, the poet drives on toward a death that is
seen necessarily from within poetry as the death of poetry
but which may only be the limit or border of poetry as it
is.

In any case, "Obedient to the light / That shone within
his soul, he went, pursuing / The windings of the dell . . ."
(lines 492–94). He follows this river to what seems the very
edge of the world where it falls into a "measureless void /
Scattering its waters to the passing winds" (lines 569–70).
Yet the poet does not, as we might expect, follow the waters
of the stream out into the void. Instead, he dies a truly
Wordsworthian death, embowered in nature, his dimming
eyes looking up at the dimming points of the crescent moon;
he is a "fragile lute" (line 667) and we are returned to the
narrator's plea at the poem's beginning: "moveless, as a
long-forgotton lyre / Suspended in the solitary dome / Of
some mysterious and deserted fane, / I wait thy breath,
Great Parent, that my strain / May modulate with murmurs
of the air . . ." (lines 42–46). It is finally the natural and not
the imaginative, aggressive, questing death that the poet
dies, against what seems the entire tendency of the poem.

But the poem does not end with the poet's death; it ends with a fifty-line lament, spoken by the narrator, which begins with a fervent wish that immortality "were the true law / Of this so lovely world!" (lines 685–86). He eulogizes the dead poet and wonders that when such virtue is subject to death, so much that is less worthy lives on. Then the narrator makes a somewhat surprising request:

> . . . let no tear
> Be shed—not even in thought. Nor, when those hues
> Are gone, and those divinest lineaments,
> Worn by the senseless wind, shall live alone
> In the frail pauses of this simple strain,
> Let not high verse, mourning the memory
> Of that which is no more, or painting's woe
> Or sculpture, speak in feeble imagery
> Their own cold powers. Art and eloquence,
> And all the shows o' the world are frail and vain
> To weep a loss that turns their lights to shade.
> It is a woe too "deep for tears," when all
> Is reft at once. When some surpassing Spirit,
> Whose light adorned the world around it, leaves
> Those who remain behind, not sobs or groans,
> The passionate tumult of a clinging hope;
> But pale despair and cold tranquillity,
> Nature's vast frame, the web of human things,
> Birth and the grave, that are not as they were.
>
> (lines 702–20)

The narrator rejects the efficacy of grief and the value of any other form of commemoration save his own poem. In effect, he demands that we dwell in this moment and in his poem by denying us the means to put it behind us. Death it seems is the quintessential poetic occasion, and his poem is privileged by its proximity. As is so frequently the case in "Alastor," the poet is made to betray himself by an echo of Wordsworth, here, of the final lines of the "Intimations" ode: "To me the meanest flower that blows can give / Thoughts that do often lie too deep for tears."

Placing these lines here, where the narrator is seeking to hold us in the pathos of his final poetic moment, Shelley reveals the pretension of Wordsworth's compensatory miracle of intensified perception, recognizing that the "Thoughts that do often lie too deep for tears" are everywhere and always thoughts of his own death. Wordsworth's extension throughout life of death's moment of loss makes our experience of nature and of the poetry that results one long meditation on the pathos of our own death. Wordsworth's poetry, Shelley seems to accuse, is built on this pathos; and the narcissistic image of the prenatal self, linked with such a narcissistic wounding as birth here becomes, makes of all poetry an enclosed meditation on the pathos of its poet's death at the expense of all else, including the reality of death itself, which can no longer be acknowledged in its reality by cries of grief or the raising of monuments. Instead, there is only a melancholy "cold tranquillity," permanently arrested in a fascination with the pathos of death, which prevents it from acknowledging the death of the poet and going on to contemplate a future in spite of it.

But this is not Wordsworth's poem; Shelley is implicated in its end and entangled in the special pathos of the poet's death, as he knows. This is why the poet "hero" can get no farther than the edge of the abyss, why Shelley's poem subsides back into Wordsworthian pathos and the myth of an intenser being—because the poetry that will carry the poet and the poem into the abyss does not yet exist, and Shelley, despite a clear and often devastating critique of Wordsworth's sublimation, is trapped within the same imaginative problematic.

As Weiskel notes, Shelley tries for the remainder of his career to free himself from Wordsworth and establish a new poetic. But as Bloom argues in his discussion of Shelley in *Poetry and Repression*—a discussion focused on Shelley's last poem, "The Triumph of Life"—he never truly succeeds.

In a chapter of *Poetry and Repression* entitled "Shelley and His Precursors," Bloom argues that "The Triumph of Life," Shelley's last poem, manages to transume the "Intimations" ode in a way none of his earlier efforts was able to do. However, Bloom continues:

> Wordsworth is a dangerous opponent to take on, and we will see that Shelley's victory is equivocal. What he gains from Wordsworth, Shelley loses to time or to language, both of which become more problematic in "The Triumph" than they are in Wordsworth. It is as though a casting-out of Wordsworthian nature demands a compensation, a price exacted both by poetic history and by poetic language.
>
> (*PR,* 98)

Bloom's reading focuses on the Shelleyan version of the Divine Throne-as-chariot vision beginning Ezckiel. This, according to Bloom, is the "transumptive image proper," common to Dante, Spenser, and Milton. However,

> as a transumptive parody, Shelley's vision in "The Triumph of Life" [lines 74–104] addresses itself more even to Wordsworth and Coleridge than it does to Milton and Dante. Shelley shrewdly implies that the Ezekiel-Revelation chariot contains the contrasting epigraph emblems of both the "Dejection" Ode and the "Intimations" Ode, the pale despair of the portent of an oncoming storm, and the image of the rainbow, sign that the storm is over, with cold tranquility ensuing. That is why, in "The Triumph of Life," the onrushing chariot is heralded by the old moon in the new moon's arms, as in the fragment of "Sir Patrick Spens" that begins Coleridge's Ode, and that begins Ione's vision in *Prometheus Unbound.* And that is why, in "The Triumph of Life," Rousseau encounters Iris or the rainbow just before confronting Wordsworthian Nature as the "Shape all light," as in the fragment of his own "My heart leaps up" that Wordsworth uses to begin the "Intimations" Ode.
>
> (*PR,* 104)

To my mind, this is a brilliant piece of poetic insight, leading to the recognition that the "life" in "The Triumph of

Life" is "what has triumphed over Wordsworth and Coleridge, that is, over their imaginative integrity and autonomy as strong poets." Furthermore, this life, the death-in-life, "is what Shelley had always feared and clearly it is what he rejects in his sublimely suicidal last poem" (*PR*, 104).

The obvious question here is why the chariot at all since it is central neither to Wordsworth nor to Coleridge. Bloom's answer is a complex and vitally important one. He points out that Shelley comes into his poetic maturity and is able to write the 1816 poems only after an intense reading of Wordsworth and, to a lesser extent, Coleridge. For him, as for all poets, according to Bloom, becoming a poet "meant accepting a primal fixation upon a quasi-divine precursor." Thus, "the problem of continuity or discontinuity with precursors became merged with the problem of continuity in and with one's own poetic self" (*PR*, 105).

Initially, Shelley tried to achieve perspective on his precursors through the metaphor of fire, the "prime perspectivizing metaphor of Romanticism," the revisionary aim of which is "to burn through context, the context of precursors and of nature." In this way, fire becomes the inside or subjectivity of the external nature and of the precursors (*PR*, 105).

The ultimate failure of fire as a redemptive metaphor in "The Triumph of Life" is decreed by an inherent weakness in the perspectivizing stance: "It is necessarily self-defeating, for all of its 'insides' and 'outsides' are endlessly equivocal and reversible. Yet post-Enlightenment poetry, as Shelley understood, was in one phase at least a questing for fire, and the defensive meaning of that fire was discontinuity" (*PR*, 106).

Thus, it was in response to an inevitable failure of the metaphor of fire that Shelley turned to the image of the chariot, by means of which he created a discontinuity with Wordsworth, whose "anti-mythological" stance prevented him from using it (*PR*, 107). Whereas fire is sublimation, the chariot is "an introjection of futurity, and a projection of lost or past time" (*PR*, 106). However, Bloom argues, this transumption leaves untouched a fundamentally Wordsworthian conception of imagination (in the guise of the metonymy "gleam"), which returns to dominate the conclusion of Shelley's poem. In a close reading of this conclusion, Bloom finds there "the end of the fire of sublimation, the hope that poetic discontinuity or autonomy could be achieved by a radical or Nietzschean perspectivism" (*PR*, 108). In the final analysis, Shelley could not apply the lesson of transumptive allusion to Wordsworth because "the primal fixation upon Wordsworth, and consequent repression of self was simply too great" (*PR*, 109).

Here Bloom seems to hover on the edge of an equivocation, almost hinting that Shelley's failure to overcome Wordsworth was the result of a psychological factor, an accident accessible to remedy. But then he closes off this avenue of explanation with a reading of the famous last paragraph of Shelley's *Defense*, the paragraph ending "Poets are the unacknowledged legislators of the world." This is true, Bloom maintains, in the sense that

> an unacknowledged legislator is simply an unacknowledged influence, and since Shelley equates Wordsworth with the *Zeitgeist*, it is hardly an overestimate to say that Wordsworth's influence created a series of laws for a world of feeling and thinking that went beyond the domain of poetry. Very strong poet that he was, Shelley nevertheless had the wisdom and the sadness of knowing overtly what other poets since have evaded knowing, except in the involuntary patterns of their work. Wordsworth will legislate and go on legislating for your poem, no matter how you resist or evade or even unconsciously ignore him.
>
> (*PR*, 111)

Thus, Shelley's chariot of life does run over Wordsworth but only because Shelley is willing to be run over as well and face the revelation that, even in his apostasy, Wordsworth is "a transumptive mirror of futurity" (*PR,* 110).

In effect, Bloom's reading of the *Defense* offers Wordsworthian terms and ideas both as the necessary foundation for an accurate reading of post-Miltonic poetry and as prescriptive of poetic possibility itself—an intersection of critical reading and poetic reality that guarantees the whole enterprise of literary criticism as we know it, including Bloom's own revisionism. In this regard, Bloom's career-long identification with Shelley represents not only a shared rejection of sublimation but also a confession of the continuing hegemony of Wordsworth and of the perspectivism at the heart of Wordsworthian Romanticism (which is to say, of Romanticism proper). At one point, Bloom remarks revealingly that Shelley's primary defense against Milton in *Prometheus Unbound* "is his characteristic and magnificent speed in and at the process of rhetorical substitution, but the defense is a desperate one, and Milton triumphs over his revisionist, because it is Milton's transumptive trope that gives coherence to Shelley's image, rather than the reverse" (*PR,* 98). Nothing could be more descriptive of Bloom's own critical gift than "magnificent speed in and at the process of rhetorical substitution," nor is a "process of rhetorical substitution" a bad general description of the process of criticism as practiced in this country. Indeed, most attempts at metacriticism or theoretical criticism can be fairly described as an examination of the process of rhetorical substitution by means of rhetorical substitution. By means of his own identification with Shelley, in a way clarified by his account of the Shelley/Wordsworth relationship, Bloom draws criticism as a whole into perspectivism, or, more precisely, he reveals the "equivocal," "reversible" perspectivism inherent in a criticism defined by rhetorical substitution.

At the most immediate level, it is easy to see that all this calls into question the reality of *the* revisionary trope, transumption, which represents the possibility offered by revisionism of a real discontinuity, a new direction, in the tradition. Instead, revisionism seems a more self-conscious form of the perspectivism underlying all literary criticism. In fact, transumption seems to represent the revisionist at his most Wordsworthian (that is, most orthodox) in its implication that a special quality of self-consciousness distinguishes the transumption from the perspectivizing metaphor it so closely resembles.

Bloom's criticism, no less than that of the hero of orthodoxy, M. H. Abrams, refers us to Wordsworth because both are founded in acts of identification, direct or indirect, enthusiastic or ambivalent, with Wordsworth. Among Romanticists, it is a well-known fact that different versions of Romanticism tend to be founded in identifications with different authors—primal identifications that serve as the critical equivalent of Bloom's "scene of instruction" and that make our conception of the period an equivocal and reversible agglomeration of perspectives. I would venture to guess that something similar is true of the criticism of other periods as well.

In the case of Romanticism, all of these identifications, like that of Bloom with Shelley, threaten perpetually to reveal themselves as de facto identifications with Wordsworth and the main line of the tradition, which makes possible a criticism based on identification, perspectivism, rhetorical substitution, and the saving superiority of self-consciousness, not only for critics of the Romantics but for a modern criticism of any period. Since Wordsworth made self-consciousness his own, placing the problematical relationship between identity and identification at the center of our tradition, his influence on the critic cannot be escaped, as Bloom tries to do in *Agon,* by shifting his identification to the "American pragmatism" of Emerson—the act of identification itself is ultimately Wordsworthian in its ambivalence.

For us, Wordsworth's is the definitive representation of the continuous relationship between the tradition of secular letters and that of Judeo-Christian letters, between the qualities of secular and religious belief. The self-limiting identity of literature and of literary criticism seems designed to confine writer and critic alike within the perspectivizing upon which that continuity depends and (or at least so it seems to us now) has always depended. The only way to arrest the play of perspectives and to privilege decisively one over the others is to smuggle in some disguised "extraliterary" standard. The fiction of an objective and rigorous criticism seeks to exclude such extraliterary considerations in defense of the ideologically central perspectivizing stance. Even where critics seek to extend the language and methods of literary interpretation into other disciplines, either criticism becomes unliterary or the discipline in question is re-presented as an aspect of the general perspectivism. From within such a conception of literature, the arrest of the play of perspectives is inseparable from the death of literature itself. Similarly, a fundamental change in the literary situation or in our conception and use of literature can appear only in the guise of this death. This helps to account for the combination of yearning for and revulsion from the anticipated end of literature characteristic of post-Enlightenment letters—an ambivalence that carries forward into the secular world the conflict between history and apocalypse in which our tradition is founded.

Looking back over all we have discussed since the beginning of this study, we can see that revisionism is founded in and ultimately confirms the continuity and authority of the tradition, even as it expresses a profound ambivalence over this fact, which is itself a central part of the tradition. In his insistence on articulating and exploring this ambivalence, the revisionist can be distinguished from the more orthodox critic, who thinks of the tradition as beleaguered and devotes himself to defending and shoring it up, implicitly seeing in its ultimate triumph an unalloyed good. These two stances, both "traditional," represent perspectives equally likely to be exploited by anyone who becomes concerned with literature. The revisionist's sense of tradition's overpowering imaginative authority refers to its continued effectiveness for anyone who identifies with and resides within literary culture. The orthodox sense of the vulnerability of the tradition, founded in its institutional and pedagogical situation, refers to literature's status in society as a whole.

A book like Abrams's *Natural Supernaturalism,* a powerful expression of the orthodox view (along with Bate's *The Burden of the Past and the English Poet,* perhaps the most powerful such expression we have), attempts to represent the persistence of the tradition as an act performed upon it by the genius of secular authors—a tactic that cloaks ambivalence in a cloud of solicitude and, roundabout, aggrandizes the redeeming power of an essential creative self. More important, Wordsworth-like, it satisfies the urge to originality through ever more severe sublimations. Such an approach yields itself up once again to the plight of the Sensibility Poets when it becomes clear that ultimately this sublimation must become so self-destructive in its severity as to be tantamount to a denial of desire itself.

The revisionist, like Bloom, yields himself up to the late eighteenth century by a different path. His tone, the entire manner of his criticism, expresses desire, even as its content confirms that the essence of literature is self-limitation. Thus, the revisionist satisfies his urge to originality by a seduction; he seduces more orthodox critics into branding him heterodox, even heretical, creating a difference or break with tradition that he is powerless to create for himself. He achieves the pleasures of originality *and* effects the defense of tradition against his own attacks, which are, after all, dependent for their significance on the recognition and exploitation of its continuity and authority. This path corresponds to the assertive outbreaks of apocalyptic imagination in *The*

Prelude, which threaten to bring the work of poetry to an end and paradoxically confirm the necessity of sublimation. As Weiskel observes, Wordsworth's most open assertions of originality are powerfully restrained by a recognition that the authority of the tradition must be preserved or else accession to that authority is meaningless.

It should come as no surprise that the nature of the literary tradition, or of tradition in general, is so conservative, converting to its own service even the most apparently radical perspective based on the reading of literature. It is perhaps a bit more surprising, certainly sobering, to recognize how ill-conceived and trivial the terms of so many supposedly crucial critical disputes really are. Our response to this situation must ultimately depend on factors outside of literature as we know it, in society as a whole and in the imperatives of life in our times. But that is another book entirely.

INDEX

Compositor: Huron Valley Graphics
Text: 10/12-point Bembo
Display: Bembo
Printer: McNaughton and Gunn
Binder: John H. Dekker and Sons